"This book delivers on its promise to help you formulate an Internet strategy. The *Corporate Internet Planning Guide* isn't just another cookie-cutter, skin-deep take on Internet strategy. [The author] delivers the goods in a well-thought-out and clear manner."

Erin Callaway,
PC Week

"This book is vital to any business trying to position itself strongly on the Internet. It provides a simplified problem solving framework for an extremely complicated process. Far and away the most useful book I've read on this subject."

Rolland Waters, Founder
RTime

"To date most companies have limited their use of the Internet to poster-like websites and e-mail, not utilizing its full potential. This book prompts readers to push the limits and focus on the strategic planning required to develop and manage a truly useful website."

Michael Fagan, Vice President in the
Information Technology Department
Morgan Stanley & Co.

"Beyond all the fad and hype, the rise of the Internet is important because it transforms how we do business. Yet the challenges it presents and how they affect business and organizational strategies have largely been ignored. This useful "how-to" guide fills that void and offers an important roadmap for creating positive change within your organization."

Steve Sundquist, Chief Information Officer
Frank Russell Company

"If your company is contemplating an Internet strategy, read this guide first. It contains illustrative and thought-provoking examples and a realistic analysis of the key elements of a successful Internet strategy. I wish this guide had been available when we got started."

Peter Wilson, Operations Manager
DealerNet

"The virtual organization can become a reality with the insight provided by Rich Gascoyne. He really understands the importance of effective communication in our evolving networked world. I'm already adopting many of his ideas into our PR strategies."

William Ryan, Partner
Niehaus Ryan Group, Inc.

"If you want to see your business thrive in the 21st century then this book is for you. More than just a textbook for technology executives, this book demonstrates the highly relevant business impact of the Internet. Any effective business strategy should definitely include a serious review of *Corporate Internet Planning Guide*."

Richard Thomas, Managing Director
Australian Guarantee Corporation Ltd.

"*Corporate Internet Planning Guide* is the first Internet book that doesn't bombard the reader with techno-babble. Gascoyne presents responsible thought leadership to empower business managers with an understanding of how the Internet phenomenon will positively impact their organization."

Chip Overstreet, Vice President Marketing & Business Development
Open Horizon

"With relentless discipline and unfailing clarity Rich Gascoyne has created a comprehensive reference for any manager or student charged with defining and maintaining an Internet strategy."

Brian Hammerstein, CEO
Infon

"Most attempts to harness the Internet liken to throwing Silly Putty at a slippery wall. Where and will it stick are unknown. Richard Gascoyne charts a path for a business to map its Internet thrust to its corporate strategy. The odds of success now soar."

J. Roger Moody, Founder and Owner
Sandpiper Synergies

Corporate Internet Planning Guide

Aligning Internet Strategy With Business Goals

RICHARD J. GASCOYNE
KORAY OZCUBUKCU

VAN NOSTRAND REINHOLD
I(T)P® A Division of International Thomson Publishing Inc.

New York • Albany • Bonn • Boston • Detroit • London • Madrid • Melbourne
Mexico City • Paris • San Francisco • Singapore • Tokyo • Toronto

International Thomson Publishing Company.
The ITP logo is a registered trademark used herein under license.

The ideas presented in this book are generic and strategic. Their specific application to a particular company must be the responsibility of the management of that company, based on management's understanding of their company's procedures, culture, resources, and competitive situation.

Printed in the United States of America

http://www.vnr.com   Visit us on the Web!

For more information contact:

Van Nostrand Reinhold
115 Fifth Avenue
New York, NY 10003

Chapman & Hall GmbH
Pappalallee 3
69469 Weinham
Germany

Chapman & Hall
2-6 Boundary Row
London SEI 8HN
United Kingdom

International Thomson Publishing Asia
60 Albert Street #15-01
Albert Complex
Singapore 189969

Thomas Nelson Australia
102 Dodds Street
South Melbourne 3205
Victoria, Australia

International Thomson Publishing Japan
Hirakawa-cho Kyowa Building, 3F
2-2-1 Hirakawa-cho, Chiyoda-ku
Tokyo 102 Japan

Nelson Canada
1120 Birchmount Road
Scarborough, Ontario
M1K 5G4, Canada

International Thomson Editores
Seneca, 53
Colonia Polanco
11560 Mexico D.F. Mexico

3 4 5 6 7 8 9 10 QEBFF 01 00 99 98 97

Library of Congress Cataloging-in-Publication Data available upon request.

ISBN 0-442-02416-9

Production: Jo-Ann Campbell • mle design • 562 Milford Point Rd., Milford, CT 06460

To Lori, for everything.

CONTENTS

PREFACE

In many ways, an Internet business strategy has little to do with the actual hardware and software that comprise the system of inter-linked computers we think of when the word *Internet* is mentioned. Rather, an Internet strategy is about *concepts* such as agility, customer intimacy, proactivity, creation of niche markets, and exploitation of core competencies in a virtual environment. In other words, the traditional human factors—*your* creativity, determination, and vision ultimately determine your success.

Success in the world of the Internet and Intranet requires the ability to see the proverbial forest through the trees. It is easy to be charmed by the sheer novelty of Internet technology, and many sites on the World Wide Web reflect this initial enthusiasm. But placing corporate reports and sales catalogs on the Internet, declaring that you have brought your organization into cyberspace, and proclaiming success are not enough. Incorporating the Internet as an integral component of your business strategy now and in the future requires careful planning, alignment, and perseverance.

This book provides a set of business, marketing, and technology building blocks with which business and technology executives, consultants, and students can formulate responsible and successful Internet and Intranet strategies. The chapters are arranged to take you through the planning and design phases to implementation and monitoring.

A note on terminology: Throughout the book the terms *Internet* and *Intranet* are used interchangeably. An Intranet is considered a variant of the "true" Internet in that the users are predefined and readily identifiable. The technology, strategic implications, and operational characteristics of the Intranet are, for the most part, identical to those of the Internet. In using the terms to refer to a single concept, I hope to break down what I believe is an artificial dichotomy.

I base my observations, conclusions, and guidance on a wide variety of empirical data encompassing actual corporate Internet strategies, both successful and unsuccessful. Throughout the book, actual case studies and hypothetical situations illustrate important points.

Another thought to keep in mind is that technology is evolving at a dizzying speed. The Internet planning horizon is quite low, and you should—indeed, *must*—revisit your strategy on a regular basis. What is offered here is a snapshot of the technical capability as it is today and will likely be one or two years hence.

As Jay Tenenbaum notes in his essay "The Internet as an Agent of Social Change," it is crucial to consider the social, cultural, and philosophical aspects of the virtual environment. The barriers that traditionally separated large business organizations from small ones are breaking down, while at the same time the gulf between the information haves and have-nots grows wider. The Information Revolution, for good or ill, is reshaping how we work, where we work, and the nature of work itself.

Thus, the challenge before you is to respect and draw upon the strengths of your existing business systems, and rules while striving to push the envelope and mold the future. The Internet can help you bring your customers, employees, products, and services from where they are today to where you want them to be.

One note of caution: Do not regard the actual Internet strategies discussed here as gospel. What works for one company is not likely to work for *your* company. In fact, I emphasize the need to break the habit of looking to the competition and instead urge you to discover *your* company's strengths and weaknesses as well as its current and future opportunities.

Leaders are those who prepare their businesses for change. This book is designed for leaders, those who welcome change rather than shun it. Enjoy the book. Interpret it. Use it as a springboard for your own ideas and intercompany dialogue.

Philosophers often wonder, "Do the times make the leaders, or do the leaders make the times?" It is my belief that in the Internet revolution, the leaders have the ability to make the times.

The following three points summarize the principal inspirations for this book:

1. An overwhelming belief in the immense value of Internet technologies as a vehicle for electronic commerce and its ability to create virtual organizations.
2. The lack of bold and strategic Internet approaches which hamper businesses and their employees, and prevent them from reaching new global markets.
3. Respect the operating reality of your business—that is, the need to be profitable, using current systems and technologies—as the first step in developing truly effective Internet strategies.

I would like to acknowledge the efforts and assistance of Koray Ozcubukcu, Keith Sheridan, Mike Wagner, and Dustin Hubbard, along with the staff of Van Nostrand Reinhold, especially John Boyd and Marc Sperber, for their dedicated guidance in this effort.

In addition, I extend my thanks to the executives and organizations that have taken the time to work with me, providing real-life examples and insight.

Special thanks go to Paul Cosgrave, Krista Wald, and the staff of Claremont Technology Group.

Most of all, I would like to thank my wife, Lori, for her patience, direction, editing, and encouragement.

Richard J. Gascoyne
Seattle, Washington
December 1996

INTRODUCTION

In deciding how (or whether) to use the Internet in their business, CEOs, CIOs, line managers, and IT managers are faced with some of the greatest challenges ever. Today's business leaders must understand more technology than ever before, while the technology leaders must thoroughly understand strategic business issues. The hype about the Internet and its genuine potential to revolutionize most aspects of business are almost too large to contemplate. The one point on which all the pundits agree is that technology management in today's climate is a HARD JOB!

Whenever a truly difficult task appears, a talented person develops a new tool to make the task go more smoothly for the rest of us. Rich's book is that type of tool. He has distilled the relevant issues of customer needs, personnel and operational constraints, technology, communications convergence, and project management, creating an invaluable guidebook for our journey into the previously uncharted territory of Internet strategy.

Through its detailed examples, Rich's work bring into focus why and how a business needs to function in today's Internet-enabled marketplaces. Rich takes readers through each portion of Internet strategy planning and implementation, spelling out key issues, opportunities, and risks at every turn.

I am pleased to write a foreword for this book, having had the opportunity to collaborate with Rich on a project to develop a global Intranet/Internet strategy for a leading financial services institution. Rich's knowledge and professionalism made the project both successful and enjoyable. He has thoroughly tested the ideas in this book in a practical setting, working with business giants, technologists, and other consultants.

Whether your business is large or small, and whether your job is technical or managerial, this book provides a useful problem-solving framework for an extremely complicated current issue: How to position your firm on the Internet for maximum competitive advantage.

Bryan L. Bell
Strategic Technologist
Frank Russell Company
Tacoma, Washington

CHAPTER 1

A CALL TO ACTION: BUILD THE INTERNET/INTRANET INTO YOUR BUSINESS

BEING EARLY AND BEING INNOVATIVE

The successful company is one willing to meet the Internet challenge immediately and to experiment with innovative strategies.

The story of how ONYX Software Corp., a Seattle-based maker of sales force automation (SFA) software, won a contract in early 1996 is a good example. Genuity, Inc., a California-based subsidiary of Bechtel Corp., sought to purchase a flexible and robust SFA software package to track customer information and other data crucial to their growing business—and tie the data to their sales, service, and management processes.

Although it had limited knowledge of SFA programs on the market, Genuity could not devote the capacity or time to an exhaustive product search, and it quickly chose a package.

On the evening before signing the contract with the selected vendor, Geir Ramleth, Genuity's president, decided to search the World Wide Web for additional suppliers of SFA software. While surfing, Ramleth came across a product called Encompass, developed by ONYX Software. He navigated to ONYX Software's public Internet site to learn more about its product offerings and registered as an online guest, provided the necessary specifications (e.g., number of employees and volume of sales), and requested additional product information.

As Ramleth explored the site further, the telephone rang. The caller was an ONYX regional sales representative following up on the request for information just received over the Internet. During their conversation, only *minutes* after Ramleth registered on the Internet site, the sales representative provided him with the information he sought. Impressed with the experience, Genuity signed a contract with ONYX.

ONYX's strategy integrates its marketing and sales operations with its Internet site. Once a guest registers, the data is directed through the Internet server and fed into ONYX's own Encompass SFA product. The company's sales team configured the software to provide pop-up alerts on its computers when current or targeted customers log on to the Internet site. The system uses standard programming logic to create a sales opportunity record for any other qualified lead. After a prospect completes a survey, Encompass automatically routes an alert message to the appropriate sales representative based on entered criteria.

To ONYX, the Internet represents a new way to showcase its products and enhance the sales process. Today ONYX challenges potential customers by requesting that they access ONYX's Internet site and see how long it takes for a regional sales representative to call back. In most cases, a guest logging on to the ONYX site will receive a fax containing more specific product information while navigating the Web site and will be telephoned within ten minutes of registering.

The ONYX sales representative is even able to determine which pages a guest has visited and therefore anticipate likely questions.

In the case of E*Trade Securities, a San Jose-based brokerage providing secured electronic trading over the Internet, being quick to market has paid off. It was one of the very first companies to offer ultra-deep discounts for trading stocks online and was named by the *San Jose Journal* as the fastest-growing private company in Silicon Valley over the period 1992–1994. E*Trade averaged 7,100 trades per day through the middle of September 1996. It is planning on offering customized pages for its 90,000 active accounts, which is growing at a rate of 10 percent per month.

Similarly, Lombard Institutional Investors, based in northern California, provides individuals using the Internet with services traditionally available to only high-end institutional investors. Investors can run multiple interday graphs, purchase stock directly over the Internet, and manage portfolios online. As a result, Lombard's customer base has grown at a rate of up to 5 percent per week.

For Andrew Klein, a former securities attorney who is president and CEO of the New York-based Spring Street Brewery, the Internet has opened up an entirely new avenue of business. The microbrewery launched its initial public offering (IPO) of 900,000 shares on the Internet in March 1996, raising $1.6 million.

After the IPO plans were announced in February 1995, the U.S. Securities & Exchange Commission (SEC) asked Spring Street Brewery to delay its stock sale until regulatory officials could complete their study and issue company-specific guidelines for the sale. Since then Klein has received over 400 telephone calls from companies seeking to carry out their own online IPOs.

Klein decided on the Internet option after realizing that small- and medium-sized companies often encounter difficulties in attracting investor interest. In most cases, the only method for such companies is to publish an offering with the National Quotation Bureau on a pink sheet, but, as Klein points out, "Stocks on those sheets don't trade very much." To assist potential investors, Spring Street also established a Web page containing information for brokers and purchasers: http://plaza.interport.net/witbeer/new_page/.

Being early to market has also allowed several companies with popular Web sites to test profit models. For example, in the first quarter of 1996, Infoseek, maker of a popular Web search engine, reportedly generated more than $3.1 million in advertising revenue on its Internet site. Similarly, Pointcast, which allows users to custom configure a stock quotation tickertape as a screensaver has reputedly achieved significant advertiser revenues. Advertising sponsors are an integral part of the screensaver; they are more creative and alluring because Pointcast has looked beyond the Internet browser and built their service to distribute via a customized interface.

In the case of Seattle-based Amazon.com, the medium itself is an advertisement. This virtual bookstore offers more than 1.1 million titles as well as innovative customer services. The company has been the object of much discussion and commentary and was profiled in the *Wall Street Journal,* as well as several other publications.

At VeriFone, Inc., a California-based firm manufacturing Internet payment software, the management realized that its best opportunity lay in filling the gap between vendors seeking to sell goods on the Internet and customers worried about giving out their credit card numbers online. VeriFone has extensive experience in traditional credit card processing through its in-store hardware and software. In conjunction with Netscape Web browser and software manufacturer Oracle, VeriFone developed a product suite for secure electronic transactions, encompassing a wallet of electronic money for end users, point-of-sale software for merchants, and back-end applications for use by banks and transaction processors.

Experts have hailed the VeriFone software as a milestone on the road to widespread electronic commerce. Some analysts believe that online shopping could account for 10 percent of all retail business by the end of the 1990s. "This is where electronic commerce will take off," notes Jim Bidzos, president of RSA Data Security, Inc., a California-based maker of data-encryption software. "It is an extension of the physical world's financial network, and that's why it's so important."

THE BENEFITS OF ARRIVING EARLY

While the businesses examined here vary widely in their size, mission, and long-term objectives, there is a common thread. They began early. The principal advantages of experimenting early with a strategic approach include:

- Ability to establish installed customer base early to gain considerable market share.

- Opportunity to develop and test profit models.

- Involvement with standards groups to drive products.

- Establishment of early alignments with optimal business partners in advance of competitors.

- Development of new relationships with customers by offering new solutions.

- Receiving favorable industry and customer press by being early to market.

- Opportunity to develop commerce's infrastructure.

- Tracking customers' daily business and personal practices.

- Learning from various business designs.

- Ability to restructure your organization for operation within new models of business.

- Refining your value proposition to customers.

- Managing both the physical world's value chain and that of the virtual marketplace.

Jim Manzi, the chief executive of Industry.Net, a product information service, and the former chief executive of Lotus Development Corp., notes, "The game right now on the Web is about rapid customer acquisition and getting people familiar with the services you provide, getting them habituated to your service."[1]

PROFITING FROM THE LEVEL PLAYING FIELD

The Internet serves as a level playing field; in cyberspace, a business with substantial resources may not necessarily have an appreciable advantage over a smaller company. Moreover, the Internet can act as a façade: the Web site of a small start-up company can be every bit as grand as the Web site of a multinational corporation or industry leader.

Notwithstanding this leveling effect, money can play a crucial role, for the companies receiving the most hits (i.e., user activity) are often those willing to spend on marketing efforts.

The experience of Sausage Software, a Doncaster, Australia-based maker of software for Internet programming, is a case in point of a level playing field. In June 1995, the founder and president, 22-year-old Steve Outtrim, decided to establish a home page on the Internet. After trying out several programs, Outtrim decided to create a more user-friendly software package. The resulting effort, dubbed HotDog, was developed in only five days.

Outtrim then used the Internet to gain valuable testing experience. He posted a casual notice on an Internet newsgroup for anyone interested in receiving an advance copy of HotDog. Within three days, 150 people in 26 countries were helping Outtrim test the product and identify problems and areas for improvement. After five weeks, more than 800 people were using HotDog.

Sausage Software used the Internet as its forum for selling the software. On June 29, 1995, the first version of HotDog was officially released for sale. Within five months of its launch, more than 12,000 copies of HotDog were sold; and orders streamed in at an increasing rate. While all of Sausage Software's sales efforts are currently conducted on the Internet, the company plans to shift some advertising to the physical world as well.

The results are impressive. Sausage Software grew from one employee in June 1995 to over 50 employees by May 1996, and adds new staff members at the rate of about three per week. Its forecasted revenue in the first year of operation is $5 million (Australian), with a net profit before tax of $1.5 million.

Moreover, Sausage Software's business is truly international. Over 98 percent of its sales are exports, and HotDog is employed in over 80 countries. Users include IBM, NASA, Coca-Cola, the U.S. Navy, and the Reserve Bank of Australia.

Outtrim believes the success of Sausage Software is a testimonial to the virtues of the Internet. His company can move faster, change direction more nimbly, and launch responses more quickly than its larger competitors.

There is a synergistic effect as well. By posting a notice on the Internet, Outtrim virtually guaranteed that news of his product would be spread from user to user. "Most effective is word of mouth on the Internet," notes Outtrim. "That amounts to one person telling 50 million people. There hasn't been much evidence up to now [that a smaller business can compete on a level playing field], but I'm living proof that it's possible, and I don't believe that I'm especially brilliant or unique.

"Large companies like Microsoft often are unable, because of their size, to act on ideas quickly," he adds. "The ability to act quickly is, I believe, one of Sausage Software's greatest strengths. To this end, I encourage a business structure and environment of chaotic anarchy that allows employees to be innovative and for the company to develop new creative products."

On the opposite end of the spectrum from Sausage Software is General Electric Plastics (GE Plastics), the second- or third-largest chemical company in the country. GE Plastics has roughly 30,000 customers consisting of manufacturing end users as well as original equipment manufacturers.

In October 1994, long before any large non-information-technology (non-IT) business considered the Internet a tool for experimental marketing, GE Plastics began to mine its customer base for data. Under the direction of Rick Pocock, the general manager of marketing communications, the company began soliciting information on the attributes their customers most valued.

GE Plastics found that its customers needed updated, accurate, and continually available technical information concerning the physical and behavioral characteristics of the company's polymers. As a result, GE Plastics began developing an Internet solution for providing customers access to its library of research data. The results: thousands of customers now use the data as part of their daily business practices, reducing GE Plastics' distribution costs, improving the level of customer service, and building customer allegiance. Special software helps customers identify the plastics for their needs.

In this case study, GE Plastics *mitigated* the effects of the level playing field by exploiting a resource not shared by its competitors: a rich database of product information. The company leveraged the advantages of the Internet—wide dissemination, ease of information retrieval, and user-friendliness—to assert a competitive advantage.

PREDICTING THE UNPREDICTABLE

We cannot predict very well where technology will lead, but we can study the lessons of the past in order to make maximal use of opportunities. The major innovations that reshape our lives generally occur decades after the fundamental technology is invented and come about as a result of a partnership between the technology and business communities.

More important, the gap between invention and exploitation can be large. Moveable type was invented by Gutenberg in the 1440s and the first Bible printed in 1456. But the impact was small; Gutenberg saw his invention only as an instrument for spreading the word of God. It was not until almost 50 years later that the enabling aspect of the technology was realized, and the first modern book was published in 1501. Similarly, it was not until the steam engine, invented in the 1760s, was put to work powering looms, ships, and trains that its true significance was appreciated.

So too with the Internet, in existence since the late 1960s but ripening into an accessible technology only in the last several years. From its inception as a tool to link defense-technology researchers it has grown into a worldwide force, changing not only the ways we communicate and do business but also how we *think* about communication and business.

As editors Alan M. Webber and William C. Taylor noted in the editorial of the premiere issue of *Fast Company:*

> A global revolution is changing business, and business is changing the world. With unsettling speed, two forces are converging; a new generation of business leaders is rewriting the rules of business, and a new breed of fast companies is challenging the corporate status quo. That convergence overturns 50 years of conceived wisdom on the fundamentals of work and competition. No part of business is immune. The structure of a company is changing; relationships between companies are changing; the nature of work is changing; the definition of success is changing. The result is a revolution as far-reaching as the Industrial Revolution. This much we know: We live

and work in a time of unparalleled opportunity and unprecedented uncertainty. An economy driven by technology and innovation makes old borders obsolete.[2]

UNDERSTANDING MANAGEMENT'S NEW CHALLENGE

In his essay *The Coming of the New Organization*, management theorist Peter Drucker notes that it is simple to state that information technology is transforming business; it is knowing what this transformation will require of companies and their managers that is hard to decipher. The capacity to expand a business's limits far outstrips the capacity of its management to explore the new opportunities presented.[3] The Internet compounds this.

The Internet does not wait for any company to prepare its strategy, nor does it belong to a particular company, industry, or country. Its impact on business can threaten traditional strongholds while creating opportunities for entrepreneurial leaders. As Internet-related technologies enable and influence new business, marketing, and systems operation assumptions, the business manager's challenge is sifting through the multiplicity of opportunities and pursuing those with the greatest chance for success. The twenty-first century will require radical new ways of doing business. Organizations and their staffs must be flexible. Teamwork will become imperative. Visualization of goals and processes will be an essential tool.

These new ways of doing business are essential because management's challenge is evolving rapidly. "Everything we know to be true about the Internet will be proven wrong over the next five years," says John Warnock, co-founder of Adobe Systems, Inc., which manufactures desktop publishing software. So how does one manage decision-making—especially Internet decision-making—in an environment of rapid upheaval and change? While much of what we hold to be true today may eventually be surpassed or even proved false, successful strategies focus on the customer and on developing a more complete solution addressing new needs and interests.

For example, Internet telephony is a service that enables customers to conduct worldwide voice communications via the Internet for the cost of a local Internet connection (typically about $20 per month in the United States). This technology is prompting non-telecommunications companies to enter the voice communications field. In March 1996, CompuServe, Inc., an Internet service provider, announced that it will allow subscribers to its online service to make free telephone calls via the Internet. IBM plans to introduce a new Internet telephony product and sponsor a consortium to solve the interoperability problems that have limited existing voice communications services. In addition, IBM's new personal computer models will be preloaded with Internet telephony capability and made secure by encryption technology. It may soon be possible to use a single telephone line to check e-mail and conduct voice communications at the same time.

Not surprisingly, the effort by computer software firms (such as Netscape), hardware manufacturers, and service companies to enter the telephony field arouses the concern of the traditional telecommunications industry. America's Carriers Telecommunication Association (ACTA), a consortium of 130 small- and medium-sized telecommunications companies, is petitioning the Federal Communications Commission (FCC) to bar voice communications over the Internet. ACTA believes use of the Internet for telephony is unfair, because the companies providing the software and services are not subject to the regulations governing communications firms. Specifically, computer service companies are not currently required to pay access charges to local telephone service providers, as do long-distance companies to the Baby Bells. Nor do software and service providers pay into the Universal Service Fund, which guarantees service to unprofitable rural and underserved areas.

The situation raises a number of telling questions. Against whom should ACTA be competing? Can the FCC regulate the telephony activities of software providers even though its regulatory mandate does not extend to software? How can regulation comport with the Telecommunications Act of 1996, which states that the official policy of the United States is to leave the Internet "unfettered by federal or state regulations"?

Another case in which the capabilities of the Internet challenge traditional assumptions, definitions, and regulations is that of the Internet Underground Music Archive, run by the University of Nevada. This Internet service allowed new and little-known artists to post digital audio tracks and provided an environment for musicians to promote and distribute their work free of the requirements of a record contract. Musicians could test consumers' reaction to their work, build an audience, and distribute products, entirely bypassing record companies.

However, the posting of sheet music on the Internet site posed potential copyright infringement and, faced with the prospect of legal action, the University of Nevada closed the site.

A discussion of the legal issues surrounding Internet-based business is in Chapter 9.

RESPECTING THE INTERNET FROM A STRATEGIC BUSINESS PERSPECTIVE

To better understand this new environment from a strategic business perspective, we must seek a deeper perspective of business integration. The Internet is, quite simply, both an enabling tool for business and a new business environment. Throughout this book, consider the following observations:

- The Internet is the most global, borderless, cost-effective, and open business application and communication infrastructure.

- The openness and platform independence of the Internet make it the most efficient application development environment today.

- Interactions and relationships between businesses and their customers are fundamentally different on the Internet.

- The Internet creates new business, systems, marketing, governmental, legal, societal, and customer models. Most are unexplored, even by business leaders and visionaries.

- A new value proposition must be developed by businesses, given the capacity to discover and monitor customers' habits, needs, and expectations.

- With the worldwide capabilities of the Internet, customers have more options than ever before.

- No one owns the Internet; it is driven simply by whomever creates the most valued tools for navigating its complexities and responding to customer priorities. Businesses that do not embrace it with a clear strategic intent and innovative products and services will find themselves in a precarious position.

WHERE THE INTRANET FITS INTO THE STRATEGY

The business uses of the Internet have been portrayed as split into two categories: general public use (Internet) and internal employee use (Intranet). In reality, the technologies are the same; the only real difference is the level of access. The term *Intranet* is used for an internal business communications network whereby an employee can access internal information sources (e.g., benefit applications, human resources data, executive information system/decision support systems).

The growth of Intranets is expected to increase—surpassing that of the Internet—over the next several years as companies recognize the benefits of an internal communications network. Once an Intranet's infrastructure is developed, additional applications may be implemented with relatively low incremental cost. Vendors of information technology are responding by providing integrated Intranet solutions. For example, Silicon Graphics developed a product called Intranet in a Box, while Microsoft, Digital Equipment Corp., and MCI formed a business alliance to develop software and hardware for the rapid deployment of Intranets. Similarly, Netscape and General Electric Information Systems formed a joint venture to provide Intranet solutions that are outsourced and capable of customization.

It is useful to remember that the Intranet and the Internet share fundamental technologies. A company establishing an Intranet can use it to provide employees with hands-on experience before developing its Internet strategy. Thus integrated thinking is needed.

YOUR COMPETITION AND HELP ARE WORLDWIDE

The rules of success within a country were traditionally related to natural resources, size, transportation routes, and location. Today, with the evolution of the Internet, countries can prosper by leveraging their capabilities. As Kenichi Ohmae notes in his work *The Borderless World: Power and Strategy in the Interlinked Economy,* "If you look at the prosperous nations today—Switzerland, Singapore, Taiwan, South Korea, Japan—they are characterized by small land mass, no natural resources, and well-educated, hard-working people who have all the ambition to participate in the global economy. Having an abundance of resources has truly slowed down a country's development, because bureaucrats think that money can solve all problems. In a truly interlinked, global economy, the key success factor shifts from resources to the marketplace."[4]

The Internet throws a global cast onto every aspect of your business: operations, services, customer base, and competition. But there is also a big plus: your avenues of assistance, partnership, and cooperation are also worldwide. If it is more difficult to compete in today's business environment, there is a concomitant increase in the ability to meet those challenges through innovative solutions.

Distinct differences exist between countries regarding the level of understanding and appreciation of the Internet and its related technologies. For example, many Australian business executives are able to articulate their visions of how business will change with the Internet. In contrast, the Internet is still regarded as exotic or unwelcome in many quarters of the U.S. business community.

Why the disparity? Traditionally, Australia, with a population of 19 million, has been quick to adopt new technologies. The rate of adoption of the videocassette recorder, mobile telephone, automatic teller machines, and other innovations has been much greater than in the United States. Over one million cellular telephones were purchased in Australia in December 1995.

The introduction of the Internet is no exception to this trend. Since 1995, when Australia's national telecommunications company, Telstra, purchased the academic network that administered the Internet, over one million users have registered. In 1995 the number of users doubled every eight months, according to local experts Brenda Aynsley and Richard Cousins. Today Australia has the highest per-capita use of the Internet in the world. A nationwide television show called "http://" explores a range of Internet issues each week.

In Asia, fundamental societal drivers may place some countries at a distinct competitive advantage. Nearly every country in Asia is removing the bureaucratic barriers that might impede progress toward an Internet-integrated future. In some nations, such as the People's Republic of China, the lack of an existing telecommunications infrastructure provides the opportunity to proceed directly to state-of-the-art wireless systems without the encumbrance of an installed base of technology.

Meanwhile, the U.S. government may be creating more barriers than it removes. Cold War-era bans on the export of encryption technology put American software companies at a competitive disadvantage. Other countries fill the gap by providing services and operating standards to conduct secured electronic commerce, and the United States may find itself a follower rather than a leader in this field.

An analysis of the Internet in Europe published in *Inc. Technology*[5] magazine in 1996 recognized that many European businesses may be well behind those of the United States in terms of adoption, by both customers and the businesses themselves. This appears to be largely due to the current state of telecommunications regulation. After European Union-mandated deregulation takes effect in 1998, operating monopolies will be dissolved and, in theory, lower prices will spur investment in Internet projects. However, other barriers may continue to exist. Some countries are impairing the commercial adoption of the Internet by requiring businesses to register their encryption keys with the central government.

Medium-sized businesses in Europe often share the cost of investing in the Internet by working together on regional projects. While sharing keeps costs down, the practice may result in a less-flexible and less-customizable approach, which is key in a business's attempt to differentiate itself from its competitors.

American companies are more willing to gamble on high-tech benefits, notes Marc-Andre Schenk, a scholar at the University of Lausanne. Technology integration specialist Giovanni Tadei observes, "Many European home pages are just a good repackaging of catalogs...or they're facts and figures...or annual reports. The paradox is that they have all of the costs of being online and none of the benefits. Many European companies put more effort into talking about their online presence than in improving it. They distribute printed press releases to announce they are on the Web, but they don't do active marketing, selling, or customer support online. While Americans try to anticipate and push new markets, European businesses wait for them...even though they're often aware of a market's potential."

WHERE IS YOUR INDUSTRY GOING?

Businesses and industries must continually redefine their positions in the marketplace and determine where their priorities, values, and interests are migrating. As customers increasingly expect value and more complete solutions, interindustry repositioning will become even more important. For example, Eric Roach of Lombard Institutional Investors says that when people ask him if he is in the brokerage business or the technology business, he replies, "What's the difference?" He must be able to offer high-tech solutions built for customers irrespective of his label.

Consider the following observation made by business scholars Victor Miller and Michael Porter:

> The information revolution is affecting companies in three vital ways—
>
> 1. It changes industry structure, and, in so doing, alters the rules of competition.
> 2. It creates competitive advantage by giving companies new ways to outperform their rivals.
> 3. It spawns whole new businesses, often from within the company's existing operations.[6]

Is Microsoft in the software business, the financial services business, the publishing business, or the entertainment business? At the present, it appears that it is in all of these fields. Is Oracle, the maker of one of the leading database products for corporate applications, in the software or the hardware business? It has invested considerable resources in building hardware to be used specifically for Internet functions.

The wave of interindustry alignments will produce interesting results. Telecommunications companies are moving into the fields of Internet connectivity, Web page hosting services, and pay-per-view entertainment. Cable television companies are moving from content to telecommunications services. Where will the two industries cross paths?

Consider also the challenges the Internet poses to manufacturers and retailers. For decades, manufacturers have used retailers as a means to distribute their products to the end user. Most manufacturers found it inefficient to develop a worldwide retail presence. Now, through the use of electronic shopping malls and Internet store fronts, manufacturers have a direct sales channel to the customer and can bypass the traditional wholesale and retail actors. For retailers, the Internet offers a new path that navigates between the traditional walk-in customer and mail-order sales.

But enthusiasm is no substitute for careful planning. Business literature abounds with case histories of companies rushing to invest in the Internet without a clear vision of what they will do with the new technology. These companies fail to understand the Internet's effects on their business models, systems, manufacturing, and sales. They do not recognize that the Internet changes not only the *method* of doing business but also forces management to answer the question of what business it is in—or should be in.

To prepare for the global realignment of industries and services, the prudent company identifies its optimal business partners and incorporates the concepts of the virtual company so as to identify and quickly seize upon new opportunities. As Kenichi Ohmae notes in *The Borderless World*, business leaders must learn what politicians and diplomats have always known:

> "In a complex, uncertain world filled with dangerous opponents, it is best not to go it alone...Globalization mandates alliances; it makes them absolutely essential to strategy."[7]

All of this depends on creative leadership. Warren Bemis, a noted authority on leadership, suggests that leaders can be defined as people with two characteristics: knowledge of where they want to go and the ability to articulate and integrate their vision into their organization. A leader must recognize where a new model will lead and prepare the organization and its staff to meet the challenge of the new destination. Early action is imperative; the recalcitrant leader will find that the luxury of defining a new path or business is gone—for it has already been set out by competitors.

NOTES

1. Booker, Ellis, "Manzi's Game Plan for Winning Web: Hurry Up Offense," *Web Week* (18 July 1996).

2. Webber, Alan M. and William C. Taylor, "Handbook of the Business Revolution," *Fast Company* 1:8.

3. Drucker, Peter F., "The Coming of the New Organization," *Harvard Business Review* (January–February 1988).

4. Ohmae, Kenichi, *The Borderless World: Power and Strategy in the Interlinked Economy*. (New York: Harper Collins Publishers, 1991).

5. Giussani, Bruno, "Why Europe Lags on the Web," *Inc. Technology* 4(1995):23.

6. Porter, Michael E. and Victor E. Millar, "How Information Gives You Competitive Advantage," *Harvard Business Review* (July-August 1985):228.

7. Ohmae, 114.

CHAPTER 2

REDISCOVERING YOUR CUSTOMER: SERVING EXISTING NEEDS AND PREDICTING NEW ONES

Ultimately, your customer has the power to determine your business success. The crucial element of a successful Internet strategy is anticipating the Internet's impact on customer habits, decision-making patterns, needs, interests, and expectations. Once you know what the customer values, it is possible to define your virtual-based value proposition. Of course, current and prospective customers' values may change over time, so you must be ready to reinterpret data and adapt your strategy to new realities.

Your goals, then, as the Internet strategist are to: (1) anticipate your current and prospective Internet customers' new values; (2) continually develop new and innovative products and services based on those values and capitalize on the new communication capabilities of the Internet; and (3) define an acceptable value proposition with regard to the customer's values and your new solution. This chapter discusses each of these three points in detail.

RECOGNIZING YOUR CUSTOMERS ARE ON THEIR WAY

As the Internet becomes easier to use and to access through television, cable systems, and specialized computers, the pace of adoption by mainstream consumers will increase dramatically in the next year or two. In addition, it is becoming easier than ever to reach *business* customers through Intranets and local area networks (LANs) offering outside access. More and more, your customers' daily practices will be accomplished through complementary online solutions.

The savvy strategist will not be sidetracked by the specific metrics of the Internet customer base. As one business leader notes, "Focusing on the number of Internet users is like debating which way the wind is blowing immediately before a hurricane." The point is that the hurricane has arrived; lavishing time and attention on discovering exactly who uses the Internet, and when, is technically impracticable and counterproductive.

Nonetheless, several industry consortia and businesses have attempted to measure the Internet's worldwide customer base. According to the A.C. Nielsen Company, several million users periodically "disappear," only to reappear months or years later. Depending on the date of measurement and the methodology used, there appear to be anywhere from 16 million users to 33 million users in the United States.[1]

The absolute number of users does not matter. What matters to you is identifying which of those users are—or could be—*your* customers, and working from the premise that the number of your customers with Internet access will continue to grow rapidly.

The technology, business, and regulatory drivers and investments worldwide will ensure that over the next few years access to the Internet and other interactive services via personal or network computer, television, pager, and high-tech telephone will become ubiquitous and so convenient that customers will integrate them with their daily business practices. Some estimates suggest that more than 200 million people will obtain access to the Internet worldwide over the next few years. With the rollout of high-speed cable and other telecommunications services by the end of the 1990s, the range of possibilities will be far greater than it is today.

New customers will be global, free to search for options and information unfettered by physical proximity, and will continue to develop new interests and expectations.

You, as Internet strategists, business executives, and management consultants, should be focused on determining how customers will make your valued solution part of their daily practice. Consumers are turning away from their television sets and switching on their computers. Surveys find people are going online to obtain information and functionality rather than entertainment. One study found that 58 percent of online users cut back significantly on their TV viewing. Consumers with access to the Internet typically spend 40 to 45 hours per month online, while subscribers to online services spend five to seven hours per month.

PREDICTING YOUR INTERNET CUSTOMERS' NEEDS

With the capabilities of the Internet, customers develop new priorities and expectations. Successful Internet strategies anticipate and address them.

For example, Amazon.com, one of the first and largest virtual bookstores on the Internet, noticed that it had many more repeat customers than anticipated. Most of the features Amazon.com offers were developed as a result of recommendations from existing customers, which might explain their loyalty.

Amazon.com's strategic focus was not on the specific number of customers on the Internet. Rather, the company focused on specific customer values, obtained through analysis of its customers' habits, buying decisions, and feedback. The company gets so much feedback and so many recommendations via e-mail that it can monitor and respond to what customers are thinking almost immediately. Indeed, Amazon.com believes that it gets more feedback in one day than a traditional bookstore might get in a year.

THE INTERNAL AND THE EXTERNAL CUSTOMER

Before attempting to anticipate specific values, it is helpful to clarify the definition of the Internet customer. Traditionally, when a business developed applications for its users, the intended audience was made up of people *within* the company. Typical applications included decision support, order entry, and general ledger systems.

With the Internet, however, there are both internal and external users. Compared with internal users, who are likely to be familiar with the workings of the business and its structure, external users expect applications to be more intuitive and localized.

THE TEN VALUES OF THE INTERNET CUSTOMER

Let's look at specific values that successful Internet strategies incorporate. As one works through this analysis, it is important to understand how these new values differ from old values, and how the new values can be addressed in an effective and efficient manner with the Internet. The ten values we will examine are:

1. convenience
2. transparency
3. guaranteed fulfillment
4. security
5. education
6. personalization
7. proactivity
8. timeliness
9. choice
10. interaction

Convenience. Our increasingly busy lives suggest that convenience will continue to be a prized quality in our business and personal transactions. Simplicity in presentation is key; studies suggest that graphically rich Internet sites do not generate as much revenue as sites with plainer layouts that are perceived to be more convenient.

American Express allows cardholders to purchase Travelers' Cheques and Gift Cheques via ExpressNet, the company's online information and travel service via America Online. With Express-Net, customers can obtain the products and information they need when they need it, in a format amenable to their lifestyles. Card-members may take advantage of special travel, retail, restaurant, and entertainment offers as well as shop for merchandise through ExpressNet Shopping. Airline reservations may be obtained through Express Reservations, an easy-to-use service that stores personal and business travel profiles so that information need not be collected every time a customer places an order or visits the site. Clearly, online services allow companies to offer convenience, instant gratification, and guaranteed fulfillment.

Transparency. Online customers may value a high degree of transparency—that is, the ability of a user to migrate from one Internet site to another almost without realizing it. A business seeking to provide value-added services should examine its ability to offer links to complementary Internet sites. For example, a real estate concern would likely seek to provide links to a mortgage broker, an insurer, and a title search company.

Guaranteed fulfillment. Customers will increasingly rely on technology to fulfill their needs. Guaranteed fulfillment is closely aligned with immediate satisfaction and, often, immediate gratification. In considering this attribute, it is useful to look to demographics: The generation now entering the workforce (people born in the 1970s and termed Generation X) grew up in a technologically rich environment heavily influenced by television. Such customers may demand instant gratification and instant fulfillment.

Security. Security of electronic transactions is of extremely high value to the customer. According to Open Market, a software company based in Cambridge, Massachusetts, and a leading vendor of high-end Internet software products, this fear leads electronic shoppers to do more looking than buying. Data suggest that fewer than 10 percent of Internet users actually purchase goods through the Internet. If electronic commerce is to become a fixture of the global economy, Internet users must have confidence in the integrity and privacy of their transactions.

Advances in security continue to be made. For example, one element of security is customer authentication (i.e., proof of identity). VeriSign, a northern California company, provides digital IDs to Netscape Navigator 3.0 customers who register and download the VeriSign software over the Internet. VeriSign issues personal digital IDs for Web and e-mail users who accurately identify themselves online. This cryptographic technique assures the authenticity of users during electronic transactions. VeriSign issues the ID and a third party performs a background check according to the ID's level of assurance. Basically, the more information to which the customer is privy, the greater the need for authentication.[2]

Netscape has developed a wallet interface for electronic purchases of goods and services. The wallet includes credit cards, cybercash, and other features. Security needs are addressed in greater detail in Chapter 7.

Education. Abundant evidence suggests that the educational element of an Internet site is a key element to its success. Consider the GE Plastics public Internet site discussed in Chapter 1. This site is a valuable resource for the manufacturing engineer, and the accessibility of the site ensures that customers incorporate it into their daily business practices. Similarly, Lombard Brokerage Inc., also discussed in Chapter 1, provides investors with educational tools over the Internet. Doing so assists customers in making informed decisions about their investments.

Personalization. The ability to individualize your Internet presence for your customers, business partners, vendors, and even employees will become increasingly important in the future.

Using the Java programming language, which provides a rich set of functions for Internet applications, Lombard Brokerage Inc. is developing Java applets (i.e., special programs designed for Internet computing) to provide its customers with alert management systems. A customer will be able to call up graphs on a computer screen and set individualized trading thresholds. Thus, when a given stock reaches the predetermined buy or sell price, a message will be sent automatically to Lombard with instructions to carry out the designated transaction. The small investor will have the computer trading ability that was once the domain of only the largest and most powerful investors.[3]

Proactivity. The ability to move beyond meeting customer needs to actually *anticipating* those needs is the hallmark of a company striving to meet the challenges of a competitive market. The Internet makes proactivity easier. For example, floral delivery services can maintain key customers' information in their databases (e.g., birthdays, anniversaries, holidays) and send reminder messages via e-mail in advance.

Proactive solutions can also embody a high degree of transparency. For example, Cisco Systems, a network equipment manufacturer based in San Jose, offers hardware products that dial in to the company's support engineers if a predetermined threshold of errors is reached. Engineers then attempt to solve the problem online.

Timeliness. A business maxim states, "Make them wait once, lose them forever." The importance of a timely response to customer inquiries cannot be overstated. ONYX Software, discussed in Chapter 1, can contact a potential customer while that customer is still browsing on the company's Web site. The swiftness of response generates goodwill and, more important, gives ONYX a competitive edge.

Timeliness was prized by consumers long before the advent of the Internet—witness the popularity of one-hour eyeglass stores, home pizza delivery, and 24-hour shipment of custom-configured computers. With the Internet's ability to link customers to a company's internal systems and perform routine tasks such as order processing and inventory searching, customers receive better service in less time.

Choice. With access to products and services from around the globe, today's customer is choosier than ever. The Internet allows a customer to collect and assess large quantities of information about specific products and services, allowing a degree of comparison shopping previously unknown. Products such as Topic Agent from Verity automate the process of searching for products, playing into the values of convenience, timeliness, and choice.

Interaction. A customer's most valued Internet-based social experience may be with other people by computer. It is reported that a substantial part of the revenues of America Online, one of the largest U.S. online service providers, comes from users who seek to communicate with others through real-time chat rooms. This social interaction should be considered a model of doing business.

Companies such as RTIME, a Seattle-based software firm specializing in Internet-based real-time applications, are enabling the

Internet to provide hundreds or thousands of users simultaneously with the ability to communicate in a real-time environment. RTIME's software tool set allows other software makers to use the Internet to coordinate the actions of thousands of users. While RTIME initially targeted its products at game developers, it represents an interesting potential for products, service, and solutions for the future. For example, shoppers could learn from consumers who have used a particular product.

Businesses can profit from the ability to bring customers together, creating visible icons and expanding on specific communities of interest. For example, REI, the Seattle-based outdoor equipment company, sees the Internet as a mechanism for bringing like-minded consumers together to discuss outdoor activities. REI views this as a natural part of its Internet business strategy, as its customer profile indicates that the potential buyer of outdoor equipment places a high value on expert opinion and real-life anecdotes. REI is a customer-conglomerate, owned by the customers themselves, bringing people together is a logical extension of its heritage.

Table 2.1 *New Customer Values*

Expectations	Description
Convenience	With increased work hours, and less free time, customers highly value convenience.
Transparency	The customer shouldn't have to be bothered with the details of how the end product, service, or solution is achieved. Effective interlinking of business and industry solutions and sites becomes essential to achieve complete transparency. Successful strategies anticipate customer buying scenarios.
	Customers seek intuitive and comfortable interfaces. The design of the business customer interface will become more critical as it begins to incorporate elements of convenience, transparency, and individualization.

(continued)

Table 2.1 (*continued*)

Expectations	Description
Guaranteed Fulfillment	Customers will increasingly rely on technology to fulfill their needs online. Complete and guaranteed fulfillment online will be expected.
Security	Customers will require and rely on more secure communication systems. Because of the amount of information that can be collected by businesses, customers will do business with companies that meet their priority of high security. Many elements to security are explored in Chapter 7.
Education	Customers value concise, relevant, timely, and well-presented information that informs them so that they feel more comfortable with their buying decisions. Empirical evidence suggests that the education content of various Internet sites is a key element of success. Businesses have already begun to offer value through the ability to access more interactive information on the Internet about their product or service.
Personalization	Most people value their individualism and will demand products and services that respect this priority.
Proactivity	Individuals will respect solutions (services and products) that proactively market, upgrade, support, and operate themselves. Lombard and flower companies have begun to develop products and services with this in mind.
Timeliness	Timely response and delivery of the product or service becomes increasingly important. Updated and immediate information becomes essential.

(continued)

Table 2.1 *(continued)*

Expectations	Description
Choice	Customers increasingly demand more options and product diversity.
Interaction	Initial evidence suggests that interaction (particularly in a community of interest) provides high value to customers.

ASKING THE RIGHT QUESTIONS

Once you understand the importance of predicting and fully exploring your customers' values, ask yourself a series of questions in order to conceptualize what your Internet-based products and services should look like.

As noted in Chapter 1, GE Plastics examined its customer base and found that users of its products had become more sophisticated about and comfortable with technology over the years. The company asked itself what its customers' priorities were and how GE Plastics could help. The potential customer base was limited by the number of trained plastics engineers in the marketplace. Since GE Plastics could not increase the number of trained people at businesses in the traditional sense, it explored ways to increase the productivity of existing engineers.

GE Plastics compiled its product information library online, encompassing thousands of research papers. However, in 1994, few customers had access to the Internet. So, GE Plastics considered how it could bring its database to its customers. By working with a small Seattle Internet browser company, Spry Communications, it developed a method for its customers to access the Internet and, in particular, the GE Plastics site. GE has now introduced education on plastics and vocational training to help its customers grow.

GE Plastics illustrates a few of the critical questions asked by successful Internet strategists. Effective management in this borderless environment requires the businessperson to pay special attention to delivering value to customers. Before everything else comes the need to see your customers clearly. Only they can provide the clues to your successful Internet strategy. The most important questions you need to ask are:

- What is the complete solution my customers seek?

- What will be my customers' new values, needs, priorities, and expectations?

- What customer values are not currently being served well by my Internet solutions?

- Are my current business and technology systems flexible enough to respond to changes?

- For what types of customers can my company offer value-added solutions?

- What interlinking business partners should my company consider in order to develop a more thorough solution for customers?

- How well does my business understand the capabilities of the Internet from a customer interaction perspective?

- Is my business able to extend and take advantage of existing information assets in order to address changing customer priorities?

The answers to these questions are likely to change over time. However, one element of business success is your ability to answer them more quickly through each new business design cycle. The more promptly you can prepare your company and understand what questions need to be continually addressed, the better positioned your business will be.

CREATING THE VIRTUAL PRODUCT

The Internet provides new ways to communicate with the customer on both content and functionality levels. Content can be presented in several formats: text, two-dimensional graphics, three-dimensional depictions, audio, and video. More important, the *assembly* of content can be personalized, generated from user-provided information, and gleaned from analyses of customer data.

In many respects these new technologies, in the aggregate, are capable of creating a new type of product—the virtual product that can meet rising customer expectations. An effective virtual product exists even *before* it is produced.

The ideal virtual product or service is one that is produced instantaneously and customized or personalized in response to customer demand. Businesses must have flexible systems to produce virtual products. For example, IBM's infoSage Information Service delivers information that is individually tailored to the customer's needs. A customer joining the service creates a profile, indicating his or her specific areas of interest. From that point on, infoSage scans a vast array of information resources to find items of relevance to that customer. The information is then delivered as a personalized newsletter twice each day via e-mail or a personalized web site.

PUSH-AND-PULL COMMUNICATION CAPABILITY

Another important concern in the business/customer Internet relationship is the push-and-pull communication capability. Information is pulled by the customer or pushed by businesses.

For example, in the customer-pull scenario, a subscriber to an Internet-based newspaper can pull information that is of interest for downloading and/or printing. The choice of whether or not to pull is entirely up to the customer.

In the push scenario, the same individual receives updates or alerts as conditions predefined by that customer—such as stock price or trading volume—occur. Lombard Brokerage Inc. pushes quotations. IBM's infoSage pushes e-mail to customers when it finds news stories that match the interests listed in individual preference profiles.

Pointcast applies many of these capabilities. It exploits its assets by making a vast amount of information available to customers. This includes the push/pull paradigm as the interface becomes integrated into the customer's screen, independent of the application being used. The tickertape is personalized by the customer and is continually and dynamically updated.

MONITORING AND RESPONDING TO CUSTOMERS' DESIRES AND VALUES

In the traditional communication model, content is marketed in a broadcast or multicast mechanism to consumers via one business. The new communication paradigm based on the Internet is different in two fundamental ways. First, businesses can unicast information to consumers; a business can conduct one-on-one marketing, product delivery, and client service. Second, consumers themselves can more easily provide content or information to businesses or other consumers.

As companies gather, synthesize, and distribute information, they have the opportunity to better monitor and respond to customers' desires and values. The Internet search engines now available, such as Excite, InfoSeek, and Yahoo, have the potential to rewrite the old model of reaching customers. A user query for information about golf might trigger an ad for a Web golf resource on the page that is returned. A search for travel information could cue an advertisement for an airline, resort, or travel agency. In addition, a search engine can provide its advertisers with information about what each person who sees a particular advertisement does after seeing it and with details of the person's Internet navigation habits.

Consider the example of Cathay Pacific Airlines. The Hong Kong-based international carrier began advertising on InfoSeek in August 1995, eight months after activating its Web page. Today more than half of Cathay Pacific's registered visitors are referred through InfoSeek click-throughs (visitors who select the advertisement on the InfoSeek screen).

Cathay Pacific ran an advertisement that read, "Win 1,000,000 Miles" and succeeded in capturing attention. The company states that impressions (those who saw the ad) exceeded one million per month over a three-month period. On an average day, the number of click-throughs to the Cathay Pacific site was about 3.2 percent of the people who saw the ad—a good response compared to that obtained from mass mailings. Cathay Pacific reserved space on the result pages so the ad would appear when certain keywords were typed in, such as *vacation*, *tour*, *airline*, and *weather*. The keyword placements generated a much higher percentage of click-throughs, as high as 15 percent.[4] DealerNet, the first automotive group to sell and market on the Internet, currently receives a consistent 8 percent click-through rate on words such as *cars* and *autos*.

Table 2.2 summarizes the capabilities of the Internet as they relate to customer interactions. Which can you exploit in the development of new products and services? Will your customers value them?

Table 2.2 *Customer Interface Model*

Capability	Description
Access to Existing Application and Information Sources	Information can be generated and retrieved from a variety of existing corporate systems such as customer and prospect databases, billing an expense databases, and existing application systems, if the corporate systems are flexible, integrated, and networked.
Rich Customer Interfaces	These include video, audio, images, and text. Additional interfaces also available, including a virtual reality interface, allowing users to visually navigate through virtual 3-D environments.
Personalized Products and Services	Information presented to the customer can be personalized based on profile or other conditions. Narrowcasting and monocasting (unicasting) schemes will become more popular.

(continued)

Table 2.2 *(continued)*

Capability	Description
	*Narrow*casting refers to the ability to customize your information in a more personalized way than a *broad*cast.
Immediate Information	The customer interface can be frequently updated with relevant and real-time information.
Active and Intelligent Functionality	Information can include business functionality to interact with the user and the business's back-end applications, database systems, and other information assets.
Secure Communications	Unlike traditional systems and paper processes (fax, carbon copies, etc.), the Internet technology set can provide degrees of security for customers. Given encryption and other security standards, businesses can now design effective security approaches. Several standards are being created (or are available) to address new security issues.
Transparent Linking	Internet technology allows customers to easily link between global business partners transparently. Businesses can develop more complete customer solutions. Customers can accomplish a series of activities thorough effective linking and design by businesses.
Push/Pull Communications	The Internet may change the user interface paradigm. The customer can now pull for information *or* businesses can push information.

(continued)

Table 2.2 *(continued)*

Capability	Description
Community-Centric Architectures	The Internet provides a unique ability to bring together communities of practices for business or social experiences.

THE VALUE OF INTERLINKING

Interlinking between business sites is an important tool in the repertoire of the Internet strategist. Seamless linkages with business partners provide customers with more-complete business solutions. Customers can navigate transparently between sites in ways that interlinking business partners, who have anticipated customers' buying habits and decision-making criteria, have established.

An effective example may be found in the case of BayNet World, Inc., an Internet-based real estate listing service serving the San Francisco metropolitan area. It provides more specific and timely information than that typically available through generic real estate publications such as free weekly listings. BayNet customers can make selections by clicking on a map, typing in a particular area, or defining a set of parameters (e.g., price, size, style). More than a dozen real estate firms are linked to BayNet's site.

Once a property of interest has been identified, the customer makes an appointment with the real estate agent via e-mail and conveniently accesses financial information from the BayNet World site. The site is interlinked to Bank of America, which provides data on interest rates, home loans, etc. The user moves seamlessly from the real estate site to a companion site, thereby ensuring a complete customer solution.

The BayNet World example can be expanded hypothetically by anticipating the possibility of additional customer needs. A customer moving to the San Francisco area from another state or city will have to arrange for cable television and telephone line hookups, register to vote, and learn about neighborhood resources such as shopping and recreation areas. By anticipating these needs, BayNet World could provide links to the appropriate businesses and services. An apartment dweller would not need a lawn service but might want information about laundromats. By contrast, the owner of a house might seek information on lawn tools, patio furniture, and pool service.

The challenge is not as much about dealing with immature technologies as it is designing integrated customer solutions. Figure 2.1 offers a potential interlinking scenario on this extension of the BayNet World example.

Figure 2.1 *Potential BayNet World, Inc. Customer Scenario*

Customer needs should drive your business positioning and interlinking. Before establishing links, ask yourself the following questions:

- What businesses should I be linked with, and how should the links be structured?

- Will interlinking address the customer's changing values?

- What needs to be done to my business design in order to recognize and respond to these changes?

- What value does my business provide; how well situated is it to provide more complete customer solutions?

- What compelling business functionality will I provide on my site?

- Should I charge my interlinking partners for each customer forwarded to its site or should the link be a valued-added service provided to my customers?

Interlinking also allows for the development of new revenue models. For example, Denver-based Geosystems Global Corp., a leading publisher of electronic maps and geographical database products, offers a product called MapQuest. MapQuest exploits Geosystems' massive geographical databases, making them available to visitors using any Web browser. Using scroll bars, directional buttons, and menu checkboxes, a user can customize the online maps, zooming in and out among street, city, regional, and national levels. In addition, the maps can be populated with any combination of points of interest—from hotels and Thai restaurants to parks and Web sites.[5]

Geosystems is pursuing two revenue models for the MapQuest site. The first calls for sponsored advertisements. In the second, the company plans to offer MapQuest Interconnect, a link for other Web-based companies to MapQuest's online maps. The link will be transparent to the user. Thus, for example, restaurants, real estate services, and banks might interlink to MapQuest in order to provide their own solutions to the customer.

EXAMINING THE NEW PERSONAL RELATIONSHIP

How will the Internet and Intranet affect relationships between businesses, customers, and employees in the coming years? Ideally their impact will be felt in the development of new, mutually beneficial relationships; many are already evolving.

Business is becoming more personal; the value of closeness—to employees, business partners, and customers—is growing. Customer intimacy is fostered by high-touch applications such as those used by ONYX Software. As Hatim Tyabji, CEO of VeriFone, has noted, "Business is personal. People commit themselves to other people, not to organizations. For all of its techno-savvy, life at VeriFone is surprisingly intimate...We constantly try to personalize VeriFone."

VeriFone still embraces the concept of face-to-face communication. Tyabji adds, "At one level, it seems strange. Why should a company that makes fanatical use of voice mail, e-mail, and video conferencing also spend $5 million per year on airline tickets and hotels? You can't look at technology in isolation from human beings. The more we use technology, the more we need to travel."[6]

Closeness is important for your business. Knowing your customer's business better than its own management allows you to create effective new products and services, foster a productive work environment, and make your company attractive to customers, employees, and potential business partners.

One study estimates that 55 million people in the United States will work from remote locations (i.e., home) by the turn of the century. In addition, more and more people are conducting home activities such as shopping and paying bills from the workplace. DealerNet reports that the bulk of its transactions come from business locations during lunch hours. Thus, the delineation between home and the office becoming less clear. This virtual environment will force new relationships.

While the virtual corporation opens endless possibilities, its very nature—remoteness by design—depends on trust and cooperation by customers, employees, and business partners. Clear and effective communication is essential. In *The Virtual Corporation*, authors William H. Davidow and Michael F. Malone suggest that it is best to talk of the virtual corporation in terms of patterns of information and relationships. Building and offering Internet-based products requires the construction of a sophisticated information-gathering network, combining it with computer-integrated design and production process, and then operating the system in a multilateral environment composed of employees, customers, partners, and businesses involved in the chain of supply and distribution.[7]

RESPECTING THE VIRTUAL-BASED VALUE PROPOSITION

The value proposition refers to a designed business opportunity between a business and a customer. A business introduces some element of value to a customer, perhaps by enhancing a product's or service's desirability, utility, or usefulness. If this satisfies the customer's decision-making criteria, a business transaction may then occur. Businesses then ensure that this value can be recaptured for profit.

For example, an automobile owner in Iceland recently used DealerNet to find a dealer in Seattle who could supply an $800 part for his Nissan Pathfinder. The customer in Iceland valued the transaction for its convenience and availability while the dealer extended his market across the world.

Respecting the value proposition requires you to place the customer at the center of your design. It means being customer-centric. You must predict customers' needs and determine how much they will value your innovative product or service based upon its ability to satisfy those needs. This interaction is depicted in Figure 2.2.

Successful companies think through their value proposition. Internet strategists must ask themselves a series of questions: How well does the current value proposition serve the customer's changing priorities and values? How well does it address the situation enabled by the Internet? Do different types of customers have different value propositions?

Technology creates an ever-more-powerful customer. Technology facilitates a customer's ability to stay informed, empowered, exacting, and individualistic. The appeal of the Internet customer comes from his lack of allegiances and thus the value proposition becomes increasingly more complex and challenging.

NETCOM On-Line Communication Services, Inc., a leading Internet service provider (ISP) based in California, recently faced the challenge of providing customers with more value in order to distinguish itself from its competitor ISPs.

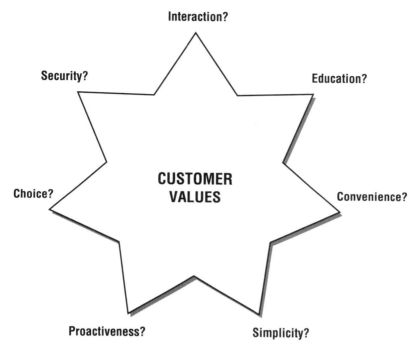

Figure 2.2 *Sample Value Propositions Considerations*

While many players joining the market attempt to attract customers with access-only offerings, NETCOM anticipates that Internet users want more than just access. It therefore provides customers with personalized access information that meets specific needs. By providing value-added service at no additional charge, NETCOM helps users find relevance in the Internet so that they continue to subscribe.

Consider the value proposition designed and developed by United Connection, a service of UAL Corp.'s United Airlines. United Connection allows customers to make their own travel reservations directly through the Internet, providing the value of guaranteed order fulfillment, interaction, and convenience. In addition, the customer receives access to continually updated information, a secure system, access to the schedules of 500 other airlines, and updated information on their United Mileage Plus accounts.

Moreover, United Connection offers customers the opportunity to earn 500 Mileage Plus miles every time a United Airlines ticket is secured through CompuServe's United Connection Forum.

The value for United Airlines is recaptured thus: potentially increased revenues as a result of mileage incentives and reductions in labor costs as a result of decreased need for reservations and ticketing personnel.

NOTES

1. "New Estimates in Old Debate on Internet Use." *New York Times* (17 April 1996).

2. Joachin, David, "VeriFone, Netscape to Link Net to Payment System," *Web Week* (February 1996):7.

3. Chabrow, Eric R., "Wall Street on the Desktop," *Information Week* (11 March 1996):61–66.

4. Calem, Robert E., "Behold! A Web Advertising Campaign That Has Produced Results," *Web Week* (3 March 1996).

5. Booker, Ellis, "MapMaker Debuts Searchable Atlas," *Web Week* (3 March 1996).

6. Taylor, William C., "At VeriFone It's a Dog's Life (and they love it)," *Fast Company* (Premiere Issue):115.

7. Davidow, William H., and Michael S. Malone, *The Virtual Corporation*. (New York: Harper Business, 1993).

CHAPTER 3

STRATEGIC OBJECTIVES: YOUR INTERNET/INTRANET BUSINESS CASE

This chapter presents the conceptual framework for an Internet/Intranet (business) strategy. The first three sections discuss the frame of mind for thinking about the Internet as a tool of change. In the next section, strategic objectives are examined and analyzed. The customer's needs and desires are discussed in the following section, while technology and related issues are the subject of the final section.

HOW SUCCESSFUL COMPANIES SET THEIR INTERNET GOALS

For successful companies, the Internet is not about technology; it is about the customer. Successful companies' Internet goal is delivering more value to the customer. These companies distance themselves from technology issues and address the real business issues, which are inherently customer oriented.

When early successful business leaders and entrepreneurs began to commercialize the telephone, they most likely did not first think about handsets and switches, copper cables, or even quantitative

41

return on investment (ROI). They probably talked about attracting new customers, improving customer service, and offering innovative products and services. These were their strategic business objectives.

An effective and successful Internet strategy first requires asking the right questions. These questions need to push you to revisit your strategic business objectives. This will lead you through the rediscovery of your core competencies and identifying areas of mediocrity. "How much money can I make with the Internet?" and "Are my competitors making money with the Internet?" are *not* the right questions. "What innovative products and services can I offer?" "Can I develop a more complete customer solution?" "Who are the right interlinking business partners?" "What relevant competence can I leverage for my Internet-based customers?" and "How can I exploit my current channels?" are appropriate strategic questions.

This chapter leads you through the right questions to prepare you for the methodology behind effective Internet strategy, which is outlined in Chapter 5.

Successful companies build their Internet business case by aligning their strategic business objectives, irrespective of any particular technology, with their Internet strategy. The business case for the Internet then becomes qualitative rather than quantitative. Bryan Bell, chief technology strategist at the Tacoma-based Frank Russell Company, which provides financial services to customers worldwide, suggests the Internet brings about evolution in business principles as well as revolution in process. Because of this revolution, the Internet is not about the ROI—at least initially it is not.

So why should you not focus on asking or understanding if your competitors are making money with the Internet? First of all, getting a good answer assumes that:

- You know who your new Internet competitors are and will be;

- You can determine whether or not they are making money with their strategy;

- Your competitors' strategies are based purely on a public presence, not a more private environment; and

- Your competitors know what they are doing with the Internet.

What relevance does this have to your business goals or strategic objectives? Of course it is useful to understand which experiments or strategies were successful for your competitors. But simply to ask this question without focusing on *your* customers, understanding the qualitative reasons for *your* case, and revisiting *your* strategic objectives is an ineffective approach to forging business strategy.

If your competitors know what they are doing, they may have already defined new products or services and it may already be too late for your business to react. Playing by the industry leader's rules is competitive suicide because you are always reacting—versus inventing—and look past customer-centric strategies in favor of competitor-centric strategies.

Ultimately, reacting to customer needs yields a better chance of success than being competitor-centric. As Gary Hamel and C.K. Prahalad note in their essay "Strategic Intent," "Traditional competitor analysis is like a snapshot of a moving car; by itself, the photograph yields little information about the car's speed or direction—whether the driver is out for a quiet Sunday drive or warming up for the Grand Prix."[1] So the two worst questions asked by an Internet strategist are perhaps the most common: (1) How can I make money? and (2) What's my competitor doing? Rather, for the best shot at success, an effective Internet strategy must be fully and thoughtfully embraced, aligned with your business strategy, and independent of competitors' actions.

An extensive and integrated corporate-wide Internet and Intranet was developed at Silicon Graphics (SGI). SGI is a hardware and software developer employing approximately 10,000 people, with offices throughout the world. Referred to as Silicon Junction, its Intranet is an integral part of the daily business practice of its employees and business partners. To SGI's staff, the Intranet and Internet are one. As users navigate through the hundreds of thousands of pages of functionality, they move across both the Intranet and the Internet and are often unaware whether they are within an SGI site or at a site on the Internet.

Silicon Junction has over 800 Internet servers networked through-out its worldwide operations. Depending on user classification or grade, access is limited to Silicon Junction functions. The CFO has access to financial results whereas a business partner does not. This concept of layered access is discussed in greater detail in Chapter 4. The range of functions currently includes:

- up-to-the-minute sales commission information
- real-time inventory information
- the latest product literature and competitive analysis reports
- order status information
- intelligent and sophisticated data-mining applications to help with prospecting
- the ability to book flights and hotels for conferences
- expert presentations through audio and video

Integrated e-mail, scheduling capabilities, links to relational legacy databases, and applications, are also available.

Let us review how SGI achieved its objectives. First, SGI fully embraced the Internet set of technologies, committing itself to the Internet's capabilities and maintaining a world-class electronic environment. Second, all its systems are focused on better serving and empowering its customers', associates', and business partners' needs.

For example, SGI's advertising agency in Seattle provides direct access to upcoming promotions and public relations material for SGI's sales force, linking directly through the Intranet. The sales team is always aware of the next advertisement and what it is focused on because they càn review it before any customer or prospect sees it. At SGI, the Internet is perceived as a success because of its strategic qualitative value and was *not* initially measured as a quantitative ROI. The company looked at the Internet as an opportunity to rethink and challenge many of its processes.

SGI's Intranet/Internet has become a showcase for the company and its sales team. It can demonstrate to customers and prospects what is possible with the Intranet firsthand. In fact, salespeople have commented that their ability to sell Intranet and Internet hardware and software solutions is facilitated by SGI's commitment to the Internet and belief in the power of an online environment as a sales tool.

WHY TRADITIONAL QUANTITATIVE GOALS DON'T COMPUTE

For many reasons, the Internet business case cannot easily be modeled in terms of a traditional ROI. First, Internet technology, its costs, its design, and the processes on which it has an impact are constantly changing. There are so many components and so much complexity involved in determining the total cost of an investment in the Internet business case that the ROI is infinitely malleable.

Second, the success of a traditional ROI analysis requires a full understanding of the future cost of operation, the design, and the business and customer benefits from those expenditures. As such, it works best in a mostly static business environment featuring known competitors, a definable customer base, and predictable development costs. Pioneers of successful Internet business strategies, such as Netscape and DealerNet, do not focus on the traditional business case as such. They see the Internet as a necessity for doing business and an instrument for achieving their strategic business objectives. They have embraced the Internet environment. Moreover, as they accept the Internet and respond strategically, they recognize the necessity of shifting the company focus to issues such as agility, customer-centric organizational models, and external orientation.

This type of *qualitative* business case is uncomfortable for many larger companies. Their bureaucracies remain focused on management models devised when innovation cycles were less frequent, technologies changed over years rather than months, and customer expectations and options were not as extensive. Bureaucracies are the bête noire of the innovative Internet business. In fact, Eric Roach, president of Lombard Institutional Investors, says that his biggest management challenge is to resist the urge to set up a bureaucracy when managing these innovative activities. He continually forces himself to think in terms of empowerment of people and other entrepreneurial management styles.

Business leaders in some larger companies have also successfully resisted this urge. GE Plastics, for instance, was one of the first non-IT Fortune 500 companies to invest strategically in the Internet. It did this when fewer than 20 percent of its customers had access to the Internet. Bureaucracy did not hamstring GE Plastics because the Internet strategy became the vision of one of their leaders, who was able to sell the case to management by saying that this was simply what needed to be done.

YOUR NEW BUSINESS FOCUS

To be successful in this new medium, your business team's focus must migrate from creating the ROI to understanding, creating, and exploring new rules of business with the capabilities of the Internet. The team's goal must shift from determining the number of customers on the Internet to anticipating customer expectations, preparing your organization to better respond to these expectations, and getting your customers online. Prediction of development costs must give way to understanding what can be developed and then building and experimenting. The Internet vision must become integral to your organization. Once you accept the Internet as a business requirement, move quickly and efficiently. The Internet rewards agility.

The pioneers embraced the Internet strategically based on a belief that there is tremendous value in being leaders in this revolution. Once you have embraced the Internet as a necessary cost of doing business, however, you've only just begun. As Fidelity's director of Electronic Services, Mary Ruth Moran, says, "All you have done so far is to buy a ticket to the dance."

I believe that companies that come late to the dance will have a harder time finding the right dance hall, finding something to wear, finding someone to dance with, and understanding the rules of the dance itself.

According to Moran, Fidelity has no plans to justify its Internet strategy with a strict ROI analysis at any foreseeable time. Fidelity's perspective is that the Internet is a necessary cost of doing business. It is effectively regarded as no less a requirement than a toll-free number for a mutual fund.

Fidelity believes that the rate of acceptance of the Internet by customers will be tremendous because they appear to adopt technologies that serve their needs more rapidly than predicted. In 1985 Fidelity managers forecasted that by 1995 approximately 20 percent of its telephone calls from customers would be handled by automated services. In fact, in 1995 over 75 percent of Fidelity's 500,000 daily calls were handled without human intervention.[2] Fidelity believes that the Internet will eventually reach similar acceptance levels and will be as integral as the telephone in delivering information to customers.

Why? The Internet can be used to address customer expectations and priorities—for example, convenience. The average American works 160 hours more per year now than in 1985. As people spend more time at work, one of their priorities becomes convenience. Fidelity promotes the use of this service to its customers by negotiating discounts with Internet service providers such as MCI and AT&T. Fidelity makes it convenient for customers to do business with the firm by helping them get online and offering account and educational information online 24 hours per day.

How do you do a traditional ROI when the number of customers is growing at 15 percent per month or more, and when technologies offer new ways to interact with customers almost every month? Eric Roach says that Lombard's growth rate is 2 to 5 percent per week. The business case mandated that Lombard create a new paradigm for investing. Roach sees the Internet as an effective way for customers to take care of their financial affairs. He developed a business design focused on providing value-added investment services. Since he embraced the Internet early, he created the rules of this new investing paradigm and reaped the benefits. Lombard sees itself as a leader in the new breed of financial services companies, providing the individual investor with services such as dynamic inter-day graphs and portfolio management systems, that were once the domain of only the largest institutional investors.

Interestingly, being the lowest-cost provider was not Lombard's ultimate business objective. It wanted to compete based on what it felt the real needs of its customer would be. While this included cost competitiveness, the company also focused on creating new services for individual investors. Its goal was delivering proactive, secure, convenient, and complete solutions with guaranteed fulfill-ment. In areas where it cannot provide value through a core com-petency to the customer, Lombard provides links to businesses or sites that have that information. It identifies exactly where it can and cannot provide value. And it does not try to fool itself or its cus-tomers. Lombard seeks only to focus on its core competency of in-novative, Internet-based customer investment software solutions.

Has it proved successful? When before could individuals receive four dynamically updated inter-day graphs on their stocks and stock quotes pushed down to their computer every few minutes? This was generally available only to institutional investors. The customer satisfaction that Lombard's services generate is reflected in the company's growth rate.

ALIGNING INTERNET STRATEGIC OBJECTIVES WITH BUSINESS GOALS

Jeff Bezos, president of the largest Internet-based bookstore, Ama-zon.com, indicates that although the company developed high-level revenue estimates when building its business case, the Internet is changing so quickly that it knew its margin of error had to be incredibly large to predict or focus on the ROI.

Instead, Amazon.com focused its efforts on building innovative customer-centric solutions in line with its high-level qualitative business objectives. How could Amazon.com have predicted what the Internet would hold for it? It is too unpredictable. How could it have predicted that it would become the largest bookstore in Guam overnight, or that in its first month of business it would sell books to customers in 26 countries?

Amazon.com looked past the thicket of unknowns and knew that being successful on the Internet required fully embracing it. The decision had to be strategic and qualitative more than anything else. Finally, all its designs, plans, and products had to be first and foremost customer-centric, catering to the new interests, expecta-tions, and needs of the Internet customer.

Pioneers of the Internet looked at their business strategy from the macro level. They chose not to identify their business environ-ment (the Internet) in the traditional sense because it was—and still is—going through massive changes. For example, the number of users is increasing by the millions each year, Internet consumer habits and decision-making processes are unclear, security standards are still evolving, marketing rules are changing, new innovations are offering new kinds of products, successful profit models are limited, and international legal issues are not resolved.

The unresolved issues aside, the Internet is an attractive medium, bringing together millions of customers and businesses with new capabilities and therefore new services and products. Pioneers cannot base their cases on known and similar models. There are few, if any, appropriate templates; they must be created. Pioneers base their decisions on high-level trends, anticipating the evolution of the Internet to an extent but focusing on the overlap of customer-valued services and products and those the Internet can provide.

For example, GE Plastics did not perform a micro business case when it developed its strategy more than two years ago. It first looked at the customer benefits and its strategic business goals, such as customer intimacy, innovative services, and making it easy for others to do business with the company. Although it knew its distribution costs were high because it relied heavily on vendors such as Federal Express to distribute documents to its 30,000 customers worldwide, it did not address those costs in detail.

Rather, the company looked past the issues of saving money on distribution costs to the higher goal of increasing service to customers. GE Plastics also recognized that its database, containing more than ten million individual documents describing the characteristics of its products, accrued high costs for storage, printing, and distribution.

GE Plastics understood that the Internet is an excellent medium for delivering information critical to its customers, and it sensed that an online information management solution would enhance its customer service, build loyalty, and generate repeat customers. It could not estimate how many of its customers would use the feature nor how long it would take to achieve the goal. GE Plastics ultimately based its decision on maximizing customer value. The Internet medium could deliver superior customer value by providing information with immediate updates, worldwide access, platform independence, and convenience.

Aside from pioneers such as Lombard and GE Plastics, IT companies are generally among the very first business entities to experiment with the benefits of the Internet. They see more clearly than non-IT companies how businesses will change. For them, the case is clear. The market is expanding globally and internationally supported standards are being created by the IT industry. They want to be part of the process and have a hand in shaping it. Other industries, however, are close behind. One example is the merchandiser CUC International. Ten years ago, CUC shifted its focus away from electronic shopping via computers to telephone-based shopping after determining that there was no viable market for PC-based shopping, even though the technology existed.

The decision proved to be correct and CUC became a highly successful mail-order business, one of the largest in the country. In 1996, however, CUC announced that it would again provide home shopping services online, this time via the Internet, through which it now offers a wide variety of products.

For Charles Schwab, a nationwide discount brokerage, the decision to move to the Internet was consistent with its existing strategic business objectives (developing innovative products and services, being easy to do business with, creating new avenues for revenue generation, and strengthening customer loyalty and acquisition). Importantly, that is also where Schwab saw its customers wanting the company to go. More than 20 percent of Schwab's customers use PC-based services to conduct financial trades. The Internet strategy was aligned with Schwab's current strategic business goals. Its business case for an Internet strategy was more about being aligned with strategic business objectives, than their estimate of ROI.

APPROPRIATE STRATEGIC OBJECTIVES

Once the conceptual hurdle of thinking about the Internet as a qualitative tool has been cleared, the prudent business manager and Internet team will map out the organization's strategic objectives. These should not stand in isolation; think of them as the building blocks of the bridge linking your core competency and the Internet's capabilities.

CUSTOMER INTIMACY

Customer closeness or intimacy is a popular business objective that is independent of the Internet. It refers to your ability to be closer to customers in the sense of understanding and therefore anticipating their needs, interests, and expectations. Your value proposition is built around your understanding of customers; therefore, getting closer to them increases the success of your proposition.

Customer closeness can be enhanced or complemented through the innovative use of Internet capabilities. Look to the example of ONYX Software in Chapter 1. This is important, because customer closeness is the differentiator in service-oriented businesses. Some industries traditionally associated with customer closeness include telecommunications, retail, and financial services. As the Internet becomes more important to direct customer communication, other industries will also see the need to get closer to their customers.

Customer closeness can build loyalty and brand equity as well. ONYX caters to current and potential customers by innovatively integrating its Internet site with its customer service systems. The ONYX sales representatives become closer to the customer in that they better understand the customer's specific needs, respond more quickly with information, and ensure that the appropriate employee deals directly with the customer. This will help ONYX better predict customers' needs and thus provide the opportunity to define and develop better products and services.

The Internet can be used to get closer with all members of the organization: customers, business partners, and even employees. Closeness with business partners can help them understand your product better and sell your products and services more effectively. Silicon Junction provides Channel City, a secured Internet site where resellers of Silicon Graphics products can review training materials, build quotes on hardware and software solutions, get help on sales activities, and communicate with various SGI departments, all through a single, intuitive user interface. In this way, SGI has used Internet technologies innovatively to bring its business partners closer. Although companies have been doing this for a long time through seminars and mailings, the Internet's advantages of speed and customization can raise communication to another level.

Other examples of Internet applications that promote customer intimacy include those that elicit more direct customer feedback, the electronic analogue of a reader response card. Amazon.com provides an excellent example of an Internet business that uses Internet capabilities to sense and respond to its customers. It encourages customers to provide feedback on Amazon.com's designs and new services. In fact, some of the most popular features of its site are the direct result of customer feedback, including the ability of customers to post book reviews to the public and their ability to receive direct comments from authors before books are purchased. It also helps determine what customers are *not* saying and to anticipate what they will say they want. You can understand the gap between what you develop and what the customer values. Thus, it can benefit your company by facilitating the development of better products and services.

One of the simplest, but most effective business cases for an Internet investment may be the e-mail application. E-mail is among the most valuable applications currently available, providing ad hoc any-to-any communication with your customers and business partners. E-mail can be linked with attached documents throughout the Internet, providing the ability to communicate worldwide, employee to employee, business to partner, and business to customer.

Many other innovative technology applications can also enhance your closeness. Another simple, effective application is Internet-enabled calendar and scheduling software. With this type of application, in the future you can set up meetings on your vendors' calendars, schedule meetings with clients, and more. Companies including FTP Software, Microsoft, and Netscape are working with the Internet Engineering Task Force (IETF) to design standards for electronic scheduling between companies on the Internet. For example, you could view your business partners schedule and book time with him without ever picking up a telephone or sending a detailed e-mail, if given access to his calendar.

INNOVATIVE PRODUCTS AND SERVICES

The Internet often rewards the first to market more than anyone. If someone else has already done it, do not waste your precious time and resources on it. Experiment with innovation. Netscape was not rewarded by the financial markets for being second to market. Netscape employees worked around the clock to be first, knowing the Internet would reward them. Who is even trying to compete with Pointcast after the release of its innovative product, the first of its kind to market? No one. Instead of competing, potential competitors like CNN are forming alliances.

The Internet is not about selling old products to old customers through a new channel. The Internet enables the invention of *new* kinds of products and services that never could exist before these kinds of technologies were in place. Scott Cook, chairman of Intuit, which makes Quicken, notes, "I believe that there is the potential for there to be new products as important to the [financial services] industry as the credit card or the money market fund. And real leaders will do experimentation in enough ways that they will truly invent new kinds of financial products and services for the next millennium."

Internet innovations are announced on a daily basis. In fact, innovation on the Internet is so rapid, that time is measured in what are termed *Web weeks*, analogous to the concept of canine years. Netscape releases entirely new versions of software every three months, with dramatic capabilities such as telephone and virtual reality browsing. New business models can be identified and implemented very quickly, if the Internet is properly understood, and the business systems are sufficiently flexible to react to these new models.

In fact, after little more than a year as an established company, Netscape became a software power almost overnight. Netscape is Microsoft's most serious competitor. Netscape's business strategy changed the traditional rules of business in the IT industry. It delivered its solution automatically via the Internet and it developed a browser that defaults to the Netscape Internet site, providing incredible marketing opportunities (e.g., advertising space). Netscape's innovative Internet site attracts millions of users per day, so now it can offer revenue generating advertising space on its Internet presence as well. For example, reports suggest that Netscape generated more than $1.9 million in advertising from its site in the first quarter of

1996 alone. It developed its own highly successful Internet technology products by strategically considering the Internet, and it now drives the Internet user interface standards, to a large extent.

But its real product innovation was a browser that opened up the Internet in a user-friendly way. Netscape's early entry, innovative products, and distribution strategy drove it to an 80-percent market share in its first year and built a market capitalization over $2 billion. There are, however, risks. Netscape's browser product is potentially the most pirated software ever.

Although many companies in the technology industry make effective business use of the Internet, business leaders in non-IT industries should not be limited to the ideas developed and used by technology companies. Rather, business leaders should push themselves to think outside the box and identify applications that are relevant and beneficial to their organizations and industries. For example, most information technology industry leaders include the following types of business functionality on their Internet sites:

- frequently asked questions (FAQs)

- product support

- software upgrades

These are extremely beneficial applications for IT businesses, but they may not be for yours. Many businesses have applied the IT industry Internet applications to their business environments rather than looked for more appropriate applications. As a result, some businesses have prematurely concluded that the Internet technology set is not relevant or strategic to their business or industry. You need to realize this distinction, look beyond IT industry examples and explore new products or services relevant to your businesses strategic competencies.

NetStock Direct, a Seattle-based company, offers an innovative alternative to the current investment/stock-brokering model, enhancing the direct investor-to-company relationship and bypassing the broker intermediary. A relationship is then established directly between public companies and individual investors.

The primary means by which Netstock Direct accomplishes these goals is an online, interactive Internet-based stock marketing and investor relations service. The service facilitates and will eventually track direct stock sales and other investment agreements between individual investors and companies that list securities and seek capital. Both parties to a Netstock Direct transaction benefit. The public companies offering this program, such as Amoco and Ameritech, pay a monthly fee to Netstock Direct for this service. The investor pays no fees for connection, usage, or transactions. For example, an individual investor who wants to buy stock directly from Amoco comes directly to the Netstock Direct site, which posts Amoco information and facilitates the purchase of stock directly, bypassing brokers and thereby eliminating commission costs.

MAKING EVERYONE AN EXPERT

Distribution of detailed product and process knowledge throughout your business can make an expert out of everybody in your company. It leverages the knowledge of one to many. Using the Internet to post presentations, competitive analysis reports, and other information from internal experts has significant benefits for many companies. SGI salespeople use Silicon Junction effectively in this way to sell the company's products. One sales representative recently flew to Alaska to demonstrate SGI's equipment to a major oil company. Although not an oil industry expert, she accessed Silicon Junction the night before the presentation and downloaded the oil and gas presentation posted by SGI's expert in the industry. She was able to download an audio file and listen to the expert give a taped presentation to a potential customer. Because the salesperson was able to respond immediately to her prospect's questions and predict its needs, she was able to close the sale promptly.

In another instance, an announcement was made by one of SGI's competitors concerning the release of a new computer model; SGI's salespeople worldwide needed information in order to formulate a response. Within a few hours of the announcement, a product expert at SGI developed and posted a thorough response to the announcement. While this could also have been done with non-Internet technologies, neither method features the same cost-effectiveness, ease, or integration into the total solution as an Internet response. The Internet approach allowed salespeople to have a consistent, well-thought-out, immediate, and proactive response to customer or prospect queries.

MASS CUSTOMIZATION AND VIRTUAL PRODUCTS

With the Internet technologies, you can leverage the concept of mass customization. As defined by management theorist Tom Peters, "mass customization is an organizational hybrid of mass production and customized production."[3] Mass customization, personalization, and virtual products are those products that generate information tailored to individual customers. Many strategic benefits accrue. The authors of *The Virtual Corporation* conclude that the closer a corporation gets to cost-effective instantaneous production of mass-customized goods and services, the more competitive and successful it will be.[4]

Many leading-edge companies focus their development efforts on providing this type of customization as part of their Internet strategy. IBM's infoSage service is an example of mass customization. Personalized Web pages are created and updated daily to reflect news stories of particular interest to the paying customer.

In this way, companies can use the Internet to extend their relationships with customers. Software tools allow firms to create highly personalized Web interfaces for customers. The more links a client clicks on, the more personalized the site becomes. Thanks to software that recognizes how a client has used a site in the past, companies draw inferences about the information of interest to that customer and present it. The goal is to personalize sites to such an extent that customers will be reluctant to change once they have modeled a particular Web site to suit their needs. You want to develop an allegiance with them through this personalization. Interlinking then complements your overall solution.

An early innovative example of a personalized site is offered by Scudder Investment Services, which manages family mutual funds. In June 1996, the Scudder Funds site on the World Wide Web became the first mutual fund company site to offer Internet users a customized "Personal Page." The site, designed for interactivity and simplicity, provides information on asset allocation, tuition, and retirement planning to users who fill out interactive worksheets. Investors can easily establish a Personal Page that presents daily price information on funds they follow. Fund performance data, from both Scudder and Lipper Analytical Services, Inc., are available on the site. "Our objective is to provide convenient, easy-to-access information, as informed investors become successful investors," notes Mark Casady, director of Scudder's U.S. Mutual Funds Group. "We believe this Web site is singular in its ability to relate to users on a personal level."

Although many investment services claim that they approach each investor as an unique individual, Scudder Funds laid the foundation for accomplishing this over the Internet through its Personal Page. For this reason, Scudder plans for the Personal Page to serve as a platform for its Internet strategy. The company will continue to build new services on top of it.

MAKING IT EASY FOR OTHERS TO DO BUSINESS WITH YOU

Several examples so far have aligned Internet strategy with the goal of making it easy for customers and partners to do business with your organization. Let's review GE Plastics and Charles Schwab. GE Plastics makes it easy for customers to do business with the company by working with Spry Software to develop Internet applications that GE Plastics sends to its customers in order to access the Internet and, specifically, to direct them to the GE Plastics site. For Schwab, its Internet service complements existing services, such as voice brokering and telebrokering. Schwab sees the Internet as part of a package of services it developed to increase its accessibility.

Amazon.com conceived its virtual bookstore entirely based on the Internet and electronic communications. It offers quick delivery of almost any book in print to customers worldwide. It also developed friendly policies toward publishers, who help create Amazon.coms Internet catalogue and make it as extensive as possible. Publishers can submit digital images of book covers and related information and have them included on Amazon.coms site. There is virtually no cost to publishers for this type of advertising.

ATTRACTING NEW CUSTOMERS AND PARTNERS WITH WIDER MARKET REACH

With its current presence in over 100 countries, the Internet can be used to reach a wider customer base, as well as to target niche customer groups. Because the size of the overall market is so large, the niche size is often significant. Nonetheless, it must be noted that the Internet presence in Second- and Third-World nations, containing many of the most promising markets, is weak.

Sausage Software, discussed in Chapter 1, developed its business case around its ability to take advantage of the Internets mass audience. It believed that a case existed for selling low-cost utility software applications over the Internet to a niche group. The strategy was centered around limiting development costs per product and providing the tools needed by software developers in the rapidly changing software business. Sausage developed software applications that could go from the drawing table to the customers hands within a few weeks. It limited development expenses for each program to approximately a few development weeks. Projects exceeding that limit were scrapped.

Today the company's strategy focuses on the development of niche application software tools so that at peak production several new products will be released each month. The risk is limited due to low development costs, and the approach reaches wider markets than were previously available. The upside potential is enormous. Pricing is typically around $50 for each application, while the downside risk is limited to the relatively low development and operational expenses. The business case proved effective on the Internet; in its first year alone, the company expects to turn over $1 million profit.

By design, the Internet establishes a business as a global company. The successful business utilizes the global opportunities and maximizes this capability by finding new business partners. In 1995 Rozet Rose Oil, Inc., a small rose oil producer located in southwestern Turkey, created an Internet public presence for marketing purposes. Its strategy was to use the Internet as a complementary marketing tool. Because of the high costs associated with Internet sites in Turkey, it outsourced the design and administration of its site to a company located in Little Rock, Arkansas. Its marketing presence was limited to a one-page introduction of the company and its products, for a cost of $25 per month. One week after the launch of the public presence, the company received a phone call from a cosmetics company in Japan that saw the Internet site. A short time later, this led to a sale of rose oil products valued at approximately $2 million annually.

Similarly, the Chocolate Factory, a confectioner in rural Bucks County, Pennsylvania, took advantage of the Internet's marketing capacity. In September 1994 the owners set up shop on the World Wide Web with the aim of reaching millions of customers around the globe. The eight-person company received more than 1,000 orders over the Internet in about a year. It ships chocolate all over the world, something that never would have been possible without the international presence of the Internet.

GETTING MORE FROM LESS: INCREASING RETURN ON ASSETS AND INDIVIDUALS

Communications, distribution, rent, advertising, marketing, product education and training, customer support, and sales all represent major business expenses. The Internet, however, provides an alternative to the traditional channels of performing these functions while significantly reducing expenses.

A dramatic example is the experience of the AP Gallery, located in Seattle. For years the AP Gallery offered an extensive collection of artwork through its store. In 1996 it determined that the bricks-and-mortar expense was too significant relative to the advantages of an online storefront. It closed its physical store and now offers its artwork via the Internet.

Amazon.com's Internet bookstore has only 39 employees but more than a million titles. By comparison, most large physical stores carry approximately 100,000 titles with a similar number of employees. Lombard Brokerage, Inc. has less than 100 employees to operate a customer service business that adds thousands of new customers each week. Amazon.com and Lombard both allow the customer to speak with a human if necessary.

U.S. corporations have dramatically downsized over the last several years, primarily because of reengineering efforts. Corporations are now forced to do more with less. If used properly, the Internet may help meet this challenge.

REDUCING TIME TO MARKET

The Internet allows companies to come quickly to market. For many industries, especially the software industry, speed to market is at parity with low cost as a competitive necessity. Many companies greatly reduce time to market with the Internet over traditional channels. For example, when Reuters announced its Internet news service, 27,000 users downloaded the Reuters NewsTicker in eight weeks. The Reuters ticker allows individuals to configure and receive their Reuters news feeds directly over the Internet. The Sausage Software case also illustrates how the Internet can be used to reduce the time it takes to get a product to market. As noted in Chapter 1, Sausage used the Internet community to test its product and get feedback in days, not weeks or months. It also used the Internet to distribute the product quickly.

Netscape capitalized on this potential for garnering assistance from customers. It offers prizes for individuals who download early beta versions of its product and find faults. Typically, Netscape has tens of thousands of people testing its products in this way within days of posting them on the Internet site.

INTERNALIZING EXTERNAL INFORMATION

The challenge of the business to manage and support internal data such as corporate financials, sales, and customer information, is significant enough, but you also need to determine how to manage the wealth of *external* data available on the Internet, such as SEC regulations, market information, industry newsgroups, and the like. Many companies offer employees little or no direction for accessing information via the public Internet. Similar to the business objective of making everyone an expert, internalizing external information benefits your business by capitalizing on the abundance of public data on the Internet.

Because of the wealth of information available, helping to lead your employees to the right sites will prove beneficial to you and your company. To this end, you can provide productivity pages for employees to help lead them to highly relevant sites. These pages can provide predefined links to Internet-based information, services, and products for your employees, such as customer and competitor sites. Since the Internet offers an astonishing array of information helpful to every organization, it is logical to consider an outbound internal site: an Internet server that employees use as a launching pad into the Internet. The outbound site should be used to direct employees to specific sites that aid in daily business practice, such as market research, sales statistics, and purchasing. Listed below are a few types of sites that could be helpful to almost any business.

- customer sites

- prospect sites

- regulatory agency sites

- business partner sites

- current competitor sites

- potential competitor sites

- legal database sites

- industry newsgroups

- research sites

- filtered news retrieval sites

- product ordering sites

- shipment tracking sites

- strategic and innovative Internet sites (a list of sites is presented in the Appendix)

Software products now available can alert users with pop-up alarms when preselected Internet sites are changed. Such tools aid users in sifting through corporate information, allowing them to work more efficiently.

Verity, a Sunnyvale, California-based company, for example, offers a useful product. As the volume of available information sources in your business and on the Internet grows, so do the problems associated with finding the right information. Verity's Topic Agent Server monitors information streams on the user's behalf and delivers relevant information to their desktops. Topic Agent Server supports personal software agents that continuously watch a wide variety of information sources such as news wires, electronic mail, and topic-indexed documents on the Internet and throughout your business enterprise. Topic Agent allows users and online providers to filter incoming information against interest profiles and send automatic alerts via personal Web pages, e-mail, or fax. Users are automatically alerted when information matching their personal profiles is found.

EXTERNALIZING INTERNAL INFORMATION

In order to better build Internet applications that customers understand, appreciate, and value, it is helpful to build and experiment with applications on your own Intranet. By using applications internally before offering them to customers and the public, you can experiment with them before turning them outside the firewall for customers to use. This allows you to better understand what customers will see once the information is released. The business objective in exploiting internal information is to help customers understand your company, products, and services.

CUSTOMER ACQUISITION AND LOYALTY

One purpose in developing an innovative Internet strategy early is rapid customer acquisition. The sooner you can get a customer familiar with the services you provide and have that customer incorporate them into his daily practices, the better your chances for keeping that customer. Once the customer has been acquired, the goal migrates to achieving his loyalty.

San Francisco-based Bank of America (BoA), one of the largest banks in the United States, attempts to acquire customers through early and innovative use of Internet technology. It continually strives to increase the number of services, (e.g., checking, bill paying, transfers, account information) customers use, effectively increasing their loyalty. Its business objective is to provide a full customer solution of financial services by providing a suite of integrated Internet services.

Beyond innovation, loyalty increases when customers' needs, concerns, and preferences are integrated directly into the product planning process. Amazon.com constantly uses the feedback in its Internet site development. Creating communities of interest centered around your product can help achieve loyalty and acquire customers. For example, Kodak enables customers to join in a real-time chat with experts during specified periods of the day.

Company newsgroups provide electronic bulletin board functionality for posting messages relating to specific areas of interest. Any user questions or comments about your products or services can post them and anyone in the discussion group can answer. In many cases these questions are answered by other users in lieu of customer service employees. Today's consumers are rapidly becoming more sophisticated and look for as much information as possible when making buying decisions.

EXPLOITING BOTH CHAINS

Studies indicate that companies attempting to do business in both the virtual and physical world are more successful and profitable when they exploit *both* their physical and virtual value chains. For example, Charles Schwab, while committed to development of online services, does not plan to reduce its number of physical retail outlets. In fact, these units are essential to the customer acquisition process. Schwab's electronic activities are value-added service used by investors after they become customers.

Your Internet strategy should exploit non-Internet-related elements of your business. For instance, c|net is both a nationwide television programming service and a worldwide online service. It provides its online members with information and opinions about general news and the Internet, exclusive lab-based computer product reviews, the latest computer and online news, free software capable of being downloaded, contests, and polls. Moreover, it provides the opportunity for Internet users to chat with other guests, hosts, and producers of non-Internet businesses.

It is important to remember, however, that rather than managing one series of value-adding processes, these companies are actually managing two. Why? Because the economic logic of the two chains is different: A conventional understanding of the economies of scale and scope does not apply to the virtual value chain in the same way as it does to the physical value chain. The virtual value chain can re-purpose information in more ways more quickly than the physical value chain. Moreover, the two chains must be managed distinctly, but in concert.[5]

The Chicago Tribune Company has experts focused on both value chains—its Internet edition and its hard copy edition. Each day journalists working exclusively for the Internet gather and edit material for Web users. While some of their work appears in the printed newspaper, most is specifically designed for use on the Web. In addition to text and photos, the Internet edition provides audio, video, and graphics to illustrate stories, and opportunities for readers to provide feedback and discussion appear on every page.

Your customers will continue to look for solutions beyond those available in the virtual environment. In many cases they expect a virtual solution to be complemented by a solution in the real world. Even Scott Cook, chairman of Intuit, the maker of the most popular PC financial planning package, Quicken, does not believe that most customers are going to organize something as important as a retirement plan solely with a box of $39.00 software. There are too many questions, too many issues. For most people, financial and retirement planning are too central and difficult to interpret. Instead, most people want a connection with somebody whose advice they trust in addition to the information they receive from software like Quicken. They will still look for someone to provide guidance, counsel, interpretation, perspective, and answers before committing to a course of action.

REVENUE-GENERATING OPPORTUNITIES

For some segments of the population, trends seem to indicate that the Internet will be a preferred channel of distribution, one with attractive revenue-generating opportunities. Fidelity indicates that Internet users are more likely to actually buy a fund than those who call in by phone; 2 percent of all Fidelity inquiries come from Internet users, who make up 3 percent of sales.

Beyond the traditional approach of looking at revenue-generating opportunities, your strategy should consider new ones as well. For example, the Internet provides a new type of revenue-generating opportunity, a different audience, potentially enabling a business to profit from small transactions because of the significant number possible.

Some groups are working on standards for transactions of less than a cent, often referred to as microtransactions. For example, Carnegie Mellon University is developing its NetBill architecture exclusively for the microtransaction environment. This is important because it may have a profound impact on what businesses will look like in the future. In essence, micromerchants would support transactions that are small but significant in the aggregate, considering the size of the market.

NetBill's business case is built around the belief that information industries dominate the economy and will continue to do so as the Internet evolves. It suggests that the current market for online information is up to $100 billion per year. The NetBill architecture assumes that in the future vendors will distribute information products varying from complex software valued at thousands of dollars per copy to journal pages or real-time stock quotes valued at a few cents each. For this to be effective, the network-based electronic commerce transaction costs must be held to a fraction of the cost of the item.

Today transactions on the Internet for typical online credit card purchases cost approximately 23 cents, on average, for processing between the merchants, customers, and banks. With the eventual size of the market (both in number of transactions and number of people by the end of century) as well as the growth of the information industry, smaller transactions have the potential to be more commonplace and provide a valued piece of the overall customer solution. Several other organizations are creating standards for micropayments, such as CyberCash, DEC, and VISA.

WHAT'S IN IT FOR THE CUSTOMER?

So far we have looked at the vendor side of the equation. Now, we turn to the other parties involved. What will it take for your customer to go online?

A MORE COMPLETE SOLUTION

Customers want complete and convenient solutions, not pieces of solutions. Simply repurposing data, the application, or the product is not enough. Repackaging is an inherently partial solution. Providing a complete solution requires rethinking the whole process or product/service. Instead of planning a vacation through a series of phone calls, faxes, and e-mail messages, customers would prefer a convenient, full solution offering them the ability to create a customized vacation from a number of options with all the information available in one place online. A hypothetical but technically possible scenario like this is well beyond the package solutions currently offered. (Therefore, a complete solution is about a new product, more flexible and customizable than ever before.) It is so flexible that it does not exist in full form until it is created by the customer through access to an online solution.

Galt, a Pittsburgh-based Internet mutual fund center, markets its NETworth site as the financial marketplace for the Internet. It is an intermediary, or *info*-mediary, between prospective mutual fund investors and mutual fund companies. It maintains a comprehensive mutual fund service where customers can search the Morningstar database of fund information, organize mutual fund data with the Mutual Fund Market Manager, and update portfolio stock quote services.

Looking at Galt as a tool that online investors would be interested in, Intuit acquired it in 1996. Now, when customers access the Intuit site, they have a more complete solution available to them thanks to the capabilities of Quicken, links to the Galt site, and more. Similarly Lombard Institutional Investors' site has external hyperlinks to the other financial sites.

When SGI designed a conference registration application on its Intranet, the company included more than the application itself. It rethought the whole process of registration on its site and provided a variety of transparent and nontransparent links to users for hotel registration, roommate preference, car rental information, and flight-booking capabilities.

The Internet will not embrace all individuals, nor will it be the sole place where customers look for complete solutions. The Internet will not totally replace the traditional means used to connect to customers. Using the Internet will be *complementary,* a value-added resource for interested customers, but it will not replace the traditional ways of doing business. Personal interaction is still better and more valued than even the best Internet product and service for certain products and transactions.

The level of human interaction needed also depends on the particular customer. For example, a person may use the Internet to find the best mortgage rate but want to meet face to face with a banker to ask about specifics of the mortgage contract. An e-mail message may not be sufficient. The most complete winning strategy will employ hybrids. It will use people, bricks and mortar, and technology, relying on the strengths of each and using their synergy to create complete customer solutions.

Some theorists suggest that the Internet will free the world from intermediaries. They suggest that the customer will always value directness to the end business. Some Internet strategies have been successful in achieving this, such as Spring Street Brewery, discussed in Chapter 1. However, there is significant value in intermediaries, the specialized business partners called interlinkers.

In fact, given time, intermediaries are likely to grow in value and number. These interlinker relationships can be established quickly and provide value by facilitating the customer solution, providing context around the solution, and presenting the appropriate options. Scudder Investment Services, Inc. presents its information on the Internet through Galt's NETworth financial marketplace, because of Galt's capability to reach potential customers. Prospective customers can link directly to a mutual fund site, or define information on their servers.

Similarly, Industry.Net has 4,500 industrial companies paying for an Internet presence on the Web to display products and services. Industry.Net provides an intermediary function, bringing together thousands of businesses in one place. Though currently providing product information, Industry.Net also has a focus on creating scaleable back-end systems to support transactions. A scaleable service can then be offered for a range of business needs, from complex transaction processing to less complex applications for smaller businesses.

HOW CUSTOMERS BENEFIT FROM BECOMING "YOUR" EMPLOYEE

The value in providing information so that customers can serve themselves has significant advantages for both parties. Service-oriented businesses must define themselves in terms of how well, and to what degree, this capability can be integrated into their business models. Dick Schaaf notes in *Keeping the Edge* that a largely untapped power exists in such customers. For a service company, delivering the complete solution entirely by itself is more time- and labor-intensive than finding cooperative partners (customers) who (1) already know what will satisfy their needs and expectations; (2) cost nothing in terms of labor (or training, management, and administrative support); and (3) become more loyal and thus more valuable over the long term as mutually satisfying relationships develop.[6]

Internet software applications can provide customers with the ability to perform, in effect, their own customer service functions. A simple, early, and noted example of this can be seen at Federal Express. By extending its existing information assets, it allows direct customer access to its mainframe package tracking databases via the Internet. This capability significantly reduces Federal Express's expenditures for customer service support, reportedly by as much as $2 million per year. Customers also benefit by the ability and convenience of tracking package status 24 hours per day, seven days per week.

SGI's Intranet has a customer-servicing application that allows employees to look up details on orders that the company has filled. Salespeople can transparently link to Federal Express to monitor the specific status of any order, even if it has left the factory.

Customer self-servicing applications can be developed for almost any service-oriented business. Customers can then better see and understand what they are getting. For the travel business, Corretti Soft, a California-based software developer, introduced an Internet application called Hotelview that allows travelers to access information, such as room availability, rates, general hotel information, and even images of hotels. Users can also make room reservations and cancellations without ever speaking to an agent, if they choose. Holiday Inn was one of the first hotel chains to enable customers to book rooms online. Many hotel chains are studying the possibility of providing 3-D walk-throughs of rooms over the Internet.

For your Internet strategy to benefit customers, you need to realize that merely giving them access to existing data on your mainframe does not deliver success. Data must be easy to use and meet customers' expectations. In the early 1980s, the banking industry tried offering access to existing data, with home banking via personal computers. This was a failure, largely because the mass of potential customers was not substantial and banks were unable to offer innovative products around the data. Thus, merely offering access to data so that customers can serve themselves does not guarantee success.

Providing customers with the option of performing their own customer service functions is often referred to as the customer-employee model. The possibilities of educating customers about products and services become much more achievable in this medium, as companies are not limited to small advertisements in printed media and brief television commercials.

Traditionally, customer support representatives spend a large percentage of their time answering the same questions over and over. Simply posting the most frequently asked questions (FAQs) on your Internet site can significantly reduce the volume of support requests. In addition, postpurchase training, such as tips on product use, can be provided, enhancing customer satisfaction. Sun Microsystems claims to have saved almost $43,000 per month in personnel costs by posting FAQs. Sun also claims to save $1.3 million per month in shipping and personnel costs by preparing and delivering user software patches (to fix bugs in a program) via the Internet. Postpurchase education and training can also be provided. Customer support, servicing, education, and training can be an expensive aspect of your business, but the opportunity to communicate directly with customers via the Internet can lead to dramatic cost savings in this area.

Additional benefits accrue to providing the customer with the self-service option. For example, the ability of customers to obtain more detailed information about a product or service may lead to more educated use of the product and therefore product satisfaction, more intelligent buying decisions, repeat purchases, fewer returns, and customer loyalty. Lombard sees the Internet as an opportunity to train investors and is considering the idea of setting up a virtual Lombard University to provide investment tools and education for its customers. With these types of value-added offerings, businesses benefit by building long-term relationships with customers, who benefit in turn from performing their own customer service activities.

You can turn your customers into employees by making them a bigger part of the design process. Amazon.com believes that it receives more customer feedback and suggestions in one day than traditional bookstores in one year. Sausage Software says that 90 percent of the original test-market suggestions for improvement were incorporated in the development of HotDog. By turning customers into employees, these companies created products that are very different from those of their competitors because they were completely driven by customer needs.

CATERING TO THE CUSTOMER THROUGH MONITORING AND RESPONDING

The ONYX example in Chapter 1 illustrates a company that can monitor and respond to customers almost immediately. Before a customer calls back, sales representatives can tell which Internet pages she explored. This helps ONYX better predict and respond to customers. As noted in the episode described in Chapter 1, both the sales representative and the president of ONYX responded to the customer. This is because ONYX built its system to alert specific people to respond to an inquiry based on the position of the prospect. In this case the prospect was a company president, so ONYX was able to respond with messages from the person with comparable authority within its own organization. Innovative use of the Internet provides you many different ways to cater to your customer through monitoring and responding, ultimately benefiting both the customer and the business.

With the Internet, you can track the exact actions of customers who access your business site either internally or externally. Figures 3.1 and Figures 3.2 show graphs generated by Internet activity analysis software. This type of software runs programs against your Internet server logs, which record all customer activities on your site. In particular, these programs pinpoint where users are coming from and track what customers did once they were on your site.

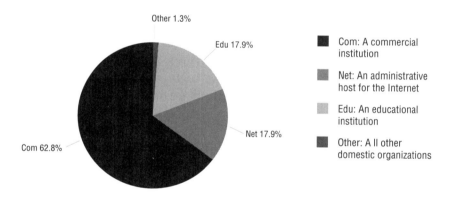

Figure 3.1 *Internet Usage Information*

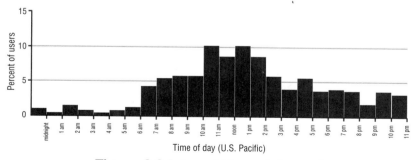

Figure 3.2 *Internet Usage Information*

You can collect several types of relevant customer data as part of your strategy, including:

- The pages or functionality most frequently accessed by users.

- The most popular times of day your site is used.

- The Internet site from which a user came through interlinking.

- The state and country from which a user accesses your site.

- The type of company or academic or governmental institution from which a user accesses your site.

The information found in Figure 3.1 and Figure 3.2 represents only a fraction of that which is potentially available. These tables were obtained from Interse Corporation's product called Market Focus. In the market focus report at Figure 3.1, 62.8 percent of the users to the site were from commercial organizations, while Figure 3.2 shows that most of the traffic was generated between 1:00 A.M. and 2:00 P.M.

It is possible to gather additional, higher-level information. For example, ONYX integrated its internal sales systems with its external Internet systems to obtain the names, titles, fax numbers, and phone numbers of users. Chapter 7 explains the type of software components needed for a Internet site in greater detail.

With user analysis software, responses to new product and service offerings or new company campaigns can be measured in a real-time mode. For example, Market Focus tracks a user's path through a site, the time spent on each page, and a host of other data as desired by an Internet strategist.

But an initial user report represents only the tip of the iceberg; the more specific values and habits of customers are below the surface. It is through the integration of applications such as decision support systems, sales force automation applications, executive information systems, and data mining applications that the real value can be found. You have to pick and choose the application most appropriate for your needs. Tools that analyze Internet logs, such as Market Focus, provide a review of your customer use. Complex data mining tools can be used to conduct more detailed examination of your activity.

Data mining refers to the discovery of meaningful new correlations, patterns, and trends by sifting through large amounts of data stored in repositories and by using pattern recognition technologies. Data mining applications help executives with decision-making by providing statistical information about customers' habits, patterns, and trends.

Owing to advances in computer processing power over the last few years, a variety of data mining applications are now available from companies like Oracle, Red Brick, and Informix. The processing power for this type of application is now becoming financially viable for medium-sized companies.

In the most successful implementations, applications based on sophisticated algorithms find previously unrecognized patterns in data. Once discovered, such patterns enable businesses to quickly anticipate buyers' needs, resolve client dissatisfaction, and keep customers happy. The greatest data-mining success stories involve businesses, often retailers, that use this process to respond to previously unrecognized patterns in customers' buying behaviors. For example, grocery chains analyzed customers' purchases and learned that buyers of cosmetics typically also purchase greeting cards. The chains subsequently increased sales in both product categories by redesigning store layouts to ensure that the two product lines are positioned in the same aisle. Some companies are even considering making available data-mining applications to customers so they can make their own correlations of data from the business.

VIRTUAL LOCATIONS FOR CUSTOMER CONVENIENCE

As enabling technologies mature, businesses virtualize their offerings, and the necessity for bricks and mortar becomes less relevant for some businesses. In other cases—for example, Amazon.com—the physical structure was never needed in the first place.

Security First Network Bank is the first full-service bank on the Internet. It says that it operates with only one third of the overhead of a regular bank of comparable asset size, although that overhead now includes a staff to provide 24-hour online support every day of the year. Benefits are given back to customers through increased money market and CD interest rates—a dividend resulting from efficiencies of service and lack of expenses incurred in a typical physical location.

Seattle's Blume Art Gallery moved from real space to a virtual Internet market space. "We are taking the gallery to everyone," notes co-owner Jeff Blume. He took the step of conducting business exclusively through the Internet for two reasons: first, the business gained the ability to reach a wider market, and second, technology made the venture feasible. In the privacy of her home or office, the customer can browse through more than 10,000 digital images of fine art and prints in the gallery. "This is, by far, the largest selection of poster art on the Internet," Blume notes.

If a customer types in the keyword *Monet*, dozens of prints available for sale appear on the screen. Or, if someone wants to see all artists whose names starts with *M*, he just types in that letter. Specific posters and prints can be located by subject, title, or a word that appears in the title. Alongside the displayed artwork is the title, artist, size, and price. Click on another button and an order form appears, complete with a selection of shipping methods. While the digital image is not as clear as an original hanging on a wall or reproduced in a printed catalog, the presentation is more than adequate to make a selection.

Even though customers appreciate the convenience and flexibility of a virtual location, they are likely to want the capability, when necessary, to go behind the virtual storefront to talk with experts. For example, the Australian subsidiary of the U.S. Citicorp., CitiBank, has begun to test virtual bank locations, lightly staffed with only those people needed to operate the facilities and perform administration services locally. However, customers can communicate with mortgage and loan officers through high-tech video conferencing systems networked to the banks headquarters.

For organizations seeking to expand rapidly and globally, setting up virtual offices is an attractive option. These offices provide a minimum local physical presence but the information resources of the full company. A number of IT companies developed hardware and software products whereby businesses can use the Internet as a Virtual Private Network (VPN). In this way, the Internet backbone itself is used to transport a company's business data between offices. These products offer security measures such as encryption to protect against theft and misuse of data. Microsoft, in its Windows NT operating system, plans to offer a technology that will enable creation of a private network over the Internet.

DEALING DIRECT CAN LOWER COSTS FOR CUSTOMERS

Internet customers benefit from working directly with Internet businesses in the form of lower costs. Pittsburgh-based USAir, for example, started selling discount fares on the Internet, as have American Airlines and Northwest Airlines. In some cases, online fares are as much as 70 percent below the lowest fares available through a travel agent or an airline reservation office. Direct Internet sales are a way to fill up some of the thousands of seats that go unsold on flights daily. By simply posting the fares and routes to customers who are willing to buy direct, airlines can improve their capacity.

Charles Schwab has always passed savings on to customers willing to use self-service functions. "Investors have come to rely on Schwab's leadership in technology and our aggressive use of technology to lower costs to investors," says David S. Pottruck, president and COO of the Charles Schwab Corporation. "As electronic trading volume grows and more trades are directed to the Internet, we'll pass the cost savings on to customers. Today, more than one in five (22 percent) of the approximately 90,000 daily trades by Schwab customers are transacted through PC-based services offered by the company, and that's about half of the entire online brokerage marketplace."

E*Trade Securities is a deep-discount brokerage firm in Palo Alto, California. It launched an Internet trading system that allows account holders to place stock and option orders, receive confirmation information, review their portfolios, and receive quotes and news from E*Trades Web site. Access to the site is free and E*Trade, offers some of the lowest commissions in the securities industry. It currently charges $14.95 for market orders of up to 5,000 shares listed on the New York Stock Exchange or the American Stock Exchange. Execution of orders placed during trading hours are normally confirmed within seconds.

Other firms, including Netstock Direct, take the idea one step further by eliminating the necessity of a broker altogether. Netstock Direct acts as an intermediary, enabling individual investors to buy stock directly from selected public companies without commissions.

Due to competitive pressures and streamlined operations, prices for services like E*Trade are expected to be eventually as low as $10 per trade. To diversify, E*Trade launched Online Ventures, which uses the Internet to find venture financing for companies with accredited investors. E*Trade tries to prequalify investors electronically before they browse through pending deals.

E*Trade is not the only firm pursuing this line of thought. IPOnet is also examining the market for online venture capital. IPOnet proposes to post notices of private offerings in a password-protected section of its site. Only accredited investors will be able to access offerings.

The following example illustrates an Internet business case that benefits the customer while achieving strategic objectives for the business, including generating additional revenues and eliminating middlemen. AND Meerschaum Smoking Pipes is located in Eskisehir, Turkey, and employs approximately 35 mostly part-time people. AND produces hand-carved smoking pipes made of meerschaum, a mineral substance found only in Turkey. The retail price for an average AND pipe in the United States is close to $400.

The local market in Turkey provides only a small portion of current sales and market potential for AND. The value of the pipes tends to be much higher in other parts of the world due to the scarcity of meerschaum and the uniqueness of the product. Ninety-five percent of AND's product sales are overseas.

AND always sought more control over sales and distribution, but the cost to market and sell its products using traditional methods was prohibitive. It relied on an export management company to purchase the pipes and export them for resale. AND's cost to produce one pipe is approximately $35. Pipes are sold to distributors for $45 each, for a profit of $10 per pipe. The pipes are exported to markets such as the United States, Japan, and Europe, where in the retail market they sell for an average of $400 each.

In an effort to gain more control over the product's pricing and distribution, AND recently hired an Internet service provider (ISP) to produce a low-cost marketing and distribution channel. The ISP developed a simple, easy-to-use storefront, displaying available models and prices. AND also provides a fax number on its site for customers interested in ordering via fax. Rather than keeping the price of pipes at $400, AND decided to offer them for approximately $150 each, providing an exceptional value to customers and a higher profit margin for AND. The company's operational costs for hosting the site are less than $50 per month.

AND's benefits of utilizing the Internet include:

- the ability to better control, direct, and manage sales and distribution

- a larger market reach

- an increase in profit margin

- significantly improved value proposition to the customers, including cost savings and convenience

- increased customer closeness, including the ability to communicate and interact directly with customers to better address their changing needs and interests (through e-mail)

- a low-cost, yet highly effective, distribution channel

Even though AND has not advertised its site except through search engines, AND is selling about 20 pipes per month. Prospects are only led to the site when they search for pipes using search engines.

TECHNOLOGY LIMITS AND OPPORTUNITIES

In general, technology is more of a driver and fundamental enabler of business strategy than ever before. The Internet technology set in particular is enabling new technology strategies that can strengthen your business case and give you reasons to fully embrace the technology set. These include network-centric computing and platform independence application development.

NETWORK-CENTRIC COMPUTING

The Internet allows you to design and build your business applications in a new manner, referred to as network-centric computing, given the maturity of its technologies. Network-centric computing is best suited when there is an open, accessible, resilient network between business partners or customers. High-performance networks are becoming available in many forms. Digital communication links are now readily available from many homes in the United States and several other countries. These digital links, referred to as the Integrated Services Digital Network (ISDN), provide the type of performance traditionally limited to commercial businesses.

The Internet offers sufficient redundancy for most forms of business commerce. Although the network cannot guarantee information delivery, the Internet was built with multiple paths to sites, and its underlying data delivery mechanisms have good operating records. From its inception as a government-funded defense project, the Internet has had a highly redundant and reliable infrastructure. In fact, Internet service providers are beginning to announce their plans to offer service level guarantees to business.

Internet programming languages, such as Sun Microsystems' Java, can be used to develop all types of network-centric applications, which can run on any platform on any PC. From a strategic corporate technology perspective, the Internet is really about an early phase of network-centric computing, which inherently relies on a robust network infrastructure for application development.

PLATFORM INDEPENDENCE

In the past, businesses communicating electronically with customers encountered a lack of control of the customer's computer platforms and of a cost-effective network infrastructure. In addition, businesses had to ensure that their customers or partners had software that could communicate with a variety of platforms, different versions of software, and a multiplicity of configurations.

Tools such as Java promote the goal of platform independence. One application can be developed and leveraged across all customers or partners regardless of platform. Moreover, the application can be distributed efficiently via the Internet and run by the client computer or the server computer. Java is discussed in greater detail in Chapter 7.

Platform-independent applications can be deployed to provide the customer with business functionality and access to your corporate data. All new corporate application development efforts should consider developing systems with platform-independent models. It is important to build in-house skills and reusable software programs that can be used over the Internet or Intranet. Although Java is often noted for its graphics capabilities, its ability to seamlessly network corporate databases is more significant for your business.

Leslie Tortora, a partner at New York–based Goldman, Sachs & Company, responsible for technology, says, "It's the Webs promised platform independence that the firm finds most enticing. With the advent of the Web and browsers, all of a sudden you don't have to care as much, because you build more applications that can run across the desktop, whether you are using Microsoft NT or Sun." Goldman uses its corporate Intranet to deliver internal information and to communicate with its clients, which include institutions, money managers, corporations, and individual investors. The Web, says Tortora, "enables the business to extend in ways that have just been very difficult in the past."

A large engineering firm had been trying to implement a timesheet submission and reporting system across its network of 900 Macs, 900 PCs, and 300 UNIX workstations for six months. The challenge was significant because of the difference in computing platforms. Developing and maintaining applications for each of these platforms was very complex. With Web standards, all browsers communicate using the same protocol, so there is no need to develop for all computing platforms. Failing to accomplish the task with the traditional development approach, the company began experimenting with Web technology. Within two weeks it had an application up and running with a back-end Sybase database. Web browsers were used to accomplish cross-platform viewing. In addition, training was minimal because the system emulated existing paper-based forms and engineers were able to assist each other even if they were using different machines.

THE OPPORTUNITY TO GET YOUR CUSTOMERS ONLINE

Many companies have found that their customers do not have access to the Internet. Successful companies can, however, use this as an opportunity, not a limitation. If your customers do not currently have access to the Internet, or if they have not yet made it part of their daily business practice, your business could be catalyst for getting them online and making your service a part of their business cycle. Assisting current or potential customers onto the Internet can provide your business with a strategic and competitive advantage, building customer loyalty as customers configure their systems with your products and services in mind. You can also work with clients to develop effective designs in order to make your site part of their daily business practice. Providing them with the proper browser software and Internet access software, which you could either give away or charge a nominal fee for, allows you to customize the browser to come directly to your Internet business site as a default. Netscape and Microsoft offer a developer's kit that extends their popular browsers for a variety of purposes. Companies can add logos and define the user interface in order to be more accessible to their customer bases.

Intuit worked with an ISP so that customers would use the Intuit site as their point of entry to the Internet. When someone buys Quicken, Intuit's financial planning software, and installs it on his PC or Mac, he is prompted to get additional information from the Intuit Internet site. The site is continually refreshed with software updates, advice, and interlinks to other appropriate financial sites, such as Galt. Galt's NETworth Internet site was developed as a mutual fund marketplace. Dozens of mutual fund companies advertise and educate customers about their products on the site. If the customer did not have access to the Internet when he bought Quicken, he can dial up a predefined ISP from the Quicken software directly and set up an account. Once the customer registers, Intuit becomes the first site he sees when entering the Internet. Intuit then leads customers through the Internet, navigating to appropriate interlinking business partners like Galt.

Fidelity Investments and Prudential Securities worked with various Internet service providers to offer discounts for those customers who want access to the Internet. Even some Fortune 500 companies have contemplated customizing browsers and sending them in place of or along with an annual report to the shareholders. Shareholders would receive the benefit of seeing more information, presented far more graphically than previously possible with a glossy annual report, and the ability to interact with the company's site.

Computer game vendors often employ a concept referred to as *Internet in an envelope*. They distribute diskettes in computer magazines or through mailings that, when placed in a PC, dial directly into the Internet and go to the game company's Internet site. New game versions can be downloaded; customers can register for support and obtain addition information.

COMMERCIAL SOFTWARE VS. CREATING YOUR OWN

The common buy-verses-build question is, "Do I create software myself or buy commercially available software?" Most businesses incline toward buying software and customizing it to fit their needs. Due to the market's focus, hundreds of Internet-enabled applications are becoming available to businesses. These include high-end, multimillion-dollar manufacturing applications such as SAP to inexpensive graphical applications than can be used to easily build Internet-compatible graphics. Internet business applications are available from vendors, including Netscape, which has developed some high-end integrated applications. Its Merchant system is a bundled package that includes a secure Web server, databases for content and customer information, and a set of supporting programs to provide credit card verification. The Merchant system allows a company, such as a retailer, to establish a cyber market with large a number of products. It supports secure communication and credit card transactions with real-time authorization. These types of packages provide retailers with an easy way to establish a full-function cybermall or cybershop without significant software development or build time.

Many software vendors provide Internet server solutions for businesses. Seattle-based iCAT Corp. provides solutions for small- to medium-sized stores. iCAT initially started building CD-ROMs for catalog businesses and realized that its product could be easily extended as an Internet server. One of its clients was able to provide its entire catalog on the Internet for under $15,000 in development costs; the server and installation took three weeks. However, its product information was already in a form that would easily fit into the iCAT product set. If your information is not available electronically in a proper format, the process will take much longer. The availability of these turnkey products will fuel commercial activities on the Internet, because some businesses will not need to build Internet server applications from scratch.

Other plug-and-play or turnkey solutions can also be used to get a site operational for much less than $15,000 in hardware and software. Source companies include Microsoft, Netscape, and Progress Software. Other operational components are discussed in Chapter 7.

NETWORK BANDWIDTH LIMITS WHAT YOU CAN DO NOW, BUT DON'T WAIT

It is important to limit development of applications to those bandwidths currently available to customers. From home this is generally 28.8 kbps and from offices up to 1.5 Mbps access shared among employees. Rich graphics are enticing but will frustrate customers who dial in from low-speed devices. Some reports suggest that even profitable sites focus less on graphics and more on functionality.

However, technological advancements make this a moving target. Cable modems, currently being tested in more than 50 trials worldwide, could become commercially viable by the end of 1997. At least 25 trials for cable modems are going on in North America alone, primarily sponsored by cable companies. Many of these are outlined in Chapter 7. Once cable modems become available, consumers will have access to dramatically higher speed links to the Internet and other online services. To appreciate the level of performance improvements expected with cable technology, consider the results of a study measuring the time to download a video whose playback time is 5 minutes 48 seconds and whose size is 55 megabytes (see Table 3.1).[7]

Table 3.1 Network Performance

Media	Duration
Telephone line at 28.8 kilobits per second (kbps)	4.24 hours
ISDN network line at 56 kbps	2.18 hours
T1* line at 1.5 Mbps	14.66 minutes
Cable modem/Ethernet at 10 Mbps	44 seconds
Cable modem at 27 Mbps	16.2 seconds

*T1 line represents a high-speed telecommunication line that can be used for voice or data traffic. Outside the United States these lines are generally equivalent to E1s.

Although Internet bandwidth at present is certainly a performance bottleneck and a limiting factor, several steps are being taken by the operators of the backbone networks, providers, and software companies, in addition to cable companies, to alleviate the problem.

The Internet backbone in the United States currently operates at a speed or bandwidth of 45 megabits per second (Mbps). This is the telecommunications network that transfers data over the Internet to local and regional networks. Companies like MCI and Sprint are responsible for the U.S. Internet backbone. The next major upgrade to the Internet backbone, referred to as Very High Speed Backbone Network Service (vBNS), will provide more than a tenfold improvement in the available bandwidth. Vinton Cerf, recognized as a founding father of the Internet and now a senior vice president at MCI, predicts that vBNS will lead to applications not considered possible because of current bandwidth limitations, such as real-time and multimedia applications. vBNS could be commercially available within the next several years.

Several telecommunication vendors are already responding with solutions to address service and performance problems. For example, Omaha-based MFS Communications Company merged with ISP UUNET Technologies, Inc. (Fairfax, Virginia) in mid-1996. A few months later, they merged with Worldcom (Jackson, Mississippi) to form MFS-Worldcom, which offers local and long-distance services. The combination of UUNET, MFS, and Worldcom networks will eventually enable the company to provide wide-ranging end-to-end

Internet service agreements. This may be done by carrying traffic as far as possible on private networks, where quality service levels can be ensured. Data will then be transferred to the Internet at the closest physical location to the Internet site. This approach mitigates risks of performance and service errors on the Internet. In fact, Alan Taffel, UUNET vice president of sales and marketing, says the company may also offer guaranteed service levels to the Intranet customer. The concept is new, so specifics are not yet worked as to how this would be accomplished. The trend of additional vendors providing more service guarantees will continue as the Internet evolves. In the future, it is likely customers will be paying for class-of-service options with the Internet and Intranet, similar to the U.S. Mail service options; time-sensitive material will be sent faster (for a price) and lower-priority bulk mail will be sent slower. MCI will also launch a premium Internet service with guaranteed network throughput and availability levels aimed at corporate Intranets.

MFS-Worldcom is getting ready to trial T-1 speed Internet access using low-cost asymmetric digital subscriber line (ADSL) technology. ADSL is a new technology standard utilizing copper cables, the same infrastructure of the current telecommunication operators. This is more than 50 times faster than the 28.8 kbps transmission typical today. Copper cables do not have to be replaced with fiber for high performance. If successful, MFS-Worldcom may adopt the technique in the United States, giving users high-speed Internet access at a fraction of the cost of an equivalent T-1 line. The ADSL service will enable users to receive data at 1.5 Mbps and send data at 64k bps.

Although these fundamental network infrastructure improvements are in the future; software vendors provide innovative solutions today to alleviate current performance problems for customers. Consider FreeLoader, the first offline WorldWide Web delivery service, from FreeLoader, Inc. Internet users simply choose which sites and at what times they want to browse their favorite Web pages. FreeLoader then collects the Internet Web information and stores it on hard drives, automatically caching the sites for later viewing by the customer. Users do not have to be present or lose productive time during lengthy download periods, nor do they have to wait for graphically intensive sites to download. Users can visit these sites at their convenience. FreeLoader can be programmed to visit the sites during off-peak hours, eliminating online gridlock. FreeLoader also has an interactive screensaver that stores preselected Web pages on the user's desktop. The screensaver also keeps users current as to when a Web page is updated or a new site launched.

Another approach to this problem is illustrated by America Online (AOL), which actually caches popular Internet sites on devices called caching servers, so that when AOL users navigate the Internet, they are often not leaving the AOL network. These servers contain copies of remote Internet server data. The advantage to AOL customers is better response time. The disadvantage is that businesses with a presence on the Internet cannot create records of all users who have visited its site; the data from the site is copied to the servers, and therefore customers may not actually enter the site.

HOW MUCH COMPUTER PROCESSING POWER DO CUSTOMERS NEED?

The current computing power available to both businesses and customers provides more than enough capacity for several types of Internet communication and is available at a reasonable cost. In addition, symmetrical multiprocessing systems (SMPs), which are becoming more available to businesses, string Central Processing Units (CPUs) together to share processing loads. This can dramatically increase speed at reasonable cost increments.

Consider the power of Digital Equipment Corporation's (DEC) Alta Vista search engine. A search engine attempts to catalog as many Internet sites as possible. A user enters in search words and Alta Vista returns with sites containing those words. With today's computing power, DEC is able to index every word of every available Web page (currently 15 billion words, 30 million pages). This enables DEC's search engine to respond to queries almost instantly.

OPEN STANDARDS

Base your technology strategy on open standards. Standards set by international groups such as W3C, IEEE, and others, as opposed to proprietary or vendor-specific approaches, provide for open international access across networks and computing systems. Internet standards reduce the cost of communication and increase the ease of application development and deployment. Non-open strategies limit your opportunities for success. Consumers actions indicate that open networks are favored over proprietary networks. Consider Apple's eWorld, an online network similar to the Microsoft Network (MSN) and Prodigy. In 1996, less than two years after its release, eWorld was shut down by Apple, and its nearly 150,000 subscribers were urged to move to AOL. Moreover, MSN in Australia, called On-Australia, shut down in 1996, less than a year after the joint venture between Telstra and Microsoft was initiated with much fanfare. The openness and power of the Internet forced Apple, Microsoft, and Telstra, among others, to rethink their strategies. In the interim AT&T, with its recognition of the value of openness, says it cannot keep up with the demand for sign-up kits for the WorldNet Internet access service it launched in March 1996. This openness is clearly where customers want online service to go.

SOFTWARE FLEXIBILITY

An important new approach to software flexibility includes object-based models, in which software can be changed quickly and components reused and integrated into other applications. Java programs are developed in an object-based architecture. As Tony Martins, a senior vice president at Claremont Technology Group, suggests "the challenge faced by business processing software today is very different from that of the past twenty years. In the past, software was an accessory, a subordinate tool; today, software faces the challenge of being an 'enabler of change,' the tool that permits service organizations to face the economic storm out there. In order to fulfill that role, the nature and properties of the software that successful organizations need is very different from what they had in the past."

The low cost and ease of access of Internet technology in many areas of the world has driven the rapid commercialization of the Internet and created many opportunities for businesses and benefits for customers. The Internet represents by far the least expensive communications service option with few, if any, exceptions relative to proprietary-based solutions, such as private network offerings from IBM. In addition, the Internet was developed with an attitude of vendor independence, openness, and neutrality. This dramatically reduced the cost of hardware and software for access and operation on the Internet. The original aim of the Internet—to link academic and research communities and foster the sharing of information—is reflected in the borderless nature of the WorldWide Web, nonproprietary development, and distribution of free and low-cost enabling software. The fate of eWorld and On-Australia demonstrate the Internet's hostility to corporate attempts to force standards and technologies.

After reading the first three chapters of this book, review the Internet's capabilities from a strategic business perspective. By now you should have a deeper respect for the capabilities of the Internet. The points in Table 3.2 were initially outlined in Chapter 1.

Table 3.2 *Key Attributes of the Internet*

Internet Attribute	Description
Global	Accessible in more than 100 countries on six continents. Navigation around the Internet is seamless between countries from the user perspective.
Cost-Effective	Unlike traditional communication models, telecommunication costs are not distance-sensitive. Customers are not limited to navigating and exploring locally.
Computer Platform–Independent	Many, if not most, computers have the ability to communicate via the Internet independent of operating systems and hardware. Customers are not limited by existing hardware systems.

(continued)

Table 3.2 *(continued)*

Internet Attribute	Description
Efficient Applications Development Environment	In many respects, applications can be more efficiently developed and distributed because they can be built without regard to the customer's or business partner's technology platform. Application updates do not have to be manually installed on computers. Rather, Internet-related technologies provide this capability inherently through automatic deployment of software updates.
Widely Adopted by the Information Technology Industry and Some Governments	Information technology vendors made fundamental shifts in their technology direction, focusing strategically on the development of Internet-related technologies and network-centric computing. Also, government agencies appear proactive in the adoption of Internet technologies, creating a greater demand for Internet services through initiatives like the National Information Infrastructure in the United States.
New Capabilities and Solutions for Customers	New types of applications can be developed that were significantly more challenging before, such as real-time updates of business information and customer access to corporate applications and information assets.
Monitor and Respond to Exact Habits of Customers	Through the Internet, businesses can monitor specific habits of customers in a real-time fashion, ranging from when sites are accessed to which sites direct or refer customers. (*Direct* in this context refers to a business site's ability to link to another business site.) Businesses can specifically identify the value of their online marketing approaches.
New Business, Marketing, Systems, Customer, Sourcing, Society, and Government Models	The Internet environment allows for more effective operating models including customer, business, information systems, marketing, and organizational, among others. Businesses are forced to rethink their competencies, customer values, differentiation, alliance opportunities,

(continued)

Table 3.2 *(continued)*

Internet Attribute	Description
	and ultimately their value proposition relative to the Internet.
Newly Enabled Customer Values, Habits, and Decision-Making Criteria	Individuals develop new values (habits, decision-making priorities, etc.) based on the capabilities of the Internet.
Interlinking	Businesses can efficiently interlink with global alliance partners to provide a more complete and integrated customer solution. Proper inter-linking partners will be integral to successful Internet business strategies.
Pull/Push Capabilities	The Internet provides an infrastructure where by information is pushed by businesses to customers or pulled by customers from businesses.

NOTES

1. Hamel, Gary, and C.K. Prahalad, "Strategic Intent," *Harvard Business Review* (May–June 1989).

2. "The CorpFiNet Interview," *www.CorpFiNet.com* (September 1996).

3. Peters, Tom, "The Boundaries of Business Partners–The Rhetoric and Reality," in *The Evolving Global Economy*. ed. Kenichi Ohmae, (Boston: Harvard Business School, 1995).

4. Davidow, William H. and Michael S. Malone. *The Virtual Corporation*. (New York: HarperCollins, 1993).

5. Rayport, Jeffrey F. and John J. Sviokla, "Exploiting the Virtual Value Chain," *Harvard Business Review* (November–December 1995):75–85.

6. Schaaf, Dick. *Keeping the Edge—Giving Customers the Service they Demand*. (New York: Penguin Group, 1995).

7. "Cable's Big Break-through," *Convergence* (February, 1996):20–21.

CHAPTER 4

LAYERED ACCESS: HOW EXTERNAL AND INTERNAL USERS WORK WITH YOUR SITE

This chapter discusses the differences—both actual and perceived—between the Internet and Intranet. The distinguishing feature is one of layered access. Your partners, customers, vendors, and suppliers all have different business needs, and it follows that their information needs differ as well. The chapter goes on to explore the types of Internet connections between businesses and concludes with a discussion of the virtual corporation.

INTRANET VS. INTERNET—LAYERED ACCESS

For the purposes of your business planning, it is important to cast aside the technological distinctions between the Internet and Intranet. The only real difference is one of *access to information*. Customers and business partners may not need to view information available to your employees. The information to which your banks, law firms, and accountants have access is likely to be different than the data your suppliers need. Similarly, you may want to offer different degrees of access to customers, depending on their interests, needs, and buying habits.

The term *Intranet* commonly defines Internet applications employed within an internal private network. The technologies (with the exception of your own internal network technology) are the same, the only difference being access restrictions by type of user: customer, employee, business partner. In general, the term *Intranet* means an internal, private business communications environment based on Internet technologies and services. A company's Internet server is typically on the other side of a device referred to as a *firewall*, that attempts to prevent unauthorized access to the Intranet from the public Internet. Typically, the firewall is both a hardware (PC- or UNIX-based) and software device that filters information packets between the public Internet and your internal network. This is illustrated in Figure 4.1.

Figure 4.1 *Traditional Internet/Intranet Definition*

Your business case and strategy should incorporate both the Internet and Intranet in a single strategy. Creating two strategies, one for each, limits your perspective. Why? Because the Internet is all about integrating Internet/Intranet technologies into your business architecture, your interactions with customers, other businesses, as well as your employees. In fact, the strict technology definition breaks down when you ask the following technology questions:

- If business partners (but not the general public) are inter-linked over the Internet, would this be described as an Intranet or Internet? Technically, it could be both, not one or the other.

- If a corporation employs application servers in several different locations to serve both internal employees and external customers simultaneously over the Internet, is this Internet or Intranet? Again, it could be both, not one or the other.

You want one cohesive and integrated strategy, not two. As you consider the questions above, the value of the term *Intranet* becomes less clear and also less relevant. The traditional Intranet definition breaks down quickly as businesses begin to strategically understand the impact of the Internet from both a business and technology perspective.

Figure 4.2 illustrates an Internet/Intranet analysis by examining the way information flows throughout a business environment. For example, remote employees can communicate over a secured private network, the public telephone network, or the Internet to access information stored on the internal corporate systems (the Intranet).

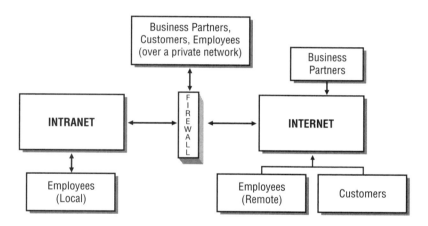

Figure 4.2 *Internet/Intranet Analysis: The Wrong Way*

Businesses will better understand and recognize the value of the Internet by considering another perspective based on *the types of business interactions* possible with the Internet. Remember, the key concepts to keep in mind are the types of business interactions and levels of access possible with your Internet business architecture. This then defines which network (public or private) you should use.

Figure 4.3 outlines types of interaction and levels of access. This may not be the exact model you want to use to build your Internet strategy, but it does represent another, perhaps more strategic perspective to consider. You may want to consider fewer layers. When striving to define the Internet/Intranet as one entity, your point of reference will be your business environment. Remember, the pyramid represents one infrastructure, incorporating both the Internet and Intranet.

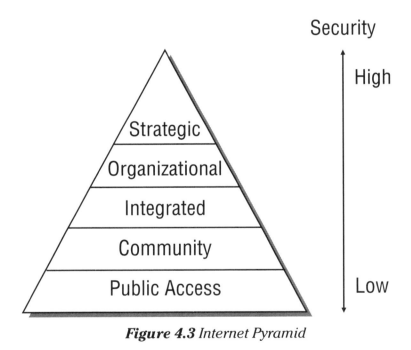

Figure 4.3 *Internet Pyramid*

Table 4.1 defines the corresponding characteristics of each layer of the Internet infrastructure.

Table 4.1 *Internet Access Layer Descriptions*

Access Layer	Characteristics	Sample Applications
Public Access Layer (PAL)	• open to the *public* worldwide • no security barriers to prevent access to Internet server information	• general marketing • generic customer service (e.g., answers to frequently asked questions) • recruiting
Community Access Layer (CAL)	• open to *certain groups* of users, such as existing customers or subscribers • moderate level of security to limit the casual user	• services/products available to registered customers • subscription-based services such as online newspapers, newsgroups, chat groups
Integrated Access Layer (IAL)	• open to *business partners* and *strategic customers* • high degree of security	• supply chain management • product planning • client/business partner–specific information services • joint project development with interlinked global partners • knowledge/ information sharing
Organizational Access Layer (OAL)	• open to the *employees* of the organization (either remotely or locally) • high level of security • depending on the degree you incorporate virtual company aspects, this may even include business partners, consultants, and other members of the virtual corporation	• employee manuals • groupware • international office communications • project management • knowledge sharing/ document management/discussion groups • human relations (HR) forms, telephone lists (e.g., employee directories)

(continued)

Table 4.1 *(continued)*

Access Layer	Characteristics	Sample Applications
Strategic Access Layer (SAL)	• open to a limited *strategic group of key customers, employees, and business partners* (internally and externally) • highest level of security	• private information sharing between executives and selected outside partners and customers such as banks, insurance companies, legal entities, government and financial institutions

This table distinguishes each access layer by the type of interaction with customers, employees, and business partners. Based on the level of access, each of these has security implications. Internet security design is discussed in greater detail in Chapter 7.

Communications between the business and customer can occur within several of the access layers, public through strategic. For example, information such as bank account balances or asset allocations may be built into the *strategic access* layer, general customer service information may be provided via the *public access* layer, and customer product planning applications could be offered through the *integrated access* layer. A base of customers needing specific data through subscriptions could be designed around solutions based on a *community access* layer. When developing your business architecture and design for the Internet, it is important to think through the type of interaction each user has with your business and the level of access each should have to your data.

The ability to communicate with business partners, customers, and employees in an integrated way is where businesses may achieve the highest business benefit. Today the Internet and networks (such as Local Area Networks [LAN] and Wide Area Networks [WAN]) within a company are thought of as the Intranet, where people collaborate very closely and internally. But the highest business value will come from the integration of two or more companies' Intranets, facilitating efficient intercompany/business partner communication. The idea of taking the Internet and integrating both the customer and supplier to get a seamless customer relationship is dramatic.

Think about relevant business processes that can be implemented at each level of the Internet pyramid. Focus on ways to provide new strategic solutions, and interlink with global business partners.

Several Internet-enabled business benefits and opportunities are already being realized with today's technology. However, typical business use of the Internet can still be characterized as limited. Most organizations utilize the Internet for passive marketing campaigns while leveraging existing marketing models and offering limited business functionality. Clearly an opportunity exists for businesses willing to consider the Internet a strategic and fundamental enabler of new business models. You need to look at new models and determine the impact on all levels of your business. At this point it is useful to expand the discussion of the Internet business architecture by outlining more specific examples of the types of interactions.

INTERNET BUSINESS CONNECTIONS

INTERNAL LINKS

Morgan Stanley links its 37 offices around the world with Internet technology to distribute data and information seamlessly on a global basis. The organizational access layer of the Internet business architecture allows it to do that. For example, the mortgage-backed securities division, based in New York, used to work until midnight each day, cutting and pasting a 100-page daily update of financial data, including Morgan Stanley's positions in a variety of bonds as well as the latest interest rates offered in Tokyo, London, and New York. The update was faxed to more than 100 traders and brokers throughout the world. The information often arrived in Tokyo after markets there opened for trading. Now Morgan Stanley's network is programmed so that most of the data is pulled from databases and assembled on a Web page without any human intervention. Traders in Tokyo get the data on time by logging onto the company's Intranet when they arrive at work. Better still, the document is updated continually throughout the day, so that traders always get the latest information.

INTERLINKING

Interlinkers represent a new type of business partner—companies that you may link to, or from, as part of an overall customer solution. Interlinking with business partners can often resolve a customer need. Examples discussed thus far include SGI, Intuit and Galt, and BayNet and Bank of America. Each interlinking partner maintains a specialization in a complementary core competency. In this way each partner offers a piece of the complete customer solution. These examples are just the beginning of what a successful strategy can employ. The Internet creates an open market with an almost endless supply of competitors and potential business partners. Organizations that align with effective business partners and interlink relevant core competencies will be in the best position to provide unique differentiation and an overall solution to customers.

The traditional business must prepare for change in order to compete successfully in this new global marketplace. In the past, businesses focused on, and responded to, a relatively limited number of competitors, generally within specified borders. Today, given the capabilities of the Internet, most businesses face not only an increase in the amount of competition but also *different types of competitors* enabled through business virtualization. These competitors have new approaches and solutions to customer needs and values. With the formation of effective interlinking business relationships, each partner brings to the table a specialized core competency, allowing you to reach customers you might not have in the past. This is referred to as the virtual organization, which has the ability to provide more complete customer solutions at a reasonable cost and the flexibility to react to the changing market more quickly than the traditional company.

LINKS WITH SUPPLIERS, BUSINESS PARTNERS, AND OTHERS

Integrating with your suppliers utilizing Internet technologies may prove valuable to your business. Using the Internet to integrate the customer and supplier to create a seamless relationship is dramatic. Several companies have already seen some of this potential benefit. For example, approximately half of the businesses with Intranets today have allowed their partners to access their Intranet information. Analysts suggest that this is not unexpected. By far the highest financial return from similar technologies, such as IBM's Lotus Notes, has been seen by companies using business-to-business communication. Lotus Notes provides for workgroups to collaborate electronically using newsgroups, databases, and other features. Scott McCready, a principal with International Data Corp., has also suggested that the bulk of the benefits from Lotus Notes applications is, in fact, due to the integration of Notes among business partners.

The German software developer SAP AG's high-end R/3 manufacturing application software suite, used by thousands of manufacturers around the world, is being extended so that it can be accessed through the Internet to handle business-to-business and customer-to-business transactions such as order entry, product pricing, and verification of product availability. Microsoft and SAP allied to support business-to-business communications over the Internet, developing products whereby two companies using R/3 can be interlinked to process orders in real time. For instance, company A's R/3 system sends an order that automatically triggers a series of events, such as inventory and price checks, in company B's R/3 system.

As use of the Internet increases, so does the ability to communicate between businesses. This can be facilitated by using Electronic Data Interchange (EDI) over the Internet. EDI is defined as the flow of information between organizations without human intervention. EDI uses standardized, structured electronic transaction sets, or messages, to replace paper or verbal information exchanges. EDI standards are developed by international standards bodies, including the United Nations, and many vendors have products that support these standards.

EDI can eliminate the expense, errors, and delays associated with human reprocessing of business inventories, frees up working capital, increases productivity, and cuts cycle times. Approximately 100,000 companies currently use EDI, and these are only a fraction of the businesses that could benefit from it. By providing tools and applications that facilitate the use of the Internet and Intranets by corporations, Netscape and General Electric Information Systems (GEIS) hope to expand the rapid adoption of EDI and other applications for business-to-business commerce. They formed a joint venture to provide cost-effective Internet-based EDI solutions for large and small companies.

Industry.Net also provides links to and from 4,500 businesses and thousands of customers. However, its approach is different from the EDI model. Its current solution offers a marketplace for large industrial companies and their customers to interact in. This consists primarily of product information. However, Industry.Net is now creating a scaleable back-end transaction service for commercial use. Scaleable services can be used by organizations of all sizes. Businesses can incorporate a variety of transaction-based applications through one site. One-on-one connectivity problems on a much larger scale are avoided.

THE VIRTUAL ORGANIZATION

Through interlinking business partners, closer communication with customers, and greater integration with vendors and suppliers, you can more easily achieve the benefits of a virtual organization. An Internet business architecture should consider the structure and benefits of a virtual organization because the Internet can enable it. Successful strategies will revisit and apply the concepts of the virtual organization with the Internet. Many businesses claim to see the value of the virtual organization concept but in reality do not apply its principles. Steven Goldman, Roger Nagel, and Kenneth Preiss, the authors of *Agile Competitors and Virtual Organizations*, suggest that there is a wide gulf between recognizing a concept in the abstract and understanding its concrete implications.

Let's review some of the many benefits of a virtual corporation. Goldman et al. find six strategic reasons that motivate companies to employ a virtual organization model:

1. sharing infrastructure, R&D, risk, and costs
2. linking complementary core competencies

3. reducing concept to cash time through sharing
4. increasing facilities and 'apparent' size (versus actual size)
5. gaining access to markets and sharing market or customer loyalty
6. migrating from selling products to selling solutions[1]

As discussed in Chapter 3, the Internet can help achieve many of these strategic benefits. The linking of complementary core competencies unites two companies in order to serve customers better. Members of the virtual organization are chosen because they bring something unique that is needed to meet a customer opportunity.

It follows that an agile company will position itself so that it is chosen by other organizations to participate in their virtual organizations. If other businesses never seek a company's participation, that company is limited to the opportunities it can develop on its own. The Internet enables a spectrum of new opportunities for business based on opportunity-pulled concepts. The Internet offers the most global, borderless, cost-effective communications and open-applications infrastructure, thus facilitating interlinked core competencies.

Ultimately, effective adoption of the Internet enables many business virtualization concepts. William H. Davidow and Michael S. Malone, in *The Virtual Corporation*, suggest that the virtual corporation began as a vision of futurists, became a possibility for business theorists, and is now an economic necessity for corporate executives. All this happened in little more than a decade. This not only underscores the inevitability of this new business model but also hints at the speeded-up sense of time that will characterize it.[2]

It is essential to understand the importance and strategic value of virtualization in the context of a competitive business environment. In a cover story on the subject, *BusinessWeek* defined a virtual company as a new organizational model that uses technology to dynamically link people, assets, and ideas.

You are urged to consider that an enabling technology set may be largely provided through Internet technology sets. Strategically implemented in a business design, the Internet technology set can force you into rethinking the components of your existing business strategy and design.

BusinessWeek identified the following key characteristics of the virtual organization:

- opportunism

- excellence

- technology

- no borders

- trust between business partners

The Internet, to a degree, provides the infrastructure to enable these five areas.

Opportunism. Unlike common organizational structures, the virtual organization is opportunity driven. It exists only when opportunities exist.

The Internet provides the potential to establish secure communications with business partners throughout the world in a highly cost-effective, immediate, and flexible manner. Businesses can use the technology to create secured virtual links between business partners and key customers. Because network costs with the Internet are independent of distance and location, businesses have more options when selecting their business partners, given more global opportunities. Customer solutions can then be delivered through the Internet.

Excellence. The virtual organization is assumed to be world class in its core competencies. Why? It is focused on these competencies; its success is dependent on the degree to which it can exploit them with global business partners.

The Internet enables the seamless linkage of core competencies by allowing global access to business partners and transparency to customers. In fact, the Internet forces you to identify your most relevant core competencies and compelling differentiation. In other words, there is a Darwinian imperative to do only that which you do well.

Technology. A virtual organization is assumed to offer world-class technology in its product service solutions. A business can offer new types of solutions to customers through the Internet's content capacity and distribution capabilities, which are more complete, convenient, and seamless than most existing systems. Existing business applications, databases, and corporate information assets can be extended in a new way via the Internet to provide world-class customer solutions.

No Borders. What makes the virtual organization concept exciting today is the growing ease with which physically separated, complementary competencies can remain geographically dispersed and still be synthesized into a coherent productive resource.

Trust. The members of the virtual organization team must behave toward each other in a trustworthy manner. If mutual trust does not exist, they cannot succeed, and customers will not do business with them.

The Internet may assist in facilitating a trusting environment by allowing various forms of communication (e.g., e-mail, voice, video). In addition, the Internet encourages individuals to utilize these forms of communication, given their cost-effectiveness and flexibility. In an analysis of trust in the virtual organization published in the *Harvard Business Review*, Charles Handy suggests that the more virtual the corporation, the greater the need to communicate and maintain personal relationships.[3] Can the Internet provide an infrastructure that supports more effective and trusting relationships? Perhaps, but with respect to trust one cannot assume that the average member of the Internet environment is more trustworthy than the average person with whom one deals face to face, and in fact there is some evidence that she may be less trustworthy. Another issue is the reliability of data found on the Internet. Unlike the world of print, with its many checks and balances, including peer reviews, that help validate data sources, it is very hard to verify Internet data unless it comes from a known and cited reliable source, and even in these instances there are errors in transcription that are hard to recognize without comparison with the original print source. Trust may be, perhaps, the most significant barrier to virtualization.

But make no mistake. Successful companies will leverage the Internet and the benefits of a virtual company. As Davidow and Malone note, "without a doubt, the new business revolution will be a shock to the system, a blow to our sensibilities. It will require new social contracts, ever-higher levels of general education, and a frightening degree of trust. But we have no choice. The virtual corporation stands before us, offering us our best chance for revitalizing the nation's economy and guaranteeing meaningful employment for our citizens. If we don't walk through its doors, our global competitors certainly will."

Elements of the virtual organization can be seen in the following examples. A group of former Novell executives launched a new venture to bring the idea of franchising to the Internet. The new company, USWeb Corporation, based in Santa Clara, California, has begun to sign small World Wide Web developers in several U.S. cities on board the franchise chain. USWeb offers the developers centralized administration, marketing, research and development, and the cooperative buying power of a large corporation over the Internet. In return, USWeb gets an up-front fee and a percentage of the developer's royalties. "The reason we chose the franchise model is that you retain the incredible creative talents of the entrepreneurs while giving them the infrastructure of a large corporation," says Joe Firmage, chairman and CEO. USWeb builds, designs, and runs Web sites for companies looking to use the Internet for sales, customer support, marketing, or any other business purpose.

It is important to recognize both the value of virtualization and the capabilities of the Internet technology set. Elements of the virtual organization concept may be the potential model for the future corporation. Degrees of virtualization vary. Some elements may not be relevant to your business. But the value of virtualization to businesses should be strategically considered in the context of the capabilities of the Internet. Organizing your business with the virtual company concepts is further discussed in Chapter 8.

Today, with the commercial arrival of the Internet, the ability to exploit the benefits of a virtual company can be realized to a more significant extent than ever before, as illustrated in Figure 4.4.

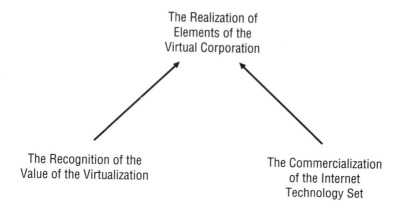

Figure 4.4 *Virtualization Drivers*

NOTES

1 Goldman, Steven L., Roger N. Nagel, and Kenneth Preiss, *Agile Competitors and Virtual Organizations*, (New York: Van Nostrand Reinhold, 1995).

2. Davidow, William H. and Michael S. Malone, *The Virtual Corporation.* (New York: HarperCollins, 1993):5.

3. Handy, Charles, "Trust and the Virtual Organization," *Harvard Business Review* (May–June 1995):40–50.

4. Davidow, et al.

CHAPTER 5

THE TEN ESSENTIAL STEPS FOR A SUCCESSFUL INTERNET STRATEGY

This chapter is arranged in two parts: The first discusses the circle of influence concept and the analysis you must carry out to formulate it. In the second part, ten steps essential to building your Internet strategy are introduced.

FOCUS ON YOUR CIRCLE OF INFLUENCE

It is clear that early, innovative, customer-centric Internet strategies lead to success, that aligning Internet strategies to business objectives is necessary, and that successful companies fully embrace and commit to the Internet business case. It is also clear that the Internet and Intranet differ with respect to levels of access and that looking at the Internet from a business perspective is more encompassing, relevant, and appropriate in building a successful Internet business architecture than looking at it from a strictly technical perspective.

To be successful on the Internet is to think beyond the solutions your business currently offers, develop new and imaginative ones, and bring them to market early. This provides the foundation on which to build your Internet business strategy. However, prior to exploring the 10 essential steps to an Internet strategy, it is important to examine one more integral part of the process, your *circle of influence*.

Circle of influence refers to the elements on which your business can have an impact—will, in fact, become the building blocks on which you build your strategy.

So, you ask yourself, what can my business have a significant impact on? What should I focus my strategy on? The most common answer all too often is the competition. Unfortunately, this could not be further from the truth. In fact, a successful strategy is not built around the competition because this implies that the competition is providing your company's thought leadership. As the philosopher Sun Tzu observed 2,500 years ago, the smartest strategy in war is the one that allows you to achieve your objective without having to fight.

Tit-for-tat responses to competitors are appropriate in some circumstances but, standing alone, they represent a fundamentally reactive approach, shifting focus away from a true business strategy. All too often companies look to their competitors when developing new business strategies even Internet strategies. They model their designs, function, and products on what has already been done. In this way competitors set the agenda for your company. Imitation may be the sincerest form of flattery, but it does not lead to competitive revitalization.[1]

Your circle of influence includes your customers, business partners, core competency, and value proposition among others. These are the elements that you can influence; they represent the building blocks of your Internet business strategy and, ultimately, your customer solution.

Look at each element in detail, starting with your customers. How can you have an impact on your customers' decisions to involve you in their solutions? Ideally, the process begins by revisiting current customer scenarios and predicting future ones. A customer scenario is the process the customer goes through to solve a problem or fill a need.

This requires understanding your customers' needs, values, and expectations on such a level that you can predict *exactly* what steps they will to take to solve the problem or fulfill the need. For example, the BayNet site might assume a customer scenario in which an individual is moving to San Francisco. The challenge for BayNet is to anticipate and influence the process this individual goes through to make the move successful and by doing so retain her as its customer. Most likely, someone moving to a new city will gather information, such as maps outlining neighborhoods and school districts, price comparisons for renting or purchasing a home, data on mortgage rates, and the telephone numbers of the telephone, electric, and cable TV companies.

The move itself, and all of the steps involved, is the problem or need that must be fulfilled. BayNet must determine what valuable part of the solution it can provide (i.e., its core competency and value proposition) and the additional elements necessary to offering a complete and convenient solution for the customer. In other words, how can BayNet provide value, and with what partners can it align to complete the solution?

The second element in your circle of influence is your business partners. Current business partners must be revisited and new ones defined in areas where your business cannot differentiate itself or maintain necessary core competencies. These partners are your customers' points of entry and departure from your site. You need to determine the proper links, transparent or nontransparent, as you want to lead the customer to them in order to complete the solution.

The businesses with which you align will significantly influence the number of customers visiting your Internet site, and vice versa. In the case of BayNet, the company might want to align with banks, newspapers, and the advertising vehicles that might attract someone looking for a home. In this way BayNet influences the potential customer's points of entry by making it easy for him to get to the BayNet site through its partners' Internet sites.

If, for instance, the individual moving to San Francisco browses through the real estate section of the *San Francisco Chronicle*, the next logical step would be to contact a real estate agency to assist with the search. If BayNet is linked with the *Chronicle*, it is easy for the customer to visit the BayNet site next, where she can set up an appointment to view homes. From there she will probably link to

Bank of America to inquire about mortgage rates. In this way, BayNet is influencing the customer's point of departure by offering her additional resources to help fulfill her need.

The third element involves redefining your relevant core competencies with respect to these Internet scenarios. You will experiment here with innovative products and services and decide what part of the solution you can best provide.

Finally, once you determine your core competencies you can define your value proposition. As you develop it, you must also define your profit or value recapture models.

Although this information may seem redundant as you begin the 10-step process, keep in mind that the circle of influence approach is meant to give an overview of elements to consider before you begin. The 10-step process will be more meaningful after reviewing and thinking through these elements, as they provide the foundation for the strategy. Figure 5.1 provides an overall view of the circle of influence, and Table 5.1 outlines the most important questions to consider before moving ahead.

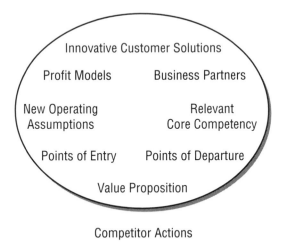

Figure 5.1 *Circle of Influence*

Table 5.1 *Circle of Influence Matrix*

	Customer	Points of Entry	Core Business Competency	Points of Departure
Responsibility	*Business* Leaders	*Business and Marketing* Leaders	*Business, Marketing, and Information Systems* Leaders	*Business and Marketing* Leaders
Key Questions	1. Who are the customers and what are their profiles? 2. What are their needs (security, proactivity, etc.)? 3. What scenarios will they be using for Internet services and what overall solution are they after?	1. What initial points of Internet entry will customers follow (search engines, business partner links, newspaper advertisements)? 2. What new business partners/interlinkers do you need to define in order to attract your customers? 3. What will lead them to your compelling differentiation and core competency?	1. What part of the overall solution are you providing? What value can you provide? 2. What are your relevant core competencies? 3. What is your compelling differentiation? 4. What is your value proposition and profit models? 5. What information, functionality, and digital assets can be created or leveraged?	1. What value can you *not* provide in a complete customer scenario? 2. What new global business partners/interlinkers need to be defined? 3. Should the points of departure be transparent or non-transparent to your customers? (Should your customer see just one business interface or several?)

THE TEN ESSENTIAL STRATEGY STEPS

You are ready to explore the ten essential steps involved in building your Internet strategy. These are:

1. Embrace the internet strategically.
2. Develop and accept new business assumptions.
3. Envision complete customer-centric solutions.
4. Predict points of entry.
5. Redefine relevant core competencies.
6. Experiment with innovative solutions.
7. Define your value proposition.
8. Explore profit models.
9. Identify points of departure.
10. Plan a phasing approach.

1. EMBRACE THE INTERNET STRATEGICALLY

Success requires embracing the Internet strategically. As comedian Woody Allen once suggested, "Eighty-five percent of life is just showing up." In a similar vein, probably 85 percent of the businesses that have an Internet presence simply show up, reacting to the Internet rather than first developing a strategic plan. Most simply place brochures and promotional materials on an Internet site. Many also accept resumes online, post job opportunities, call it a success, and move on. This is a nonstrategic reaction to the Internet, putting up a presence just for the sake of being there. Little or no thought is given to the opportunities that the Internet presents. Instead, it is viewed as simply another marketing vehicle or distribution channel.

An Internet strategy is much more than taking selected business processes from the past and applying them to the Internet or Intranet. There is much deeper business value in these technologies. Fully embracing the Internet means redefining your core competencies, developing new relationships with customers, and interlinking with new business partners to offer more complete solutions. Truly successful companies look at the Internet as an opportunity to redefine the rules of business and the roles they play in providing new and better solutions.

In short, you must look beyond short-term, tactical responses to deeper strategic approaches, align your business goals with your Internet strategy, and act early.

By not developing a responsible, thorough, and strategic Internet plan, your company will be unprepared and vulnerable, with little time to respond to new customer needs and business models. Consider the consequences of the reactive versus the proactive approach, as illustrated in Figure 5.2, below.

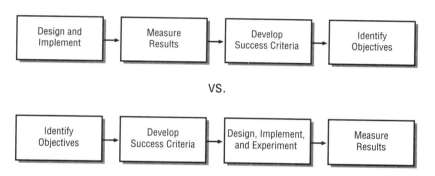

Figure 5.2 *Nonstrategic (top) vs.*
Strategic Internet Strategy (bottom)

The defensive or nonstrategic Internet strategy is unfortunately all too common. It is the typical approach of most businesses today. The results of a nonstrategic approach will clearly place your business in the precarious position of not knowing its objectives until after the plan is implemented! As farfetched as it sounds, many businesses find themselves in just that position. They race to beat the competition without taking time to incorporate their existing business objectives into their plans. No thought is given to experimentation or strategic planning. It's like signing a contract before it's been read—you may find yourself agreeing to something you didn't count on. Without an Internet strategy, you limit your options and could be forced to react to keep from sinking.

The more effective approach is also illustrated in Figure 5.2. Here the Internet strategy is first aligned with business objectives. The Internet plan is strategically incorporated into the existing business context. This allows clear identification of your success criteria and provides well-thought-out direction for design, implementation, and experimentation. This approach does not limit the focus of experimentation; it simply bases the experiment on a clear understanding of objectives. In the nonstrategic approach, experimentation is often based on what the competition has done, leaving no room for innovation and no consideration of the circle of influence.

Embracing the Internet strategically requires identifying the appropriate senior members of your business, technology, and marketing groups to sponsor and direct the Internet business strategy and execution. The Internet team ideally should consist of executives as well as front-line managers, all of whom understand the implications of the Internet. The effort must be more than endorsed by senior management. While many companies easily obtain an endorsement, this alone is not sufficient and in fact can actually contribute to ineffective strategies. Along with the endorsement, it is critical that senior management offer strategic direction.

Your strategy team must understand the company's real value propositions and differentiation in the context of the Internet. Team members must have the ability, vision, and influence to develop new alliances, business partners, and interlinkers so as to provide more complete solutions to customers. It is, after all, the completeness of the solution that will be a key differentiator for businesses that succeed.

Strategists appreciate the necessary steps to providing a valued solution. The team must look beyond online brochures and annual reports and anticipate how the Internet will fundamentally change the business. With this mastery, your company is in a position to leapfrog the competition.

Before moving to step 2, ask yourself the following questions. Is your business moving in the wrong direction as the Internet changes the assumptions of business? Do you have the business and technology skills to understand where you need to be going? More important, are you sufficiently informed to determine the proper strategy? Do you have the appropriate team in place to guide you? Have you embraced the Internet strategically, securing direction as well as endorsements from management?

These questions will challenge you to better understand your business, where it is currently, and where it has the potential to be. At this point, your perspective of the Internet's capabilities should be shifting to a deeper business viewpoint.

2. *DEVELOP AND ACCEPT NEW BUSINESS ASSUMPTIONS*

After you embrace the Internet strategically it is important to understand your new operating environment. You need to develop new business models and assumptions, comparing and contrasting the old with the new, to determine the foundation on which your business is and will be based. Only then can you fully appreciate the differences and interpret how they affect your business design. Looking at the capabilities of the Internet, as discussed in Chapter 2, and extrapolating the implications relevant to your business is helpful. This is a critical process. If you get it wrong, then you misunderstand your operating environment and the foundation of your strategy. If you get it right, then you understand your environment and your chances of building a successful Internet strategy greatly increase.

Table 5.2 presents examples of potential new operating assumptions. For instance, one of the assumptions is that access to market, for many industries, is much easier. Depending on the business, this could imply a leveling of the playing field. Determine which assumptions are different in your new environment. The table is meant to assist you with the development of your new operating assumptions.

Table 5.2 *New Business Assumptions*

Assumption	Old Model	New Model
Access to Market	Limited playing field	Leveling of playing field/ Access to market for both businesses and customers significantly increases
Barriers to Entry	Significant barriers to entry	Low barriers to entry
Agility	Agility is recognized as important, but its incorporation is slow	Agility becomes essential through recognition of proper relationships between customers, partners, and employees
Virtualization	Virtualization is an idea	Degrees of virtualization are realized
Core Competency	Initial recognition of strategic value of core competencies	Strategic focus on core competencies is paramount due to increasing competition and ability to interlink with others
Value Proposition	Value proposition for the customer changes slowly	Value proposition for the customer constantly changes with innovative products and services
Ability to Change	"Need to change" is recognized	Continuous change must be realized to grow
Strategic Drivers	Marketing drives business strategies to a significant extent	A combination of technology and marketing enables the new business strategies/The marketing function changes fundamentally

(continued)

Table 5.2 *(continued)*

Assumption	Old Model	New Model
Quality vs. Time to Market	Quality of products is important	Time to market, in addition to quality, becomes more relevant/First to market with compelling differentiation provides dramatic competitive advantages
Internet Adoption	Internet business and systems strategy is a small piece of the business solution	Internet is a complementary business design element essential for a variety of business activities
Competition	Moderate number of competitors	Larger number of and more global competitors/Competitors come from new industries
Customization	Products are regionally customized	Products are individually customized/Global localization and personalization is a recognized success factor for business
Design Perspective	Company-designed products	Customer-designed products (virtual products)
Internet's Perceived Value	Internet seen as another another distribution channel	Internet requires managers to rethink their business processes and create new kinds of customer solutions
Business Partners	Formal alliances, mergers, and acquisitions common	New types of partners, interlinkers, who specialize and complement your value/Less-formal alliances are necessary for inter-

(continued)

Table 5.2 *(continued)*

Assumption	Old Model	New Model
		linking/They become opportunity based
Software Success Factors	Ease of use	Architectural flexibility in the systems becomes the key business success factor
Customers	Needs and expectations change slowly	Needs, expectations, and priorities change constantly as new services, virtual products, and choices become available

Do not be limited by the models presented here. This table represents only some potential operating assumptions of the Internet. Subsequent chapters offer a perspective on new marketing, technology, organizational, success, and legal models, among others. Develop your own conceptual models by exploring how your business will operate in the future. Accept them as part of your business vision and make a conscious effort to appreciate them as you develop your strategic plan. Many businesses unconsciously understand these assumptions, but they must be actively and deliberately accepted into your business.

As technologies race to the future, the need to think about Internet-enabled models becomes more critical, particularly so for traditional information technology personnel. They need to fully understand the new business, marketing, and technology models in order to develop systems consistent with the company's strategic direction.

According to James J. Cash, Jr., professor of business administration at Harvard Business School, "Many IS professionals are well trained in structured problem-solving but poorly trained in unstructured thinking, which is vital when assumptions need to be challenged and plans redirected. New technology can give rise to new opportunities—if employees are creative enough to identify them."[2]

You then need to develop models in your business context that challenge your current operating assumptions. For instance, Table 5.3 illustrates what a newspaper business could look like in the future.

Table 5.3 *Newspaper Industry Models*

Assumption	Old Model	New Model
Content Timeliness	Point-in-time editions are produced at periodic, predefined intervals	Dynamic—incrementally updated rolling editions produced progressively as news evolves
Time to Market	Hours to days	Minutes
	Distribution to end users is time-consuming and labor-intensive, thereby introducing further delays between production and consumption	
	Distribution to all consumers is immediate, thereby enhancing the relevance and value of news content	
Publishing Principle	Broadcasting	Narrowcasting
	Same product (content) sold to all consumers regardless of individual interests or requirements	Subscriber's individual interests and requirements are catered to by tailoring published material
		A layered Internet NewSpace allows subscribers to selectively mine for information as required. Ultimately, intelligent network agents enable subscribers to create individual newsfeeds from material sourced on the Internet.

(continued)

Table 5.3 (continued)

Assumption	Old Model	New Model
		Filters set within a subscriber's browsers can be individually customized so as to flag important news updates or selected subject updates immediately to subscribers.
Content Type	Static	Dynamic
	Text and still images constrained by fixed page size, layout, and advertising ratio requirements	Integrated set of information-related services including video, audio, 3-D rendered images (VRML), photo and news libraries, in-depth analyses, tutorials, reference aids, and related historical data
Information Sources Available to Consumer	News reports and analyses	News reports and analyses
	Features	Features
	Limited historical sports and business data	Extensive historical data
		News archive and library material
		Related background and reference material
		Interactive tutorials
		Automatic cross-reference to encyclopedia, dictionary, atlas material, etc.
		Taped interviews

(continued)

Table 5.3 *(continued)*

Assumption	Old Model	New Model
Readership	Limited (geographically)	Extensive, typically global
	Compromise between coverage of local, regional, and global news	Enables both regionalization concurrently. Content is not limited by page size and count, so space is given over to local, regional, and global news as required.
		Many types of profiles (different solutions depending on profile)
Reader Interaction	Generally limited, e.g., letters to the editor after days of delay	Potentially extensive, e.g., facilitated discussion groups whereby subscribers participate in discussion on a given story or subject, perhaps with the journalist/author/subject expert
Advertising	Static	Dynamic and interactive, incorporating links to advertiser's own Internet material, and supporting Internet transactions
		Targeted
	Limited collection of marketing information	Ability to collect accurate marketing information
		Facilitates statistics gathering and usage pattern analysis to enable targeting of subscriber preferences

3. *ENVISION COMPLETE CUSTOMER SOLUTIONS*

The most successful Internet strategy offers a more complete, convenient, and timely solution for the customer than that available today. Your business may not be able to effectively provide the full solution alone. In the BayNet example, Bank of America offers only a piece of the complete solution—a financial services component, including loans. The individual moving to San Francisco still faces a vast number of other tasks before the solution is complete.

To envision new customer solutions, develop scenarios of your typical customers in their daily practices, incorporating your products or services into the picture. What part of the complete solution can you offer, and how can you facilitate better solutions to keep your customers coming back? This approach will eventually force you to understand and define your relevant core competencies and customer value within the context of the Internet.

Galt markets its NETWorth Internet site as a one-stop shopping center for mutual fund information. The site attracts a large number of visitors, partly because it offers free access to a Morningstar database on the performance of roughly 7,000 funds. Intuit, the parent company of Galt, recognized that mutual fund information, along with the ability to buy and sell funds on the Internet, was part of a more complete need that its customers had.

Intuit found that investors value the ability to access this type of information when they perform personal financial analysis or investigate investment opportunities. Intuit acquired Galt to continue its strategic business objective of building a complete customer solution for the millions of Quicken users. Quicken is a software package that specializes in personal banking solutions and portfolio management. Although this example features a formal acquisition, interlinking partners do not have to be acquired.

Consider a newspaper business in the context of the Internet. The business can align with international newspaper partners to provide a more complete solution for the customer. The interlinking with partners enables customers to link to news anywhere, worldwide. They can search out international perspectives on a variety of topics or stick to local issues. Moreover, interlinking with businesses in other industries can facilitate the availability of new types of services to newspaper customers, such as linking to newspaper advertisers offering products and services on the newspaper site.

This is an example of offering a complete solution, allowing a customer to perform a variety of tasks with the navigation being anticipated by the business. Customers could register on the newspaper site; the registration or customer information can be transferred when the customer links to other partners, alleviating the need to register on every site. This information can be shared to dynamically create personalized screens for customers. The newspaper industry's business, marketing, information systems, and customer assumptions are changing, as are its relevant core competencies and the value it provides.

Reuters, an international news service known for its coverage of international sports, acquired a stake in SportsLine USA to develop a more complete solution for customers. SportsLine is among the first online services dedicated to sports information, entertainment, and merchandise. The service includes proprietary sports news content from its own editorial staff as well as dozens of popular American sports writers, and has rapidly become a premier Internet site for American sports coverage.

SportsLine offers regular sports news and scores from all major sports news services along with in-depth current and historical statistics. It also offers conversational features for members, gaming odds on sporting events, and online sports-related shopping. SportsLine is a company that strategically embraced the Internet early on and literally created a new service. Its agreement with Reuters contains provisions granting Reuters the exclusive rights to distribute SportsLine content as part of the Reuters sports news service and allows SportsLine access to Reuters' extensive coverage of international sports and sporting events for its Internet site. If implemented correctly, the Reuters-SportsLine alliance should benefit sports enthusiasts worldwide.

This visioning of complete scenarios is the responsibility of business and marketing groups. In the new medium there are a thriving number of interlinkers who, in aggregate, provide complete, convenient, and valued solutions. The Internet's ability to monitor the habits of consumers can be used to facilitate a better understanding of customer needs, values, and expectations. For example, if you track statistics showing that 50 percent of new customers come from a unforeseen source site, take time to repeat the exercise of envisioning customer scenarios. It may suggest you define or develop new business partners. The Internet environment necessitates the constant need to change or modify your solutions to keep customers loyal.

4. PREDICT POINTS OF ENTRY

Points of entry are all of the possible routes potential customers might use to get to your site. They could be business partner (interlinking) sites, other product- or service-related Internet sites, or advertisements (both online and offline). Your site is also the point of entry for other sites.

Points of entry initiate the customer scenario: the manner, method, site, or path the customer follows to get to your site, content, functionality, and value proposition. For example, BayNet is one point of entry to the Bank of America site. Together, the two sites provide a more complete customer solution for those in the market to buy a home. Intuit is a point of entry for potential Galt users.

Identifying points of entry is one of the critical tasks of the marketing group. The better points of entry are defined, the more successful your business can be because the more qualified customers you have coming to your site, the better you can anticipate and serve their needs. Depending on the situation, identifying potential points of entry may require new business alliances. If the envisioning is correct, the points of entry will fall out of the customer scenario in step 3.

Look at the example of GE Plastics, which developed a "Home of the Future" in Massachusetts. People can walk through this fully functioning model home and see the different types of plastic used throughout. Taking advantage of the work that has been done on the house and the designs, the company is now developing a Web site to allow visitors to take a virtual tour of the home.

In short, GE Plastics is taking advantage of one of its existing digital assets, but it is also effectively becoming a point of entry for its business partners and customers, for whom it will provide links. In the future when a visitor spots a component in the virtual Home of the Future, such as an Andersen window, he may link directly to the Andersen Windows site. GE Plastics, then, is a point of entry for Andersen Windows.

What relationships unfold as you define your points of entry? How formal are they? With interlinking partners there may be no formal contract, no buying and selling of equity, and few, if any, binding provisions. The relationship can be fluid, dynamic, and evolving. There may be guidelines and expectations, but currently no one expects a precise, measured return on the initial commitment.

The Internet is so unpredictable at this point that these relationships are seen as mutually beneficial for all parties concerned. Ideally, they encompass two or more companies which each believe they are stronger together than on their own. Each believes that the other has unique competencies it lacks; when brought together, they each provide a piece of the puzzle, resulting in complete, innovative customer solutions.

5. REDEFINE RELEVANT CORE COMPETENCIES

Redefine your core competencies from the perspective of the Internet customer. Your competencies depend on the evolution of business and technology. For example, the newspaper and periodical industry may recognize that its relevant core assets in the context of the Internet may actually be the wealth of historical data available in libraries and archives, and the ability to provide customized information. Thus, a company's most relevant core competency, from the customer's perspective, might be one thing today, but something else tomorrow. The *Chicago Tribune* recognized this during the launch of its Internet strategy in March 1996. A press release stated, "Today we start on a long, exciting road...We'll be adapting our offerings based on changes in technology, changes in demands for information and changes in the way we gather the news."

Refer to Figure 5.3 for an illustration of core competency as seen by customers. Notice how it might change over time. In this example, *A* might refer to a newspaper's ability to provide detailed, in-depth coverage, and *B* might refer to its ability to print and distribute dailies.

A senior publishing company executive said recently, "Instead of publishing travel books, we're going to be a travel information provider." From the customer's perspective, this solution provides more relevant value.

As you redefine your relevant core competencies and assets, your compelling differentiation will become clear. A differentiable solution is based on your strategic competencies. This is the essence of what you will provide to the customer and can come in two ways: either by *creating* new services through redefined, prioritized competencies relevant to the Internet now or by *exploiting* existing information and assets. Currently, smaller companies tend to create new services while larger ones tend to exploit existing information assets.

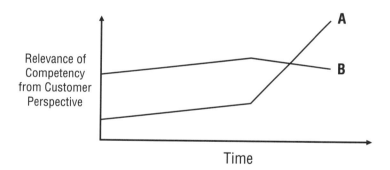

Figure 5.3 *Relevant Asset vs. Time*

Internet pioneers such as Lombard Institutional Investors are creating new services. Lombard developed an application allowing a user to run four graphs simultaneously on a screen. Lombard won a prestigious technology innovation award for this. Its customers can manage their accounts through real-time interaction over the Internet. As Eric Roach, president of Lombard, says, "In reality, we are not leveraging any physical asset, we are creating new solutions." The competency Lombard is leveraging is intangible. It is its nimbleness, the ability to provide customers with high-value services quickly and efficiently.

This step goes almost hand in hand with step 8, Experiment with Innovative Solutions, because you can best understand your most relevant competencies when you look at your business from your customer's perspective. By experimenting with innovative, customer-centric solutions, you experience the solutions in the same manner as the customer does.

Some companies revisit and exploit their competencies to build the Internet infrastructure. VeriFone has two decades of experience in credit card transaction processing and maintains key relationships with merchants, banks, and other players. Thousands of merchants worldwide use VeriFone devices to process credit card transactions. The company offers a track record of proven technology for credit card authorization. Customers and merchants expect to see VeriFone on the Internet because they are familiar with it.

VeriFone realized this and developed the first secure Internet product for merchants, customers, and banks. Its product consists of three items: vWallet, an electronic virtual wallet for the end user; vPOS, a virtual point-of-sale application for the merchant; and vGate, a software gateway that allows the credit card processor to accept transactions from Internet storefronts and process them in their existing host systems. Because VeriFone was early with a solution and provided parts of the infrastructure, and because merchants and customers are familiar with VeriFone, the company has a strategic advantage. VeriFone did it right the first time—started in early, leveraged core competencies, and took advantage of its already established reputation.

Businesses can offer products and services in both the physical and virtual worlds, and take advantage of their competencies to the mutual advantage of each. CUC International, Inc., the billion-dollar telephone home shopping company, now provides its services on the Internet as well. CUC is exploiting its existing relationships with business partners, suppliers, and customers, and capitalizing on the experience gained from its telephone shopping operations to provide a wide range of products through the Internet. Without a significant customer base, existing suppliers, and fulfillment skills, smaller companies could take much longer to come to market. CUC is not creating a brand-new service but rather is exploiting its current competencies and comprehensive relationships with business partners and extending them to the Internet.

The Regional Bell Operating Companies (RBOCs) in the United States represent another example of larger companies taking advantage of current information assets and competencies. By selling advertising space in the Yellow Pages, the RBOCs have long standing relationships with almost every local plumber, auto mechanic, and architect who advertises. Smaller companies have no comparable relationship. The RBOC's advantage is knowing their advertisers' marketing needs.

In the future, RBOCs may even be able to move in on foreign carriers' traditional monopoly. Assuming regulators will permit it, an RBOC could expand to offer worldwide Internet Yellow Pages with local listings from Sydney to Stockholm. For example, the Nynex Interactive Yellow Pages has more than 16 million national business listings. The directory lists business type, company name, address, and telephone number. Nynex's online advertisers create a brief business profile for approximately $100. Telecommunication carriers in other countries are also exploiting their information assets and experimenting with products. Telstra (formerly Telecom Australia) offers a site containing the entire Australian White Pages listings.

Forces outside your industry may require you to revisit your primary core competencies and redefine your compelling differentiation. Intuit is doing this with banks. Intuit is setting up an interface between Quicken and a third-party processor that will serve as a switch to any bank seeking to participate in home banking through Quicken. Intuit has acquired a bank processing company, NPCI, to facilitate this. Future versions of Quicken software will have an interface to NPCI.

Microsoft also wants to serve as the front end for customers doing banking over the Internet, through Microsoft Money. Microsoft and Intuit may charge banks each time a customer comes through the third-party processor's switch to her own bank. Thus, in the future, all banks may look alike; a particular bank would face the new challenge of differentiating itself from its competitors. If Intuit and Microsoft provide the context, how will banks provide value and differentiation?

6. EXPERIMENT WITH INNOVATIVE CUSTOMER-CENTRIC SOLUTIONS

There are business problems that Internet technology can solve, and, more important, business opportunities it can create. For example, the Internet facilitates communication with suppliers, but it also creates new opportunities by offering more personalized and complete solutions to a global audience. It is important to recognize the difference between these two concepts, because you need to experiment with solutions to optimize and reengineer your business as well as with new solutions that customers will value.

As you evaluate your relevant core competencies, you need to explore new products and services opportunities. For instance, the U.S. Postal Service (USPS) is considering becoming a certification authority, providing registered digital IDs so that businesses and individuals can be protected in electronic commerce. In this way, the USPS could authenticate any customer in an electronic commerce transaction. A business could use USPS to verify customer identification. The Postal Service believes it may be well suited for this function because of its customer relationships and its other core competencies.

RTime, Inc., a Seattle-based software developer, evaluated its core competencies in the context of the Internet and developed innovative solutions. RTime architects originally developed SIMNET which the U.S. Army uses for training tactical units in a real-time field exercise simulation accommodating thousands of soldier-trainees in a single cyberspace exercise. With the success realized from its work on SIMNET, RTime rethought its value and is experimenting with innovative products on the Internet.

RTime believes its software applications provide a clear competitive advantage over other companies offering multiplayer simulation packages. RTime adds real-time response, memory from session to session, and sharing of data among thousands of Internet users. It develops and markets off-the-shelf software products that allow software developers to link thousands of participants together in a real-time environment over the Internet. This allows applications ranging from game playing and entertainment to process control and air traffic management. The technology also provides an environment for hundreds of individuals to shop and ask questions of sales personnel and to make bets at far-off horse racing venues.

The Internet is about new paradigms; you must think this way when experimenting with new solutions. Consider the current model of the broker-client relationship in stock trading. The traditional method of purchasing stock is to use investment brokers, who provide advice to investors and generate fees through both the purchase and sale of securities. By contrast, Netstock Direct enhances a direct investor-to-company relationship, bypassing the broker intermediary. It improves industry financing by facilitating direct investment relationships between companies and individuals investors. Any company with a direct stock purchase plan can participate. The primary means through which Netstock Direct accomplishes these goals is an online interactive stock marketing and investor relations service. The service assists, facilitates, secures, and tracks direct stock sales and other investment agreements between individual investors and companies that list securities and seek capital.

Both parties to a Netstock Direct transaction benefit; Netstock Direct plans to derive the majority of its revenues from fees paid by companies for investor relations and direct investment services. The investor will pay no fees for connection, usage, or transactions.

Information and services are often given away, free of charge, on the Internet. Services such as stock quotes, historical analysis, and personalized news information are available nearly everywhere online. Clearly, information is in oversupply and consequently customers have high levels of expectation. They need no longer tolerate incomplete solutions. If you don't provide a convenient, timely, and highly valued solution, someone else definitely will.

Demand is created only for the most innovative products and services; therefore, you must analyze demand-side strategies. This will force you to better understand your customers and to create a solution or part of a solution that will become part of their daily practice. With an Internet strategy, you must identify your value in an information-based product. Be proactive; experiment with innovative strategies and become part of your customers' routine before the competition does.

7. DEFINE THE VALUE PROPOSITION

The value of your Internet offering to the customer must be clear. Is the product or service secure, interactive, educational, or proactive? As you develop the value proposition, continually review customer expectations and priorities. What do you think your customer will value? Chapter 2 contains a discussion of customer values analysis as well as an assessment of what the Internet can offer in terms of added value. Determining the right value proposition to offer the customer is critical to the Internet strategy.

Figure 5.4 presents customer priorities important in defining the value proposition.

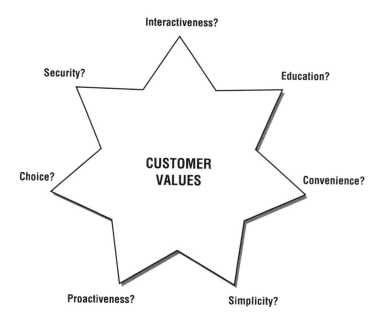

Figure 5.4 *Customer Priorities*

Eric Roach of Lombard notes that the company had to make a decision when developing its Internet strategy: Would it follow the lowest-cost provider route and become strictly a transaction-based business or would it try to add value while being cost competitive? Although Lombard believed that customers' values include cost competitiveness, it also believed that the educational and proactive qualities of its solutions would be more valued by customers than lowest cost.

Following this determination, Lombard decided to focus on delivery mechanisms and proactive, innovative solutions that were never before available to the individual investor. It planned and designed a solution to meet those needs. Stated simply, customers want to buy stocks appropriate for their needs and risk profiles, and to have a rich set of tools to monitor them. Lombard now provides option quotes, unlimited access to historical graphs, inter-day graphs, and other tools. The value proposition offered by Lombard is apparently successful. It has developed a significant installed base of customers who trade millions of dollars in stocks over the Internet each month.

The processes for creating value in the physical and virtual worlds are not the same. The most successful Internet value propositions take into account four components: (1) relevant core competency (in your customer's eyes) and compelling solution differentiation; (2) the value of interlinked business partners; (3) customers' changing needs and expectations; and (4) Internet-enabled business capabilities. This is depicted in Figure 5.5.

FreeRide offers the Internet equivalent of redeemable Green Stamps with its novel value proposition. The company offers free Internet time to customers buying consumer products offered on the site. FreeRide profits by selling traditional products over the Internet. From the customer perspective, the value proposition is attractive: Purchase any of the products on the FreeRide menu and get time credits applied to the Internet service provider (ISP) or on-line service of your choice. To cash in, a customer saves proofs of purchase from the products and send them to FreeRide, which issues online a credit statement to the designated online service or ISP. The service is free to end users; the selection of products is extensive.

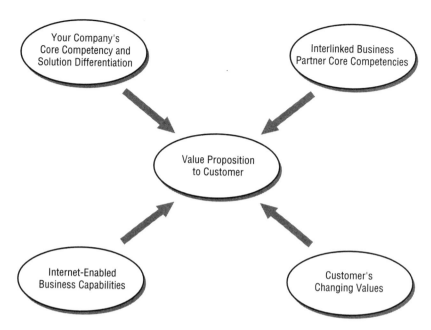

Figure 5.5 *Internet Value Proposition Equation*

You must ensure that businesses in other industries that enhance your product or service are also part of your value proposition analysis. Identify the industries that can market your core competencies optimally and exploit information assets for the mutual benefit of providing better customer solutions.

Identify your value in the interlinking industry models. IBM says the key to its success in subscription-based solutions is serving as a broker between the consumer and the business offering the product. IBM is not a competitor but rather a partner, facilitating transactions and helping customers bring their products and services to the marketplace. It wants to be an intermediary between banks, insurance companies, manufacturers, distributors, media companies, and their constituencies. In fact, IBM's online motto is, "The way we put it all together is what will set us apart."

For example, IBM created World Avenue, an Internet server providing retailers and others a way to sell their products online. IBM takes a commission of 5 percent of sales. World Avenue adds value by providing merchants with sales data through searching tools and intelligent agents. Data-mining tools provide instant feedback to companies on market conditions, purchase volumes, and site usage patterns. Intelligent agents record browsing and purchasing habits—with the customer's consent—to help retailers give customers more personalized views of merchandise.

8. *EXPLORE PROFIT MODELS*

The Internet is often characterized as the world's first zero-billion-dollar industry. Everyone is convinced there is money to be made, but few are successful in making it.

How will you recapture value and profit on the Internet with these innovative customer solutions? Will value be recaptured through expert advice, new information, or possible leads that you bring to other businesses via the Internet? Will it be recaptured by linking with appropriate business partners? Will it be recaptured through the non-Internet channels? Many questions need to be explored but, essentially, your goal is to see where you fit into customer solutions, where and how you can and should provide value, and how to recapture that value.

The appropriate profit models for your business will most likely change over time. However, they must always be based on the value added to enrich the customer solution. It is natural, then, that the customer pays based on that value. Finding the right profit model for your business rests with customers; therefore, make a concerted effort to understand them. In fact, profit models may be specific to different types or profiles of customers. The authors of *Agile Competitors and Virtual Organizations* state that the customer enrichment dimension of agile competition suggests that if a company knows its customers well enough to provide them with solution products, it also knows the enrichment value of those products to the customers.

In such a context, it makes good marketing sense to charge the customers some fraction of that enrichment value. It is customary to think that the same product should have one price for everyone, that it is not fair to sell it at different prices. This idea is not valid for the solutions of tomorrow. The value of a solution is contextual, even with regard to the same customer, and will vary according to the circumstances of the customer's purchases. It is likely that the same solution has different enrichment values for different customers even under the same circumstances.[3]

From the examples discussed thus far, several profit model options unfold. These might be classified in the following ways:

• advertising space (Netscape)

• links to partners (BayNet)

• providing a more complete customer solution (Geosystems)

• electronic agents (Verity)

• customized solutions (NETCOM)

• information/knowledge provisioning (IBM infoSage)

• innovative products/services (NetstockDirect)

• transaction fulfillment (IBM InfoMarket)

• provision of qualified leads (InfoSeek)

• subscriptions (*Wall Street Journal*)

• selling side strategies (Industry.Net)

• intermediaries (IBM WorldAvenue)

Significant revenues have already been generated by Internet advertisements. Advertising revenues in this medium were almost nonexistent one year ago. Table 5.4 offers revenue estimates (although controversial) from popular advertising sites in the first quarter of 1996.

Table 5.4 *Advertising Revenues*

Site	Q1 1996 Advertising Revenue
Infoseek	$3,107,500
Lycos	$2,622,200

(continued)

Table 5.4 *(continued)*

Site	Q1 1996 Advertising Revenue
Yahoo!	$2,190,000
Netscape	$1,908,500
c｜net	$1,330,500

Beyond ads, Internet businesses can make money through other means. It is possible to recapture a small piece of the overall solution for a company. Recall that Geosystems says it will pursue two revenue models for its MapQuest site. In addition to sponsored advertisements, it envisions a new revenue model from MapQuest Interconnect, a service for other Web-based sites. Through MapQuest, companies can link to online maps for geographic views. MapQuest will host this data, transparently linking a company's business products and service data with the relevant maps, providing a timely and seamless solution for the customer. MapQuest can recapture value through each link to its information.

Note that the provision of leads to other business partners can be a profit model as well. One company today gets $0.50 per customer lead generated.

The Internet is still a new economic model. Do not look to traditional profit models for comfort and solutions; experiment with new ones. For example, Internet newspaper subscriptions may not be an appropriate (value recapture) model because the Internet newspaper is not a newspaper in the traditional sense. People do not use online newspapers for the same purposes as a hard-copy paper. Reading online newspapers is usually done with a specific purpose in mind. A banker in Australia seeking information about a Seattle startup company may want to search through the Seattle newspaper's archives but is not interested in the region's cultural affairs.

In this example, a pay-per-view model may be more appropriate than a subscription-based approach. It may not make sense for the banker to subscribe to the Seattle newspaper, but it does make sense for the paper to generate revenue by offering services to a global audience. Perhaps customer needs would best be met by setting up a search service for news articles relating to a specific subject, or by offering the option of ordering a single paper rather than a regular subscription.

Other models are being tested. For instance, AT&T Personal Online Services is testing HealthSite, the first of the AT&T consumer unit's paid sites. "We think the model is comparable to the general-purpose magazine model," says Caroline Vanderlip, president. She notes that the site will have a "thin level" of promotional content designed to pull in subscribers as well as a variety of "premium services" accounting for 10 to 15 percent of the total site. Other sites, such as ESPNet's SportsZone, take a similar tack, offering a certain amount of content for free and charging for premium services beyond that.

Table 5.5 summarizes the Internet strategy approach thus far, using the example of a newspaper.

9. *IDENTIFY POINTS OF DEPARTURE*

At this point, you have completed much of the strategy analysis and determined the circumstances in which customers will enter your circle of influence. However, you must still consider how a customer will *exit* your Internet-based product or service. Points of departure represent new interlinking business relationships that complete your vision (step 3) of the customer solution.

Consider the following questions:

- What can't you provide, or what can someone else provide better to complement your service or product?

- To complete their solution, where would users naturally want to go next after they received value from your site?

- What new partners or interlinkers do you need to develop?

- Do you want transparent or nontransparent linking from your site?

- What customer information, if any, will you forward to your interlinking partner?

Table 5.5 Sample Internet Business Strategy

New Assumption	Product/ Service	Customer Value	Value Proposition	Profit Recapture
Customized News	Customized electronic newspaper delivered to your e-mail address	Convenience Individualization Proactivity Timeliness	Time savings Better knowledge gathering on special interests Newspaper alerts you for special-interest news Instantaneous delivery	Larger audience Cost savings on printing and distribution Offering more value, therefore higher customer costs Pay per view
Customized Advertising	Customized general and classified ads	Convenience Individualization Proactivity Timeliness	Time savings from the elimination of unrelated ads Better knowledge gathering on products of interest Ads are proactive; they reach you when you need them Ads reflect the current offerings and relate to news content	Better segmentation and higher accuracy for advertisers lead statistics Optimal return on advertisers increases value recapture for newspapers
Virtually Unlimited Content	Detail-on-demand news	Convenience Education Proactivity Timeliness	Time savings—when you need details you can get the full story and interlink to relevant topics Since newspapers are not limited by physical page size, long details can be provided for better general education	Better utilization of the information already collected; more relevant content would be highly valued by customer
Virtually Unlimited Advertising Space	Detail-on-demand advertising Newspaper never has to show all the ads to all customers	Convenience Timeliness Proactivity	Customer can review the ads he is interested with and get details if needed. He can buy directly using newspapers acting as a transaction clearing house	Virtually unlimited advertising opportunities. No tradeoff between the amount of advertising and customer satisfaction with content

10. PLAN A PHASING APPROACH

A phasing strategy is a necessary part of your Internet business strategy. Why? Because you need to be early to market with an innovative solution, and phasing allows you to accomplish this. The Internet customer does not reward the second to market. The momentum generated by the first-to-market company can be a tremendous competitive obstacle for other companies.

But being early to market is only the beginning. The company that establishes customer allegiances before its competitors but is content to rest on its laurels courts trouble. While a "version 1.0" application has the power of novelty and first-to-market recognition, it more than likely does not offer a complete customer solution.

You should plan and develop a phasing strategy designed to reach your business objectives and achieve your success criteria in stages. A successful phasing approach provides stepping-stones toward fulfillment of the ultimate objectives.

After the conclusion of each step or phase, the assumptions of your Internet business strategy should be reviewed. Measuring success at the end of each step will help tune your strategy, guiding you in the most successful direction. When developing your phasing approach, remember:

- Begin with the end in mind and make each phase bring you a step closer to where you want to be. However, do not be limited by the number of phases; the three-phase approach presented in Figure 5.6 is only an example. Given the rapid evolution of the Internet, shorter, rather than longer, time between phases will be less risky for your business. In this way you can determine if and where you need to shift course.

- Phasing allows you to identify where you want to go and develop checkpoints to assess your progress. It limits your risks by ensuring you do not err too far before your solution and assumptions are tested on the Internet. It provides flexibility, so that lessons learned from one phase can be incorporated into the next. Commercialization of the Internet is moving so rapidly that new capabilities, regulations, laws, and business drivers may affect your objectives. Phasing your approach deflects the impact of unforeseen changes.

- Be clear on what you expect to achieve and learn from each phase. At a minimum, briefly outline the objectives, success criteria, and underlying assumptions for each phase.

Figure 5.6 illustrates a phasing approach.

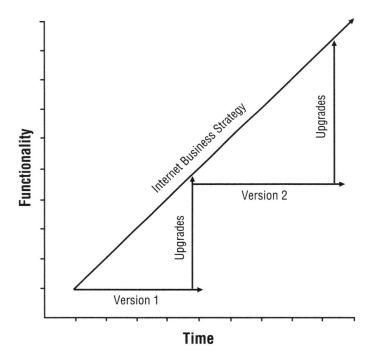

Figure 5.6 *Potential Phasing Strategy*

To design a phasing strategy, you need to outline business, marketing, and systems objectives for each phase and for each relevant access layer. Align each phase with the key business strategy steps, such as profit models, core competencies, and assumptions. A basic phasing strategy might look like the example presented in Table 5.6

Table 5.6 Phasing Example

Phase	Business, Marketing, and Technology Objectives	Levels of Access	Summary of Key Business Strategy Elements	Success Criteria	Assumptions
1	Generation of marketplace awareness, development and testing new of marketing, business, and technology models	Public	Highly dynamic site, leveraging existing information assets to provide high usage volume	20 leads per month, operationally robust system, flexible software architecture, high usage volume from links from new business partners	A and B will be the most relevant customer values. Technology Z will be matured by Z date. Key business partners are D, C, and E. Relevant core competency is Z.
2	Electronic delivery to key clients and partners	Public, Community, Organizational	Highly interactive, intuitive, and educational for public, customers, and business partners	200 leads per month, operationally robust system, more flexible software architecture, customer serves herself 75 percent of time online, customer base grows 30 percent internationally	A, B, and C will be the most relevant customer values. Relevant technology XX will be matured by XX date. Key business partners are F and G. Relevant core competency is Z.
3	Electronic communication with clients, integration of systems with business partners	Public, Community, Organizational, Integrated, and Strategic	All of the above, plus transparently linking with key partners	1,000 leads per month, operationally robust system, 90 percent of customer service requests over the Internet or other online environment, customer base grows 50 percent internationally	B, C, and D will be the most relevant customer values. Relevant technology GG will be matured by X date. Key business partners are G and H. Relevant core competency is AA.

The steps outlined in this chapter may seem straightforward and commonsense. Many businesses, however, do not put these steps into practice. When was the last time you identified your relevant core competencies from your customer's perspective? When was the last time you identified changing customer expectations? These are fundamental elements of any strategy, irrespective of the Internet. The Internet simply gives you a chance to review them in a new context.

Keep in mind that reviewing your circle of influence is a *process*, not a one-time project. Think of it as a continual experiment. Customers change, as do their expectations and needs. Your organization changes as well. Therefore, the nature of the solutions that you offer should change. The nature of your solutions will be influenced by external factors as well. Keeping abreast of technological developments and the emergence of new and attractive potential business partners is crucial.

NOTES

1. Ohmae, Kenichi, *The Borderless World: Power and Strategy in the Interlinked Economy.* (New York: Harper Collins Publishers, 1991).

2. Cash, James I., "Take To The Seven Cs" *Information Week* (February 5, 1996):86.

CHAPTER 6

REINVENTING MARKETING: STEPS TO IMPLEMENT INNOVATIVE MARKETING STRATEGIES

REINVENTING THE MARKETING FUNCTION

For your Internet business strategy to be successful, marketing must become a top—and possibly even the first—priority. But you must revisit, change, and reinvent the marketing function itself. The marketing function changes in many ways. For example, the marketer's role migrates from convincing customers that they need a product to determining innovative ways to meet their needs, such as allowing customers to build products themselves (virtual products) or to test a product online before buying it.

The marketing change comes about because the Internet offers the ability to target customers, identify and cater to new niches, better understand your customers' behaviors, personalize, develop complete solutions, and reach a massive international audience. Successful marketers take advantage of this. Moreover, this type of marketing is technology- and information system-enabled; its keys to success rest with creating customer-valued solutions through technology and your corporate information systems.

143

Many businesses do not recognize the fundamental need to reexamine the value and role of the Internet marketer. Current marketing strategies reflect that. These businesses believe that Internet marketing consists of placing annual reports, statements by top managers, job listings, and press releases on the Internet. This is not a new marketing approach, nor is it reinventing, nor will it ensure success. This approach has nothing to do with virtual products, better understanding your customer, or reaching a new niche group. It will only ensure that the marketing function remains underutilized.

For companies to be successful, marketing professionals must embrace the new paradigm shaped by the Internet.

GRASPING THE INTERNET MARKETING MODEL

Internet marketing is not created in a vacuum; it draws on the strengths of traditional marketing models. Print media and television are often used effectively to market Internet media. It is natural that a synergy be generated between Internet and traditional techniques. A business can exploit its traditional marketing channels to the benefit of its Internet channel. In some ways, marketing is still the same. As Rick Fernandes, executive vice president of interactive services for CUC International, Inc., suggests, "It's still about getting customers. You constantly need to experiment, test new assumptions, offer online auctions, scavenger hunts, and more." CUC should know, perhaps more than any other vendor doing business in an electronic environment. It began selling merchandise through electronic services such as CompuServe, Prodigy, and others in the late 1970s. It built up almost 300,000 online subscribing customers and expects to double that by the end of 1997.

Traditional and Internet marketing are, however, fundamentally different. To reinvent the marketing function you must first force yourself to think outside the box. A new model is necessary because the Internet allows for different types of solutions, different customers, and different types of interactions with customers. In fact, Internet customers expect to encounter nontraditional forms of marketing precisely because the Internet offers new capabilities.

The differences can be viewed from four perspectives:

1. How is the new environment different? (the new marketing function)
2. What are new success factors of successful companies? (marketing success factors)
3. Where does marketing best fit into your organization? (organizational position)
4. How should the marketer perceive the customer? (customer perspective)

Table 6.1 summarizes the comparisons into these categories.

Table 6.1 *Marketing Operating Assumptions*

Category	Traditional Assumption	Internet Assumption
The New Marketing Environment	Marketing rules of engagement are relatively clear, defined, and constant.	Marketing rules continually evolve, driven by technology advances.
	Market is bound by countries and regions.	Market is borderless, by default.
	Market niches are difficult to identify.	Market niches are generally larger, thereby creating additional niche business opportunities. They are also more easily identified and catered to.
	Corporate-push marketing (the business defines the time and place) dominates.	Customer-pull marketing (the customer will define the time and place) dominates.

(continued)

Table 6.1 (continued)

Category	Traditional Assumption	Internet Assumption
	Higher-cost advertising.	Lower cost advertising.
	Light information systems-enabled marketing.	Highly information systems-enabled marketing, more conscious integration with IT, and marketing groups become important.
Marketing Success Factors	Awareness of product and services is considered a success.	Awareness often already exists for customers. Perceived value is essential to success.
	First to market rewarded by customers and maintains advantage over second to market.	First to market creates phenomenal global customer momentum and maintains significant competitive advantage over second to market.
	Alliances not essential to marketing.	Interlinking partners are essential for marketing success, as links provide more complete customer solutions. This allows a marketer to get more into and influence customer practices and routines.

(continued)

Table 6.1 (continued)

Category	Traditional Assumption	Internet
	Creativity is important for differentiation.	Innovation becomes essential for differentiation as number and type of competitors increase. Internet offers dramatically different ways to innovate, such as through personalization.
	Limited customer interactivity.	Significant customer interactivity.
	Promotional and partially relevant entertainment.	Educational and intellectually entertaining.
Organizational Position	Marketing drives product development.	Marketing and information systems drive product decisions.
	Marketing groups exist as umbrella organization.	Marketing groups become integrated with other business and technology groups.
Customer Perspective	Customers are less knowledgeable and informed.	Customers are more aware and informed. Their feedback can be more immediate and easier to access.
	Customer behaviors and expectations are relatively predictable.	New customer behaviors, expectations, and interests are being created and can be better monitored.

(continued)

Table 6.1 (*continued*)

Category	Traditional Assumption	Internet
	Customers are considered as a group or sector.	Customers are considered more individually and products are customer-defined (virtual products) and customer-specific.

INTERNET MARKETING RULES FOR SUCCESS

Your marketing strategy is critical to the implementation of your overall Internet business strategy. Innovative advertising approaches, being first to market, creating customer-centric solutions, and coordinating the functions of marketing with IT are hallmarks of successful marketing approaches. Determining innovative ways to meet customer needs, exploiting niche marketing opportunities, better understanding your customer's behaviors and anticipating their values, personalizing complete solutions, and reaching an international audience are at the heart of the marketer's new role.

Ten specific Internet marketing rules of success are:

1. Be first to market with innovative solutions.
2. Align and coordinate marketing and IT groups and information systems.
3. Employ targeted and innovative advertising strategies.
4. Exploit existing niches and create new niche business opportunities.
5. Integrate your solution into your customer's daily practice.
6. Create a more complete customer solution.
7. Capitalize on the massive global audience.

8. Select complementary interlinking business partners.
9. Allow customers to create, define, test, and market products themselves.
10. Learn from customer behaviors and habits.

1. BE FIRST TO MARKET WITH INNOVATIVE SOLUTIONS

As noted in Chapter 1, global, innovative, customer-centric strategies lead to success. Your marketing challenge is to define innovative solutions and to focus on customers' values. You must understand your customers so well that you can anticipate the values they most respect around any product. The final part to the equation is that your product or service must be first in the market. The market share difference between first and second will most likely be substantial with the Internet. For example, Netscape and DealerNet were the first products of their type to be introduced and remain leaders today.

Galt's NETworth mutual fund marketplace was first to market. In fact, it was one of the first thousand nonacademic sites on the Internet. Because it was the first of its kind, it generated enormous customer momentum both from end customers (individual investors) and mutual fund company customers. Galt's NETworth mutual fund marketplace now gets two million hits per day and 1,250 new registered users; even Fidelity and Vanguard are reportedly ready to sign up. Rob Frasca, president and CEO of Galt, says being first to market on the Internet reminds him of the COMDEX Effect. COMDEX is the world's largest and most famous computer trade show. Because it was the first worldwide show, COMDEX has no significant competitors, and its momentum is growing. The exhibition features 2,000 exhibitors and 10,000 new products, drawing 200,000 attendees from 100 countries. Being first may allow you to achieve the COMDEX effect.

Being first to market a solution and first to achieve a threshold volume enhances the case for the theory of increasing returns, which contradicts that of decreasing returns. With the increasing returns theory, the more market and mind share you have, the more you can increase your business with incremental investments.

2. ALIGN AND COORDINATE MARKETING AND IT GROUPS AND INFORMATION SYSTEMS

A new relationship is emerging between marketing and IT groups for successful Internet companies because the traditional organizational lines between marketing and technology groups continue to blur. Internet marketing covers a much broader range of activities than does conventional marketing.

Successful marketing groups understand the technology of the Internet. They force themselves to recognize what they can do with it. Technology is the driver and therefore must be understood in order to be used effectively. Successful marketing groups work closely with IT groups because as new customer needs are defined, new information system-enabled products must be developed quickly. Internet marketing strategies are measured by the speed with which they determine new customer needs and translate them into new product opportunities.

An effective user interface is necessary. This increases the need for marketing and IT to work together. Information systems will increasingly be built not with the internal company employee; but rather the end customer in mind.

This is a radical perspective for some businesses; ability to adapt varies. Businesses in the IT industry, for example, have long focused on accessing and manipulating information and are well acquainted with the process of designing products for the end user. In addition, IT businesses have a long history of integrating their marketing departments with their technology systems. A prime example is ONYX Software, profiled in Chapter 1.

Marketing groups should work more closely with technology groups to develop access systems or user interfaces. With the ability to access the Internet from television and other appliances now coming on the market, this will become even more critical, as customers expect easy-to-navigate systems.

The most effective marketing strategies are information systems—enabled. Marketing information systems are necessary to collect and analyze Internet-generated data. Internet activity analysis software costs from several hundred to a few thousand dollars and is widely available. A list of vendors is in Chapter 7. Chapter 3 offers an example of the material that can be obtained.

In addition to buying and implementing such third-party solutions, you also need to integrate customer information and other Internet data obtained into your existing systems, such as sales force automation (SFA) systems, decision support tools, and data-mining applications. As illustrated in Chapter 1, ONYX integrated information obtained over its Internet site into its SFA systems.

3. *EMPLOY TARGETED AND INNOVATIVE ADVERTISING STRATEGIES*

Internet marketing rules are continually evolving. As the technology evolves, new options and approaches become possible. Successful companies take a leadership position with respect to creating these new rules. For example, consumer goods giant Proctor and Gamble (P&G) took the initiative to develop a customized and targeted advertising solution on the Internet using with the popular Internet search tool Yahoo!. Working with Yahoo!, P&G defined a value-based advertising approach that had never before appeared in the industry on that scale. Under the system, P&G paid only for Yahoo! customers that both saw the P&G advertisement *and* selected the advertisement. These advertisements link to various P&G sites. In this way, P&G pays by value (number of qualified customers) it gets from Yahoo! By working with companies like Yahoo! that provide advertising space, a marketer can obtain almost immediate response to a campaign and discover how many users selected the advertisement.

Other innovative approaches developed by Internet search engine companies ensure that marketers receive qualified leads on the Internet. Advertisers can reserve keywords on some search engines. (Keywords are words that users enter into the search query tool, which returns a list of sites associated with that keyword.) In this way, an advertisement appears only when the prospect enters in the reserved word in the search box.

For example, if a hotel chain reserves the word *hotel*, its ad is displayed for any customer who types in *hotel* in the search field. Many companies report high hit or click-through rates when they use this advertising approach.

It is possible to link into the search engine's back-end systems and see how often the reserve word was used and how often the advertisement was selected by prospects. Some search engines can even change or cycle an advertisement quickly if it does not prove successful.

Internet costs for advertising are generally much less than for other approaches. Internet advertising is usually charged at a cost-per-thousand model, or CPM. In Internet parlance, any time a user sees an advertisement is an exposure, and in this model the advertiser pays each time the ad is displayed. It may be possible to negotiate the position of the ad within a site and the length of time it is available on a site, as well as the reserve words that trigger its display.

To introduce a significant product, you may want to generate a short-term, high-volume advertising campaign. Internet advertising solutions can help you achieve this. Some popular sites guarantee that one million users will see your advertisement in less than one month. This is possible because some sites—for example, Netscape —have extremely high hit rates. Netscape reports 80 million hits per day, which corresponds to more than 10 million users per day, as Netscape estimates about 6 hits per site user.

The Internet home page itself is seen as a relatively cost-effective way to market. Table 6.2 compares traditional advertising models to the Internet.

Table 6.2 *Advertising and Marketing Costs per Thousand Exposures*

Category	Cost
network television	$3–4
targeted business print ad	$50
direct marketing/direct retail	$500
complex mailing	$2,000
internet home page	$2.75

Source: Lucent Technologies GBCS (Internet home page assumes $1.3 million per year and an average home page hit rate of 50,000 per month, 15 minutes per transaction, at $0.15 the cost of the Web server.)

Some marketers sponsor events on the Internet, bringing thousands of people to their sites. For example, Sun Microsystems sponsored the 1994 World Cup Soccer games. It listed the scores and provided information about the teams. Its home page became one of the most visited sites during the games. Finding an activity, such as a sporting or cultural event, that suits your corporate marketing goals can be an effective way of encouraging traffic and establishing name awareness.

Hachette Filipacchi New Media, a division of Hachette Filipacchi Magazines, formed a cyber-network of its media properties for advertisers. On the Internet, Hachette's presence includes Web sites for the magazines *Car & Driver, Elle, George,* and *Premiere.* Marketers are offered the opportunity to purchase advertising for the total network, specialty networks, or individual titles. "Our sites' special-interest content serves as a filter of the cyber-audience as a whole," says John Dawson, Hachette's publisher. "By attracting consumers who are interested in this specialized content, marketers are discovering that our focused audiences are more receptive to their related products and services, which leads to high response rates from better quality leads." Dawson notes that SeaDoo, a maker of personal watercraft, switching its online advertising from a generic Internet news site to *Boating Online,* experienced a significant jump in traffic and brochure requests. SeaDoo reported a 12 percent conversion rate from brochure requests to product. Moreover, consumers with an interest in boating spend, on average, almost six minutes on its site—much more time than the generic advertising site drew.

Thus, marketers that know and cater to their customer profiles can be most successful. Nissan Motor Corporation discovered this by tracking the conversion of brochure requests to closed sales. Advertising through *Car & Driver* and *Road & Track* on America Online delivered the largest group of buyers.

Before paying advertising fees, ask the site's manager to provide you with the following information:

- number of exposures the site receives each day
- Internet connection speed
- user demographics

Ask specific questions, as the possibility of misleading or misunderstood information is high. A cyber-network of sites may quote an overall number for hits, thereby failing to provide specifics on the site or page you are most interested in.

Dozens of search engines are on the Internet now, many of which are industry specific. You need to ensure that you are registered in as many as appropriate. It has become relatively straightforward to submit your Internet address and site description to multiple search engines, newsgroups, and mailing lists. Tools like iTool's Promote-It, a compilation of the Internet's best publicity tools, facilitates this process.

One caveat: Many search engines analyze the frequency of words used. This can be misleading, for if your business does not use a wide variety of key search terms, it may not come up in many searches. Some innovative marketers have gotten around this limitation by including words in black color on a black background so that the customer does not see the keywords, but the search engine's robot, which is constantly searching pages and updating indexes, does see, and index them.

4. EXPLOIT EXISTING NICHES AND CREATE NEW NICHE BUSINESS OPPORTUNITIES

While the prospect of competing head to head with large organizations may seem attractive to smaller companies, there are actually other ways to capture market. One prime method is through niche marketing, by which specific communities of interest of reachable market size are defined as significant business opportunities. Innovative marketers find ways to cater to existing niches as well as develop new ones. For example, Sausage Software, profiled in Chapter 1, and New York–based Paper Software, cater to existing niches, namely high-tech computer programmers. Niche marketing has always been an interesting and profitable way for large and small companies to participate in the global marketplace. There are more Rolls Royces per capita in Hong Kong than anywhere else. Why? Although the potential market size is small, through effective marketing strategies the British car maker targeted and reached likely purchasers, and today it has an extremely loyal following in Hong Kong.

Small companies can perhaps best exploit the possibilities of niche marketing. Companies that survived beyond the startup phase usually do so because they perform some facet of their business significantly better than their larger competition, or they simply serve a segment of the market that is unknown to, or ignored by, other market actors. The Internet provides an interesting opportunity for smaller organizations to export their specialization to larger firms that may not perform a particular function well. The two companies may work together in a partnership or interlinking business arrangement.

Small companies, because of their nimbleness, are inherently suited to catering to existing niche markets. The Internet provides an even more exciting opportunity: that is, the ability to discover, target, and nurture new niches.

As George Bekier, founder of the Red and White Company, a Hong Kong–based wine retailer that plans to sell over the Internet, says, "Most people think the Internet in Asia is about mass marketing and reaching a mass audience. But the world, and especially Asia, is individualistic. In Asia you have to focus on niche marketing." Asia's huge size, and its panoply of cultures, languages, and religions, is fertile ground for Internet-based niche marketing.

The Red and White Company believes that the Internet provides the opportunity to grow and cater to a small niche. According to Bekier, in Hong Kong, as well as the rest of Asia, interest in wines is increasing. His company recognizes that although the niche is small and nascent, the Internet can cater to, shape, and nurture it.

This raises an interesting question: Can *anybody* cater to niches, independent of location and context? Could a U.S.-based Internet wine company cater to the Asian wine consumer? Perhaps, but the advantages of proximity to, and familiarity with, local markets cannot be dismissed.

5. *INTEGRATE YOUR SOLUTION INTO YOUR CUSTOMER'S DAILY PRACTICE*

Success requires understanding how to integrate your first-to-market, innovative, customer-centric solution into the customer's daily practice. Microsoft recognized this early. In 1979, Microsoft's stated goal was "to be on every desktop and in every home."

Microsoft's current slogan for their Internet products and services is "Where would you like to go today?" It identified a key success factor—getting into its customers' daily business practices. So
must any company with an Internet strategy. Yahoo! kicked off a
$5-million advertising campaign with television commercials that
ask "Do you Yahoo!?" and are intended to explain how the Internet
can fit into daily practices.

Amazon.com is getting into the daily practices of customers by
encouraging sites to link prospective purchasers to Amazon.com. It
just launched a service promoting this through the offer of revenue-
sharing opportunities. A linking site receives a share of the profits
realized from a book.

Thus, for example, if NetStock Direct wanted to provide a more
complete customer solution by offering educational information to
direct investors in the form of bestselling books on money management and building portfolios, it could interlink customers to the
Amazon.com site, thereby directing them in the purchase of the
book.

Like Microsoft, Netscape wants its site to be a part of the daily
practice of Internet users. Seeking to ensure that users continually
see its new services and products, the company developed a
PowerStart service whereby users customize an Internet launching
pad. Customers build a custom interface to the Web; the interface
lets them send e-mail, monitor newsgroups, link to key Web sites,
and track selected stocks with a live, streaming stock ticker.

Frank Russell Company, based in Tacoma, Washington, provides
financial services to institutions and individuals. One of its core
competencies is leadership through research about investment
managers and financial markets. Russell has differentiated these
core competencies in many ways, including the development of
dozens of financial indexes, used by money managers throughout
the world.

One of the business challenges facing Russell is that although
these indexes are prized by many institutional investors they are
not well known to the general public and therefore not widely used.
To foster incorporation of its information products into customers'
daily practices, Russell decided to offer daily updates of its equity
style benchmarks on the Internet to the public. By monitoring

Internet access logs, Russell determined that many visitors go directly to this information, bypassing the welcome page. This suggests that visitors bookmarked the Russell indexes on their browsers and are making them a part of their daily practices. Internet activity analysis software can determine, in many cases, the types of business that made the index review a part of their common practice.

One question marketers ask is, "Do I need to focus on slick graphics to get my product into a customer's daily practice?" While a significant focus on cutting-edge graphics in business functionality exists, several successful sites provide significant value with few, simple, or limited graphics. As discussed in greater detail in Chapter 10, research shows that Internet users recognize current bandwidth limitations and prefer approaches that focus on content.

It would thus be unwise to focus on graphics in place of technology infrastructure, systems, virtual products, and other services customers value that can make your solution part of their daily practice. Yes, the user interface is important. In fact, it may be critical in satisfying the customer's need for an easy-to-use product. But the marketing management focus needs to be on the value proposition and providing a complete customer solution.

Successful marketers create a society around their Internet presence to foster getting into a customer's daily practices. The Internet infrastructure supports the creation of ad hoc communities sharing interests and/or objectives. These communities have been around since the inception of the modem but have blossomed with the advent of the Internet. They are usually found as bulletin boards, forums, and chat groups. In the fields of sports and entertainment they have become extensions of fan clubs and memorials, and usually do not carry official affiliations. Available software tools help build communities of interest.

America Online indicates that a sizable part of its revenue comes from chat forums. ESPN's Sportsline Internet service generates traffic, builds brand equity, and entices customers to make the site part of their everyday practices by offering ten to 20 interactive forums on sports-related subjects. A sports executive leading an Internet strategy for his Fortune 500 company says, "There is a window of opportunity for businesses to absorb these communities into sanctioned groups catering to the communities' needs, and in return having access to a targeted audience for commercial activities."

The new marketing function can help promote your customers. Although this is possible with other media, it is much easier, quicker, more interactive, and often less expensive on the Internet, as your site provides a limitless marketing space. Netscape links to several of their key customers from intriguing online stories illustrating how their customers innovatively use their products. This serves two purposes. It promotes Netscape products as well as increased volume to Netscape customer sites. Considering that Netscape has 80 million hits per day, this represents a potentially valuable service for Netscape's customers.

6. CREATE A MORE COMPLETE CUSTOMER SOLUTION

When customers visit an Internet site they should, ideally, find all the information necessary to make a buying decision. You must create a complete customer solution serving customer values such as convenience, educational marketing, transparency, and guaranteed fulfillment. For instance, a site could offer tools to make comparisons between your product and your competitor's.

Customers are usually prequalified when they come to your site, which should provide functionality *beyond* the traditional marketing content. Such functions includes pre-sales supports, decision-support assistance, and customized communication. The Internet changes the concept of marketing by expanding the scope of activities not traditionally considered part of the marketing function. The marketer must identify these new needs of customers.

GE Plastics uses its site to offer new product tips. Eventually GE Plastics may let customers provide information themselves. This may mature into a full-scale community of interest. In addition, software can be downloaded to help customers select from the thousands of products available. This is the essence of educational marketing. Internet users are generally more informed about many products, as more data are available to them and they have elected to visit a particular site. They can differentiate sites offering valuable, unbiased information from those offering strictly sales-oriented material.

Marketers must look to provide the most complete solution, that which is most convenient for customers. This can be done through interlinking businesses (typically done by small companies) or through grouping all relevant business units into one integrated whole.

For example, CUC wants to be *the* single online shopping center serving the gamut of customers' needs. In 1997 CUC will launch perhaps the most comprehensive shopping experience in the world. Over the Internet, CUC will offer the ability to make travel reservations, find and rent apartments, buy cars, purchase and sell mutual funds, and much more.

How can CUC offer these services? Before the Internet, using telephone sales and online services such as Prodigy, CUC was already one of the top five travel agencies, one of the largest car dealers, one of the largest sellers of mutual funds, and one of the largest sellers of electronics.

7. *CAPITALIZE ON THE MASSIVE GLOBAL AUDIENCE*

The commercialization of the Internet presents brand-new global opportunities. Small businesses can now reach the global marketplace as multinational companies have done. This global reach forces marketers to think in new ways.

Review the experiences of the companies discussed in previous chapters. Sausage Software made innovative use of the Internet's capability when introducing HotDog by getting 150 people from 26 countries to test the software over a three-day period. Amazon.com sold books to customers in 26 countries its first month of business.

Paper Software developed WebFX, its first major product in 1995. WebFX enables users to display and manipulate 3-D objects over the Internet. A Web page developer maps layers of data onto a 3-D model, allowing users to zoom in on a portion of an image for greater detail. Working with a limited advertising budget but cognizant of the worldwide potential of the Internet, Paper decided to distribute free copies of the software in order to build name recognition and customer loyalty in a short period of time.

The strategy worked. Within six weeks, more than 100,000 people downloaded it. Eventually Paper interlinked its site with Netscape, and in November 1995 it placed an advertisement on Netscape's opening Web. In less than three hours after the advertisement was posted on Netscape, Paper's site had more than 200,000 hits. By giving away its product to nearly three million users during a promotional period, Paper Software built a global customer base and became a recognized vendor of virtual-reality software in no time.

8. *SELECT COMPLEMENTARY INTERLINKING BUSINESS PARTNERS*

The level playing field created by the Internet offers exciting possibilities to smaller companies. Alone this does not guarantee success, and a hasty overreliance on a single element may inhibit the smaller organization's success.

While the ability to appear larger than actual size may be appealing, façade marketing risks placing a small company in a situation it is not equipped to handle. Customer service capabilities, flexible and timely order processing systems, manufacturing capabilities, warehousing capacities, distribution and import/export channels, and administrative support functions cannot be fabricated. It may take only one or two unexpectedly large orders for a small company to collapse.

The small company marketer must be honest about the business's capacity. An accurate appraisal of core competencies, the solutions needed by customers and their expectations for fulfillment, and the potential for interlinking alliances with other companies should be your guides.

If the small company leverages the principles of virtualization, then it can take advantage of the level playing field and lessen its exposure to the risks of façade marketing. Achieving this requires carefully selected interlinking business partners and a clear understanding of your business specialization.

The marketer must also determine the site's points of entry and departure. As noted in Chapter 5, they must be identified and incorporated into your complete solution through interlinking or business partnerships.

When considering a site as a point of entry or departure, ask the following questions:

- What is the typical profile of the site (e.g., academic, government, or business)?

- Where are users coming from (e.g., country, state, business sector)?

- What do they expect from your site?

- What part of the complete customer solution are you solving and what part are your interlinkers solving?

To be successful means that someone else (a customer or business partner) sees your value. Other sites link to yours either knowingly or not. In a conscious link between two businesses, you have many options to better market, serve customers, and share revenues. Customer profile data can be passed. You can link directly to specific areas of interest. Links that you do not knowingly define with your business partners are sites that place a value in what you offer.

This can be good news for a smart marketer because it shows that the owner of another site has seen value in your site. The marketer, sensing opportunity, needs to be thinking, "Why are these sites linking to ours? What does this show me about my customers?"

You need to understand that value and exploit it. For example, Galt reports that more than 1,000 sites link to Galt's mutual fund marketplace.

9. ALLOW CUSTOMERS TO CREATE, DEFINE, TEST, AND MARKET PRODUCTS THEMSELVES

The Internet marketing function is different because customers define the time and place of the marketing they are exposed to. Generally speaking, Internet users control where, when, and how much marketing they allow. To the innovative marketer, the Internet is ten miles wide and ten miles deep. It is ten miles wide as a result of target advertising and interlinking opportunities to attract people to your site. It is ten miles deep because once customers are acquired, an effective marketer can keep them, influencing what they see by building an interactive approach that anticipates their needs and desires. As discussed in Chapter 2, your ability to be effective and provide value to customers depends to a very large extent on your customer analysis.

Consider CUC International's customer experience. CUC has learned much from 18 years of electronic shopping history about what its customers expect, namely cost competitiveness, convenience, choice, security, and educational information. The company developed a solution centered on these values.

- **Cost competitiveness**: Through its long history of business efficiencies in selling online services and establishing relationships with manufacturers as well as customers, CUC can offer prices significantly lower than those of its retail competitors.

- **Convenience**: Customers have access to an easy-to-use query tool for identifying their best options in their price range. For example, customers can enter a query for stereos with specific features in a certain price range.

- **Choice**: CUC's site offers more than 1,700 brands and 250,000 products.

- **Security**: The site is secured and available only to customers.

- **Education**: Gathering purchase-related information is a preferred Internet activity. Customers feel educated and therefore more comfortable with their options and decisions.

Marketers can offer innovative ways to market a product online. By letting customers test products online before making a purchase, the seller offers virtual test drives.

The test-drive approach is employed by technology companies to market equipment and services. The Massachusetts-based Digital Equipment Corp. (DEC) allows potential customers to upload and run their own software programs on computers located at DEC's headquarters. The customers can see and feel the performance of a DEC computer directly before making the decision to purchase one. Some software companies, notably Netscape, have also implemented test drives for their software.

The marketer must provide an environment for customers to create their own products. This is the essence of virtual products, which are built by customers on demand using the information assets offered by the seller. You must ensure that the customer interface and systems are sufficiently flexible to allow customers to build what they want with your data. You must also understand flexible and potentially customer-specific pricing approaches.

At Amazon.com, the marketing challenge is to make visiting the site fun. It is difficult for an online service to compete with visiting an actual bookstore—the pleasures of browsing, interaction with other customers and sales staff, background music, comfortable sitting areas, and coffee bars. Clearly, an Internet site can never match this experience.

But dwelling on physical attributes ignores the paradigm that Internet marketing requires. The central question is: What can an online bookstore offer that a physical one can't? Amazon.com allows customers to contribute to and browse in a database of book reviews from around the world. In this way customers market to other customers by fostering a community of interest around different subjects. In addition, Amazon.com's search engines allow customers to register for updated information on authors they are interested in. When a new book by a customer's favorite author is released, an e-mail message is automatically sent to alert him. In short, Amazon.com capitalizes on the possibilities offered by the electronic marketplace that physical bookstores cannot match.

The Discovery Channel's Internet site has traditionally catered to the educational values of its customers. The company developed a strategy that allows customers to search for articles on interesting subjects and to read through these materials. Updates on the topic are e-mailed to the user. Discovery Channel uses the Internet's proactive potential to provide a rich technology solution. In essence, customers create their own products and define their marketing experience.

10. LEARN FROM CUSTOMER BEHAVIORS AND HABITS

Ensure that customer and supplier feedback is fully encouraged and easy to acquire. By designing systems encouraging customer or business partner feedback, purchasing trends can be identified and acted upon swiftly.

The reports that can be generated using the Market Focus software, discussed in Chapter 2, represent only a portion of the obtainable information. Some measurement packages can track a user's path through a site, the time spent per page, and a host of other data sought by a site administrator. Additional elements of the Market Focus reports are featured in Figure 6.1. You can determine which businesses are most interested in your value and where they came from. This can help determine how effective an advertising strategy has been, whether a product is targeted at the right customers, profiles of visitors to a site, and the geographic regions where potential customers are located.

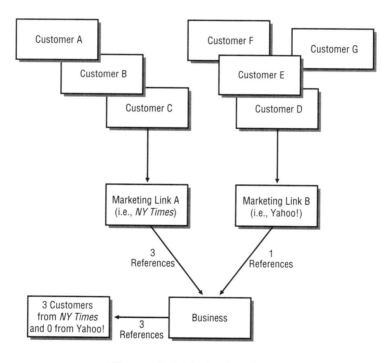

Figure 6.1 *Marketing Links* *

NY Times and Yahoo! are only used as examples.

Market Focus reports are generated from Internet access logs to assess user activity. In Table 6.3, out of a total of 191 users in one week, 88 users came from Amber Manufacturing, representing 46 percent of the total.

Table 6.3 Sample of Market Focus Internet Reports *

Organizations with the most users	Number of users	Percent of users
Amber Manufacturing	88	46.1%
MKG Cosmetics	24	12.6%
Spike's Dog Supplies	18	9.4%
Global Net Marketplace	15	7.9%
Lori's Books	12	6.3%
Lynn Partners Limited	10	5.2%
Robert's Culinary Academy	7	3.7%
Manches Munchies	6	3.1%
Tass International	6	3.1%
Sue's Sweet Shop	5	2.6%
Total	191	100%

City	State	Number organizations	Percent of requests
New York	New York	40	20.9%
Chicago	Illinois	30	15.7%
Columbus	Ohio	2	1.0%
Seattle	Washington	2	1.0%
Tacoma	Washington	2	1.0%
Cambridge	Massachusetts	2	1.0%
Pittsburgh	Pennsylvania	2	1.0%
Cupertino	California	2	1.0%
Maplewood	New Jersey	1	0.52%
Bellevue	Washington	1	0.52%
Other		107	56.0%
Total		191	100.0%

Fictitious business names used.

Do not set one strategy, implement it, and assume that it will need no maintenance. It is important to continually evaluate your marketing success and take corrective action as necessary. New customer behaviors and expectations can be monitored. Internet technology offers the opportunity to gather market intelligence and monitor consumer choices through customers' revealed preferences in navigational and purchasing behavior.

The success of your marketing strategy may be more apparent on the Internet than in traditional media because detailed information can be obtained more quickly. As the case of ONYX Software, discussed in Chapter 1, demonstrates, monitoring customer inquiries in or near real time can be invaluable, enhancing the image of the company as nimble and customer-centric.

A mechanism for evaluating the marketing effort should part of your Internet strategy. Consider asking visitors to rate your site via a user questionnaire. Encourage customers to work with you in developing your site in the way that offers the most value to them, as Amazon.com. does.

The online bookstore makes providing feedback easy. Asking for input may seem less confrontational in cyberspace than it would in the physical realm. Be open to ideas from your existing and potential customers. Collaborate with them on site design and marketing efforts during customer conferences or other events. This promotes your presence and provides immediate guidance on changing customer values.

Nielsen Media Research's I/Pro service takes an unique approach to providing site owners with user data. Customers preregister for an I/Pro account and use that whenever a site asks for their I/Pro information. If your site is designed for I/Pro numbers, all visitors that provide them are identified. You can then use the I/Pro service for specific customer information.

The benefit to the business is that it gets specifics on customer demographics, much more than it could get without registering users. Customers have only to enter their code on each site, making registration convenient.

Online advertisements can receive relatively high click-through rates relative to other forms of advertising. Cathay Pacific Airlines reports that depending on the position of its advertisements they receive between 3 and 15 percent click-throughs. The *Wall Street Journal* reports that 3 to 5 percent of those who view advertising banners on its site click on them.[1] Dealernet sees a click-through rate as high as 10 percent for banners placed in certain search engines.[2]

Ensure that processes are in place to measure leads supplied by your advertising links. You can track whence your customers come and thus measure the value of each link or referring site. Refer to Figure 6.1 for an illustration of this concept. Many advertising sites let you know how many users selected to view your advertisement, but you should track whether or not users become customers.

NOTES

1. "WSJ Set Pricing for Web Edition" *Web Week*, (March 1996).

2. Stuck, Bart W., "Internet Transactions Still Yield Small Change," *Business Communications Review* (July 1996):51.

CHAPTER 7

INTEGRATING TECHNOLOGY: MAKING IT WORK IN YOUR BUSINESS

This chapter is the most technology oriented in this book. It is essential to understand the mechanics of the Internet technology before implementing an Internet strategy. After reading this chapter, you may want to review the concepts outlined in Chapters 3 and 5.

BEING PROACTIVE, LEARNING, AND INTEGRATING THE TECHNOLOGY

If marketing opens the door to new customers, the technological back-end systems deliver the solution and close the deal. Integrating the Internet's technology set with your business is critical to the success of your Internet strategy.

Therefore, your IT group needs to explore how your business's systems must mature with the evolving capabilities of the Internet. The group must be proactive, understanding not only how to exploit existing technology but also anticipating new technologies fit with your overall plan. Being proactive and learning to integrate technology' is more important than ever before.

Online shopping giant CUC International originally outsourced its Internet development to a local company. CUC felt that its scope of Internet activities was well defined and that external experts could complete the work. Over time, the top managers of CUC changed their minds—dramatically.

They realized that CUC's information systems were a clear differentiator, setting CUC as the industry leader, and that the company's own IT personnel needed to understand the business mission. Contractors and companies retained on an outsourcing basis do not necessarily have an intimate knowledge of the business. Moreover, CUC's Internet technology activities became so pervasive that the company simply could not farm out all of the work in defined packages. So CUC bought the Internet company and is building skills internally; business knowledge stays inside the company.

IT is becoming a essential component of the overall customer solution and its differentiation. As Geoffrey A. Moore states in his book *Inside the Tornado,* which analyzes the high-tech marketplace and the role of IT, "These days, you simply can't generate a high-margin product or service that doesn't have a significant IT component. To out-customize your competitors, you have to beat them on IT."[1]

Flexible IT business systems, already vitally important, will become even more crucial to business success because their effectiveness will be judged not against static goals but against highly dynamic criteria. IT will have to cope with both evolutionary and revolutionary changes. Very few aspects, if any, of business operations are expected to be designed for life, and as a successful organization is constantly adapting to change, so should IT.

Vast technical resources detail the technical concepts of the Internet. The challenge, however, is to provide the link between technical concepts and the information necessary to develop innovative and practical business applications. To do this the basic Internet technical concepts must be reviewed from a business perspective.

APPRECIATING INTERNET TECHNOLOGY

REALIZING THE HISTORY

The Internet itself has its origins in a late-1960s Department of Defense program to devise communications capable of surviving a military attack. In 1969 the first version of the Internet, then referred to as the Advanced Research Project Agency network (ARPAnet), connected four host computers. The ARPAnet was based on a networking standard that ensured high resilience and availability. In the late 1970s new networking standards were introduced to provide for increased robustness, connectivity, and performance. In 1983 global connectivity and internetworking was formed and the Internet Architecture Board (IAB) was established. Later that year the ARPAnet split into the Military Network (MILnet) and ARPAnet. The MILnet provided military communications and the ARPAnet allowed for an experimental research network. Eventually the ARPAnet generated what we now know as the Internet.

The Internet is run today by the Internet Society Operating Committee (ISOC), a voluntary membership organization whose purpose is to promote global information exchange through Internet technology. ISOC, in turn, appoints a series of volunteers to the Internet Architecture Board (IAB), which meets regularly to pass standards, such as HTTP, and allocate resources.

The performance of the Internet backbone in the United States has migrated from 56 kilobits per second in 1983 through 1.5 megabits per second (Mbps) to 45 Mbps today. In fact, some providers are rolling out 155 Mbps today. Research groups are developing standards for the Internet backbone to support substantially faster communication speeds over the next few years. Other network media, such as cable and satellite, will be employed for the provision of online services, including the Internet. These services are being tested today and are expected to be more widely rolled out in late 1997. They all promise to offer significantly higher performance and easier access to the Internet; bandwidth improvements will allow the introduction of new services, products, and marketing strategies.

The term Internet is used to cover many services and technologies. The World Wide Web (WWW) is the service that currently has the most applicable communication protocols and technology for business on the Internet. Other Internet services include electronic mail (e-mail), file transfer (FTP), Internet Relay Chat (IRC), newsgroups, Gopher, and Telnet. New services provide voice transfer capabilities (Internet telephony). Although in its infancy, this technology shows great promise, allowing long-distance calling for the price of a phone call to your Internet service provider. For example, IBM's Internet telephony products will be able to use a single phone line to check e-mail and conduct voice communications simultaneously and to conduct conference calling. A computer user can get audible technical help while allowing a technician remote access to her computer's functions.

Existing Internet services and technologies are continually evolving. The underlying communications protocol (IP) on which many of the Internet services are based, is undergoing revisions to enhance security and to support real-time traffic flows and expanded addressing capabilities so that more users can access the network. The WWW technical protocols, such as hypertext transfer protocol (http), are being revised for better performance and security.

The WWW brings graphics, interaction, and interlinking (technically referred to as hyperlinking) capabilities to the Internet and allows for multimedia content such as voice and video. The WWW has generated the most commercial excitement of all the Internet services as a result of these capabilities. The traffic levels of the WWW are growing much faster than any other Internet service.

A common mistake is to think that the Internet and the WWW are one and the same. A Web strategy is *not* an Internet strategy, and vice versa. Rather, a Web strategy is a superset of an Internet strategy.

The FTP service provides a mechanism for sending and receiving files on the Internet. When you download files (e.g., text or pictures) from a WWW Internet site, in many cases the Internet's FTP service is invoked. IRC provides real-time text-based communication for qualified groups of users—the communication protocols for the thousands of Internet discussion groups. Businesses leverage the IRC service to establish discussion groups for customers, business partners, or vendors in a real-time format.

For example, Kodak customers can join in a real-time chat with experts during specified periods of the day, as can ESPNet customers. These technologies can be used to build brand equity and customer loyalty.

Newsgroups provide electronic bulletin boards on which messages can be posted, reviewed, and responded to. Businesses can use a secured version to communicate electronically with clients and business partners.

It is important to recognize the value of discussion groups as a customer service tool. Any Internet user with a question or comment about your products or services can post a question and anyone in the discussion group can answer—in many cases, other users. This can reduce your support cost and create a more loyal customer base. Netscape offers newsgroups for customers to post product questions and receive comments from both customers and Netscape engineers.

Gopher is a service commonly used by the academic community that provides text-based Internet users a method of searching for information throughout the Internet.

The Telnet service enables the Internet user to access and execute operations on remote Internet computing devices.

RECOGNIZING ITS POWER

The combination of Internet protocols, services, and products presents strategic advantages for businesses, some of which are highlighted in Table 7.1.

Table 7.1 *Internet Technology Advantages*

Internet Capability	Business Advantage
Platform Independence	More customers, remote offices, and business partners can exploit your information assets electronically. You need not be concerned with developing applications for different computing platforms if you devise proper network-centric solutions.

(continued)

Table 7.1 (continued)

Internet Capability	Business Advantage
Active Content Capabilities	Software programs can provide local and customized content and functionality that integrate into your enterprise wide systems.
Communication Costs Insensitive to Distance	Reduced global communication costs with remote employees, customers, and business partners.
Support for Open Standards	Businesses that adopt internationally supported Internet standards can easily maximize the capabilities of the Internet using existing architecture.
Widespread IT Vendor Support and Integration	Software products such as Lotus Notes provide cost-free interfaces to the Internet, so that Lotus Notes documents can be obtained directly from Internet browsers. With products like @Mezzanine, document management systems can be reached directly by Internet browsers.
International Access	More than 100 countries on six continents have access, which increases global access to potential partners, customers, and niche markets.
Transparent Distribution of Software	Software distribution can be designed to be inherently automatic. Businesses deploy software (e.g., Java) in one location (Internet server) and client workstations can automatically use it when they access the site.

Maximizing its business advantage through use of the Internet's capabilities, Kodak is designing systems to better serve its customers through an effort called Project Anthenaeum. Using a Java-based system (Java will be discussed later in this chapter), clients can search through Kodak's many digital image libraries. The Java applet (Java-based software application) is a component of the overall Kodak application permitting advertising agencies, motion picture studios, and other customers to search through Kodak's database of digital images of potential film sites, props, costumes, and the like. Kodak may eventually expand the applet functionality by adding zoom in and out, filters, and color management to optimize a display. Rob Aronoff, director of product marketing for Kodak's Digital and Applied Imaging Division, says, "We can get to a very large audience very easily without actually having to distribute anything. When you need it, the applet will come down over the Internet and run on your computer locally. That whole paradigm works for us."[2]

In launching Project Athenaeum, Kodak broke out of existing thought patterns and looked at the Internet as a *strategic* tool. Its business advantage stems from the technical capabilities the Internet offers, including:

- platform independence (only one version needs to be supported)

- communication costs insensitive to distance (customers throughout the world can access for low rates)

- international access (wider range of customers may be reached)

- transparent distribution of software (maintenance costs reduce)

DISCERNING THE OPTIMAL COMPONENTS

It is important for all associated with an Internet strategy to understand the components of Internet architecture. This will lead to an understanding of how to leverage these technologies for strategic advantage. However, identifying the right components to use is a challenge even for the technically inclined.

Sorting out all the new software products is a dizzying task. Figure 7.1 depicts a high-level Internet technical architecture—in technical terms, a topology diagram. To understand the subsequent sections it is necessary to appreciate the technical architecture components illustrated in this figure. Table 7.2 summarizes the associated options offered in Figure 7.1, as well as typical component selection criteria for businesses. Review these to understand a typical Internet infrastructure.

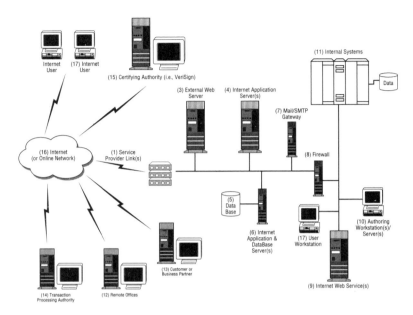

Figure 7.1 *Basic Technical Architecture*

Table 7.2 *Technical Components*

Component	Description	Some Available Options	Principal Selection Criteria
Connection to the Internet backbone (1)	Communications link between the Internet backbone	Analog or digital modem to public telephone network, and the Internet business site	Performance Reliability Cost ISDN, Fractional T1/E1, T1/E1
Connectivity Equipment (2)	Equipment that converts between Internet backbone and business communications environment	Driven by the type of connection to the Internet backbone. Options include TA, NTU, DSU/CSU	Connection Type Reliability Manageability

(continued)

Table 7.2 (continued)

Component	Description	Some Available Options	Principal Selection Criteria
Internet Server Hardware and Software (3)	The software and hardware platform that serves and manages business information through the Internet	Software available for wide variety includes: Microsoft's Intel-based NT platform, SGI, Sun Sparcstation, DEC Alpha, IBM (several platforms), HP, Apple, LINUX/ UNIX on IBM PC	Product Availability Supported Standards Performance Cost Security Extensibility Resiliency
Application Server (4)	The hardware and software to run Internet applications such as IRC, newsgroups, teleconferencing, database, and to process customer requests	Software available on a wide variety of platforms: NT on PC, NT on DEC Alpha, Sun Sparcstation, SGI Indy, IBM AIX, LINUX/UNIX on PC	Performance Cost Security Product Availability
Database System (5)	Software that manages the back-end databases to serve and collect information	Oracle, Sybase, Microsoft SQL Server, Gupta SQLBase	Performance Cost Supported Standards Functionality

(continued)

Table 7.2 (*continued*)

Component	Description	Some Available Options	Principal Selection Criteria
E-mail Gateway (7)	The device that manages e-mail traffic between the business environment and the Internet	NT on PC, NT on DEC Alpha, Sun Sparcstation, SGI Indy, IBM AIX, LINUX/UNIX on PC	Functionality Supported Standards Performance Cost Security Product Availability
Firewall (8)	Software and/or hardware that protects the internal corporate network from unprivileged access	Variety of options available that generally requires expert recommendation and installation	Reliability Functionality Performance Ease of Administration
Internal Server/ Intranet server (9)	The hardware and software that serves internal Internet information (i.e., Intranet)	Same as Internet Server	Same as Internet Server
Authoring Server (10)	The hardware and software used to develop and test the Internet systems (content, functionality, etc.) and applications before deploying into the production environment	Same as Internet Server	Ease of Use and Administration Programming Tools Available Cost

(1) CONNECTION TO THE INTERNET BACKBONE

In the United States, national Internet service providers (ISPs) include MCI, PSI International, NETCOM Online Communication Services, and UUNET Technologies, Inc. Local service providers are also available but may only provide access from specific regions. Before signing up with an ISP, make sure the service is reliable reviewing potential vendors' operational performance statistics as well as the level of technical support required. When negotiating a contract, ask the ISP for this information.

Many national providers recognize that their customers want international coverage as well so that global businesses or several business partners can use the same provider. Traveling employees can dial local numbers wherever they are and access the corporate site or the public Internet.

The type of connection required for your business depends on the amount of traffic in and out of your system. The more traffic, the more bandwidth needed. Unfortunately, there are currently no established benchmarks for number of users per hour with type of connection. However, vendors such as UUNET Technologies offer burstable services, whereby you pay only for what you need at any given time. This means not having to continually predict the level of traffic; the bandwidth of the line expands dynamically as the number of users increases and contracts as the number of users goes down. This is also referred to as Just-In-Time (JIT) bandwidth. Bill Branson of the Frank Russell Company suggests that JIT bandwidth is a fundamental part of the successful network vision of the future.

Connection types include the analog asynchronous modem line, the Integrated Services Digital Network (ISDN) line, and the high-speed dedicated digital line, (such as T1 or T3, or a fraction of a T1). ISDN is a reasonable and commonly utilized option for companies that need sufficient bandwidth for moderate volume applications but have stringent budget restrictions. With additional software, ISDN lines can be combined (inverse multiplexing) to gain bandwidth.

Fractional T1 or T3 and full T1 or T3 are leased lines with higher bandwidth, 1.5 Mbps, and 45 Mbps, respectively. If you expect high traffic, consider one of these options. ISDN can also be used as a reasonably priced backup line in the event a T1 fails. Backup lines are important to consider for mission-critical sites. ISDN can be configured so that you are charged only when you use the line.

(2) CONNECTIVITY EQUIPMENT

The type of connectivity equipment needed depends on connection to the Internet backbone. The equipment can vary from digital switching units/channel switching units (DSC/CSU) to routers to ISDN adapters and is necessary to make the data conversions between communication channels and your internal network. Service providers either lease this equipment or refer to specific products. Outside the United States, telecommunications companies often provide these components as part of their service.

(3) INTERNET SERVER

The server is the heart of the technical architecture, receiving requests from Internet users, retrieving the information locally or from networked devices, and replying. Selection and sizing of this machine is a critical task, typically presenting a tradeoff between performance and cost. Wide price ranges and supporting software availability further complicate the issue.

The two basic options are (1) UNIX-based platforms (Silicon Graphics, IBM, Sun, and Hewlett-Packard); and (2) Microsoft NT-based Intel platforms. UNIX is currently thought to deliver better performance than NT platforms for transactional-based support. This is a result of both the maturity of the UNIX operating systems and the hardware architecture. However, Microsoft's NT is now scaleable, and multiple processors can be tied together, as in UNIX operating systems, to improve performance. Microsoft platforms generally cost less than UNIX systems. Currently, most Internet sites are UNIX-based and most Intranet sites are Microsoft-based.

UNIX is a more mature operating system than NT. As a result, it delivers better performance for the same hardware configuration. UNIX administration, however, requires more complex skills. For example, the same security features that give UNIX an edge over NT also present security holes if not administered properly. If you do not have in-house UNIX expertise, investing in an UNIX-based server may require a large maintenance cost.

The initial investment is generally lower for NT-based Intel or Digital (DEC) Alpha platforms than for UNIX. As UNIX-based platforms are more proprietary for certain hardware platforms, the cost of the add-on products (hardware or software) is also higher. Another consideration is the availability of Internet server software products.

Most of the new Internet software products first became available on UNIX platforms. As the Internet forces vendors to push the technology to its limits, they usually prefer high-performance platforms to introduce their products. Merchant System and IStore, Netscape's bundled high-end electronic commerce systems, were first made available for UNIX platforms. It might be easier to choose your software first and then look at the hardware platform options. Some evidence suggests that this trend is changing, as the NST operating system becomes more prevalent in organizations.

To measure the performance of Internet servers, most vendors use a performance benchmark developed by Silicon Graphics called Webstone. However, major Internet server manufacturers are working on new, independent benchmarks. A beta (initial) version of a benchmark suite called SPEC Web, from the Standard Performance Evaluation Corp. (SPEC), is being tested. At the present, however, you are limited to the server performance analysis offered by the manufacturer or through Webstone.

Internet server software selection is relatively easy. Most of the server software on the market is based on industry standards and shares similar features. As a manager of a major manufacturing company's electronic services notes, "We try to focus less on vendors and more on selecting the interfaces and standards they support."

If your business involves sending and receiving secured communications, you need to implement secure communication software. Netscape's Secure Socket Layer (SSL) protocol is implemented by several vendors and is the industry's first de facto standard. Several other security standards are becoming available. Credit card vendors and IT vendors Microsoft and Netscape have significant incentives to ensure that the Internet can be secured in order to promote standards for online purchasing and make their products part of the everyday practice of customers.

(4) INTERNET APPLICATION SERVER(S)

Internet servers often perform initial user processing and then network to other servers for functions such as application services. Among these applications, FTP, newsgroups, IRC, audio transfer, and teleconferencing are the most common candidates for a separate Internet application server. Some, including transactions and teleconferencing, may require intensive processing power. Hardware and software selection depends to a great degree on the type of the application and its level of expected usage.

(5) DATABASE SYSTEM

Back-end databases are often used to support interactive capabilities such as customized information on demand and subscription services. A wide range of databases is available; technically, these are referred to as database management systems (DBMS). If your corporate site will feature a high level of interactivity, you should implement a DBMS. Most vendors offer the software necessary to develop programs that link directly from an Internet server to information maintained in databases. Therefore, consider the DBMS in which you already have experience. Turnkey Internet solutions with bundled DBMSs in the package are also available. These include Netscape's Merchant and Publishing Systems, which are targeted at large retailers and publishers. Microsoft's Internet Information Server is integrated with its DBMS, known as SQL Server. DBMS vendors like Sybase are building tools so that Internet sites can be developed which generate pages dynamically, based on information received from the database.

Internet sites can require a significant amount of back-end programming, used for back-end marketing systems, usage tracking, and customer service—programs that often require substantial database interaction.

(6) DATABASE SERVER

The database server—the computing hardware that runs the DBMS—directly affects the performance of an Internet site. The Internet server may serve both the Web and the database, if lightly accessed. Three important considerations for hardware servers are (1) processing power; (2) memory; and (3) storage space. These considerations are especially relevant for database servers which, on heavily accessed sites, are often the performance bottleneck. Experts should be involved in the sizing of this equipment.

(7) E-MAIL SERVER

The e-mail server and gateway processes e-mail requests from Internet users and distributes them to internal mailboxes. It also forwards mail to the Internet from internal e-mail users, generally using an Internet mail transport standard called Simple Mail Transfer Protocol (SMTP), to communicate with other systems. Its performance is not as critical as the Internet server or database server, as e-mail is not a real-time communication tool. Many e-mail server products are in the market that now offer the capability to transfer embedded HTML files and links as e-mail attachments.

(8) FIREWALL

The firewall is typically a hardware/software combination that controls the traffic between your internal network and the public Internet. Although a firewall can be directly incorporated into an Internet server, it is most commonly a specialized computer. With it, internal users can access the Internet while unauthorized entry from external Internet users is prevented. The configuration of the firewall is a challenging task and should be performed by experts. Several turnkey solutions on the market offer protection against potential intruders. Devices such as SOCKS and proxy servers can be used to enhance the security of sites.

Proactive steps should be taken to ensure that security architecture meets your business requirements. Additional hardware, software, and procedures may be necessary. These issues are further discussed later in this chapter.

(9) INTERNAL INTERNET SERVER

The internal Internet server is built for a company's network users and can be an effective tool for distributing information across the organization. If you do not need all the functionality of a large-scale workgroup product like Lotus Notes, an internal Internet server offers an inexpensive and flexible alternative. However, there are two hidden expenses to this alternative: First, everyone to be connected will need a Web browser on his workstation; Second, the amount of data (traffic) flowing over the internal network may substantially increase, forcing an upgrade to accommodate more bandwidth. This can be a costly exercise.

(10) AUTHORING SERVER

The purpose of an authoring server is to serve the applications and utilities to develop (author) Internet content pages, graphics, and applications. Although documents can be authored on the production server, a dedicated authoring server mitigates the risks of production problems (which can involve recording and/or recompilation of software programs). Most of the utilities used to manipulate graphics and multimedia material are resource-intensive and can easily drain the power of the Internet server.

The authoring server can also be used to provide a test environment in which developers can generate different visual and functional scenarios before moving them to a production environment. Many technical benefits accrue to obtaining authoring and production servers from the same vendor. It is important to ensure that the authorizing and testing environment is the same as that of production. Authoring is also commonly performed on a local PC and published to a development/authoring server for testing.

(11) INTERNAL SYSTEMS

The term *internal systems* refers to those business information systems that contain internal company data. This information usually is not open to Internet users and must be protected from intruders. A proper firewall is crucial for protecting internal systems.

The integration of internal systems and the Internet server becomes vital as companies exploit their existing information assets for customers and business partners using Internet technologies. A variety of software approaches can retrieve internal systems information to an Internet server.

(12) REMOTE OFFICES

The Internet may provide a cost-effective way of connecting remote offices. Although the Internet does not provide military-grade communications security, several software techniques can provide varying degrees of security. Available products and standards can enable a company to use the public Internet infrastructure as a private virtual network. In fact, this capability is built into Microsoft's NT server operating system. Other options are highlighted below. With these approaches a level of security sufficient for most routine business activities can be obtained. Using the public Internet as a backbone for connecting your offices, however, is frequently not a responsible decision because of the inherent performance and reliability problems.

(13) GOVERNMENT AND SUPPLIERS

Effective communication can streamline operations, decrease costs, and increase revenues. Many government organizations, both state and federal, are already on the Internet and offer a variety of Internet services. In the future, even more government services will be available online. Governments are looking to the Internet as a vehicle to reduce their support costs. Today it is possible for individuals to download software from government agencies (such as the Internal Revenue Service) and file taxes online. The IRS's Frequently Asked Questions page, for example, offers enormous potential cost savings.

Increased communication with suppliers has proved an effective way of managing inventories. However, integrating all suppliers in your supply chain, regardless of size, may not always be cost effective, given the expenses of establishing proprietary networks. The Internet provides an opportunity for companies to establish communication with their suppliers regardless of their size, because of its openness.

(14) TRANSACTION PROCESSING AUTHORITY

Credit card transactions in nonelectronic commerce are handled by clearinghouses. Visa and MasterCard are in partnership with

Microsoft, Netscape, GTE, and IBM, among others, and have developed secure electronic transaction (SET) processing specifications. Netscape is also working with FDC, the largest U.S. transaction clearinghouse, to establish a method for authorizing credit card transactions over the Internet. Several companies already developed solutions for electronic transactions. CyberCash, E-Cash, and virtual bank accounts are early innovators, although it is not certain that any of these methods will prevail over the long term and become the standard for electronic transactions. It is, however, safe to say that there will be ways to transfer money between Internet nodes. Perhaps the most promising will be based on the SET specifications.

(15) CERTIFYING AUTHORITY

A secure connection between an Internet server and a user requires a trusted third party that can verify the identity of the server and, in some cases, depending on the level of security required, the customer also. VeriSign is currently the major certifying authority.

If your server uses the most common security protocol today, Secure Sockets Layer (SSL), you need to apply for a digital certification. This is an electronic key that identifies your company over the Internet. The certifying authority verifies that the server party is actually who it says it is. There is a one-time, up-front charge, plus an annual fee. It can take several weeks for a company to obtain a certificate.

The U.S. Post Office is considering entering the business of providing certificates or digital IDs for customers.

Businesses can also certify customers themselves, but becoming a certification authority is a complex and costly endeavor.

WHAT TECHNOLOGY DO YOU NEED?

PRODUCT CATEGORIES

New technical terms and product concepts have evolved with the Internet. New products with new capabilities continue to be offered. Table 7.3 outlines software product categories.

Table 7.3 *Internet Technology Components*

Product Category	Description	Product Examples
Browsers	Provides Internet browsing.	Netscape Navigator Microsoft Internet Explorer Spry Air Mosaic Delrina Cyberjack
Internet Servers	Serves browser requests.	Netscape Suite Spot Microsoft Internet Information Server OR&A WebSite Open Market WebServer Oracle WebServer Internet Factory Commerce Builder
HTML Editors	Facilitates Web page design and development.	SoftQuad HotMetal SGI WebMagic Quarterdeck WebAuthor Microsoft FrontPage Adobe PageMill Netscape Navigator Gold
Graphical Site Development Tools	Provides visual site development; requires minimal technical and graphics experience.	Asymmetrix Web 3D DigitalStyle WebSuite
Site Management Tools	Manages hyperlinks and site structure.	Interleaf CyberLeaf Netscape Livewire Pro Microsoft FrontPage
Analysis Tools	Analyze site usage, access logs, and other statistics.	Interse MarketFocus Open Market Web Reporter
Commerce Systems	Integrated commercial turnkey application packages.	Netscape Merchant System Netscape Publishing System Netscape Istore Open Market OM-Transact ICAT Software

(continued)

Table 7.3 (continued)

Product Category	Description	Product Examples
Internet Application Development Tools	Facilitates rapid application development for Internet software applications	Silicon Graphics' Cosmo Bluestone's Sapphire Borland's Latte
Internet Database Connectivity Tools	Middleware products that allow Internet applications to access internal back-end databases.	Open Horizon's Connection Suite Allaire Cold Fusion
Firewall Software	Filters the traffic between internal networks and the Internet; attempts to prevent unauthorized access.	DEC Digital Firewall Checkpoint Firewall-1 Raptor Eagle Harris CyberGuard IBM NetSP
HTML Converters	Converts word processing documents or other common office automation products into HTML files.	Microsoft Internet Assistants for MS Word, Excel, software Powerpoint, etc. WordPerfect Internet Publisher Lotus Notes' Domino
News Servers	Provides newsgroups functionality.	Netscape News Server
News Readers	Facilitates newsgroup information access.	Spry News Reader Netscape Navigator
IRC Servers	Serves internet relay chat sessions.	Netscape Chat Server
IRC Clients	Necessary for Internet Relay Chat sessions.	Netscape Chat WinIRC
SMTP Gateways	Transfers e-mail messages between internal e-mail systems and the Internet.	Postal Union Netscape Mail Server Microsoft Exchange

(continued)

Table 7.3 *(continued)*

Product Category	Description	Product Examples
Voice Chat Servers	Serve Internet voice chat sessions.	Xing Streamworks Progressive Networks RealAudio
Voice Chat Clients	Allows Internet voice chat sessions from PCs.	Iphone CyberPhone NetPhone Progressive Networks RealAudio
Filter Software	Prevents access to predetermined sites (can exist on clients or servers).	Webster WebTrack Netscape Proxy Server
Internal Search Servers	Acts as a librarian to internally cataloged HTML pages.	Netscape Catalog Server Microsoft Index Server

TECHNOLOGY IMPLEMENTATION STRATEGIES

As you develop innovative Internet approaches, applications must provide increasing functionality for more complete, flexible, customer-specific transparent, and secure customer solutions. Internet business applications move through phases as they integrate with business information systems. This section reviews four potential phases of Internet business applications. This should encourage you to think about where Internet technology and applications are leading.

- **Phase 1.** Static and informative marketing-oriented applications that focus on creative visual appeal.

- **Phase 2.** Interactive functions, initial transaction-oriented processing, and light integration with back-end databases and applications.

- **Phase 3.** High-level interaction, greater user control, and acceptance of the Internet as a two-way interactive medium with Java business functionality allowing integration into enterprise systems. High-level transactional processing with more secure solutions such as authentication and encryption.

- **Phase 4.** Software agents, development of expert systems, and tight integration with multiple global business partner's information systems. Virtual reality interfaces and real-time interaction (this phase is currently significantly less technically mature than prior ones).

Figure 7.2 outlines the general path through these four phases of increased functionality, and Table 7.4 outlines possible applications.

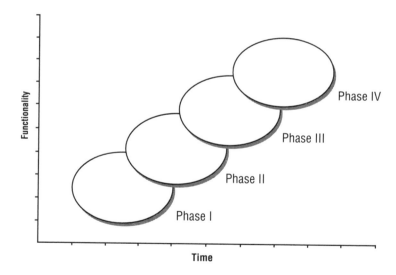

Figure 7.2 *Four-Phase Application Evolution*

Table 7.4 *Capabilities of Internet Computing*

	Phase I	Phase II	Phase III	Phase IV
General Phase Characteristics	Static information; focus on visual appeal.	First versions of interactive functionalities and transactional processing applications evolve.	High level of interaction. Greater user control and customization. Transactional processing applications become more common over the Internet.	Software agents and robots become popular, along with expert systems.
Business Applications				
Recruiting	Home page ads, Internet resumes accepted online. Internet searches based on location and job type.	Search capabilities based on prospect qualifications. Employee questionnaires transferred over the Internet.	IRC chat recruiting sessions. IRC chat interviewing. Internet applications and search agents review jobs and candidates, reporting directly back to business managers.	Recruiting agents become popular, matching qualifications with openings and maintaining profiles. Effective and widespread use of teleconferencing.
Orientation	General information about the company, such as corporate overview.	Employee manuals and similar static information.	Internet orientation fill-out forms navigating user throughout all steps of interview process.	Orientation software agents follow up the status of the forms, make arrangements with other parties such as ordering desk and computer for the new employee.

(continued)

Table 7.4 (*continued*)

Phase I	Phase II	Phase III	Phase IV	
Training and Education	Static training and educational materials.	Interactive training and educational materials.	IRC chat training sessions with experts.	Training agents and teleconferencing (voice telephony) become popular.
Presentation and Promotions	Static home pages. Focus on graphics and presentation.	Interactive questionnaires, online publications, newsletters, direct e-mailing, static event sponsorships.	VRML 3-D animations, real-time animations.	Direct participation event sponsorship; direct chatting with experts. Online contests become popular.
Pre-sales Support	Static product information.	Downloadable demonstrations, e-mail support.	Real-time online demonstrations, user newsgroups, user group IRC chat sessions, search utilities in databases.	Roundtable discussions with experts, IRC chat question-answer sessions with engineers and designers.
Sales Automation	E-mail–based feeds. High human involvement required.	Automated reply mechanisms. Sales material delivered to the user via e-mail or customized Web page.	High mobile sales force support. Telnet access to back-end systems. Catalogs, customer profiles, account information credit checking.	Integrated electronic sales agents with all the functionalities of human sales agents. Demographically sensitive, multilingual.
Customer Support and Service	Static white papers, operation tips, online manuals, e-mail support service, FAQ.	User newsgroups, online upgrades.	Customer-specific upgrades, recognition, and support based on recognized value of customer; IRC chat sessions with experts and service personnel.	Software service agents become more widespread. Direct diagnostic capability via the Internet. 3-D product training.

(continued)

Table 7.4 (continued)

Phase I	Phase II	Phase III	Phase IV	
Public Relations	Static press releases.	General and organization-specific information, releases with direct links to relevant background information, and e-mail links to names referenced.	Internet interviews and press releases with IRC chat; customized press releases based on specific press needs.	Voice connections, interviews, real-time global press conferences.
Supply Chain Management	E-mail based alarms. Human involvement.	Two-way e-mail–based alarms. Ordering and invoicing applications. Human involvement.	Two-way automatic ordering and invoicing applications.	Third parties tied to the process (banks, credit-checking organizations, shipping and trucking companies). Negotiation agents.
Product Development	Static information about product design and functionality. Some problems reporting from customers.	E-mail feedback from customers about design improvements and problems. Newsgroup users on product development.	Customer interactions on design issues and product development through virtual tests of online prototype.	Multimedia tools used to suggest design improvements.
Groupware	Information sharing through Web site. Static information. E-mail communication.	User group postings, private chat sessions, early voice chat implementations, distributed Web sites.	Resource sharing through Telnet. Screen sharing, simultaneous voice and data transfer.	Teleconferencing. Secretary agents.
Project Management	Static information about the status of projects.	Customized information about private projects, links to deliverables and team members.	Interactive joint project management.	Project manager agents access status and report back to management or other agents.

(continued)

Table 7.4 *(continued)*

Phase I	Phase II	Phase III	Phase IV	
Order Processing	E-mail requests.	Internet forms, automated feeds to back-end systems, initial level of transaction processing and credit checking.	Tools provided for customer-specific designs, product specification generation, and work order generation.	Integrated software agents handle custom order acceptance, specification generation, work ordering, transaction processing, and accounting functions.
Purchasing	Internet information search for product information. E-mail inquiries.	Detailed nonlinear catalog searches.	Product customizations after nonlinear catalog search (virtual products).	Purchasing software agents. Automated bargaining, discount calculation, negotiation, and decision-making based on your needs and historical decision-making.
Executive Information Systems/Decision Support Systems (EIS/DSS)	Industry general statistical analysis and forecasts.	Customer-specific executive analysis.	Access to EIS/DSS servers for complex modeling. Integration and access to data-mining and warehouse applications remotely.	EIS/DSS agents continually alert management.
Document Management	Static document sharing via Web site.	Document on demand with request forms. Delivery via e-mail in text format.	Document on demand and storage on demand. Search capabilities in SGML Format.	Librarian agents. Extensive search and index capabilities.
Accounting	Basic information gathering; currency rates.	Customized client account information. Internet transaction processing, and online credit checking.	Electronic cash recognition. Internet links to third parties (banks, tax authorities, investment agencies).	Global accountant agents perform accounting management activities.

HOW SECURE IS INTERNET SECURITY?

Security is perhaps the primary concern for both businesses and customers when approaching Internet commerce. The absence of mature security standards and products is one of the biggest risks today. This barrier must be overcome before Internet commerce can reach its full potential.

Even with secure systems, the risk of fraud can still be high. CUC International, Inc., saw higher-than-expected fraud rates associated with its Internet-based shopping service and had to develop expert systems to better predict and prevent fraudulent practices.

The greater barrier may be the *perception* of insecurity in the minds of customers—an unfounded fear, for the potential for fraud exists in all aspects of everyday commerce, from paying for gas by credit card to ordering theater tickets by telephone. However, credit card issuers developed standards to protect Internet customers from credit card fraud and to limit their liability.

For the present, customer preoccupation with security is a significant barrier. However, this may have a positive side: Media focus and scrutiny on the Internet and security should force vendors to respond with genuine solutions.

Few businesses and customers fully understand the current state of the security situation. Try to answer the following questions:

- What constitutes a secure system?

- What standards and applications are necessary?

- What level of security is right for you?

Many businesses perceive security as a binary concept—that is, either you have it or you do not. In fact, there are no absolutes in security; even secured military communications have been broken. Security should be understood on a continuum, such as the one presented in Figure 7.3.

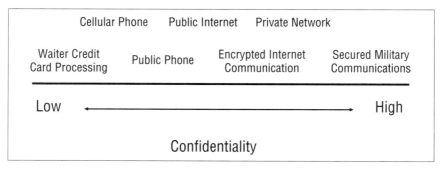

Figure 7.3 *Security Continuum*

From the security continuum it is clear that first, there is no such thing as foolproof security. Fraud has—and will likely continue—to occur everywhere. It is a cost of doing business. Second, many traditional forms of communication are less secure than current protected Internet communications. Rates of cellular telephone and traditional credit card fraud are six to seven times higher than those of online fraud. Third, even with today's standards, a moderate level of security—in particular, confidentiality—can be achieved with the Internet.

A conscious, premeditated approach is required to break into secured Internet systems, as are time, money, and other resources, but these are not insurmountable obstacles to would-be thieves. As a panel of computer scientists noted in a study issued in 1996, "Advances in computing power keep making it easier for individuals and organizations to attack encrypted information without the expenditure of unreasonable resources." The study's authors— among them Whitfield Diffie, who developed public-key encryption, and Tsutomu Shimomura, who achieved fame for tracking down infamous hacker Kevin Mitnick—noted that current encryption systems using 40-bit keys "offer virtually no protection," and that secure systems in the future will require 75- and 90-bit keys.

You must determine the optimal level of confidentiality for each type of business communication. The good news, according to Blaze et al., is that the cost of very strong encryption "is not significantly greater than that of weak encryption." In many cases a company needs only to keep casual Internet users from accessing a subset of information. Different levels of security can be achieved for each business communication requirement.

Systems designed to operate on strategic access layers (SAL), discussed in Chapter 4, should implement the strictest security mechanisms. These solutions may require arrangements with users of the system, such as coordination of ID numbers to authenticate access privileges. As the number of the users involved in a SAL is usually limited, however, this may not be difficult. Generally, the tradeoff is between cost, security, and performance. Note that additional security layers may slightly impede performance.

Consider security in the context of the Internet Access Layer (IAL) model introduced in Chapter 4. Applications in the IAL or organizational access layer (OAL) may require substantial security steps—for example, channel (or communication) security mechanisms such as SSL (Secure Socket Layer) or SHTTP (Secure Hypertext Transport Protocol). SSL is a protocol developed by Netscape and others and currently used by Netscape's server and browser products. It has three security aspects:

1. authentication,
2. data integrity, and
3. encryption.

SSL encryption uses a pair of public and private digital keys to encrypt and decrypt messages. The public key may be thought of as the padlock and the private one the key to unlocking the security features. Key length affects security level; a longer key containing more bits, offers greater resistance to unauthorized access than does a shorter key with fewer bits. The U.S. government currently restricts the export of products that use encryption with more than 64-bit keys (128-bit encryption used within North America). This vestige of the Cold War may soon be lifted by Congress.

Data integrity and authentication are included within the SSL specification. Data integrity ensures that no one tampers with messages in transit and authentication ensures that Internet sites are genuine. Other measures, such as digital time stamps and digital IDs, ensure the integrity of message transmission and that of senders, respectively.

SHTTP, now in development by an industry consortium, may offer a better long-term solution than SSL because it addresses document security and digital signatures as well.

Internet security is much more than encrypting files. An effective security strategy is more than authentication, certification, and data integrity; you may find the need to consider internal system security, which regulates users on your end. This is generally performed through access control lists (ACLs) for each application. Nonrepudiation, or proof of receipt, is necessary in some cases to ensure that the customer has in fact received the receipt.

The final aspect of security to consider is availability, which assures users' access to a system. This is necessary because unauthorized users can flood a network with traffic, thereby preventing authorized users from gaining access. Proper firewall and network design provides some protection. A large number of firewall system vendors offer robust solutions. Be aware that proper installation of the firewall system may be far more important than which firewall product is selected.

Vendors can assist you in discovering weak spots in your information security system by attempting to break into your internal corporate environment through your Internet site. Third-party software packages can also be purchased to test for holes and to monitor files that may have been subject to tampering. These security concepts are outlined in Table 7.5.

Table 7.5 *Security Levels*

Type of Security Addressed	Description	Potentially Applicable Internet Access Layers
Channel Security		
Authentication	Ensures that both parties (business and customer) are who they say they are.	Organizational, Integrated, and Strategic
Data Integrity	Ensures that data has not been altered or tampered with during transmission over the Internet.	Organizational, Integrated, and Strategic

(continued)

Table 7.5 *(continued)*

Type of Security Addressed	Description	Potentially Applicable Internet Access Layers
Encryption	Ensures transmission is encrypted so only intended recipient can read message.	Organizational, Integrated, and Strategic
Technical Architecture		
Availability	Ensures availability and integrity of corporate systems is intact through proper firewall and network design.	All
Application Architecture		
Authorization	Ensures only proper users of corporate systems are allowed in.	All
Nonrepudiation	Ensures proof of receipt.	All
Digital Time Stamp	Ensures the integrity of message transmission.	All
Digital Signature	Ensures the integrity of senders.	All

No matter how secure a system is, its weakest link is typically internal. Employees often write down their passwords and private encryption keys. Most reported security breaches are committed by employees. Any company that considers the Internet a strategic component of its infrastructure must implement a companywide internal security policy.

The U.S. Department of Defense's *Orange Book* is an excellent source for implementing an effective security policy. It is published by the National Computer Security Center and is formally known as the Department of Defense *Trusted Computer System Evaluation Criteria*. It introduces a systematic approach to developing a robust security policy.

SECURED ELECTRONIC PAYMENT METHODS

As Internet commerce grows, reliable online payment methods become more critical. Using credit cards on the Internet has been possible since the beginning of commercialization in early 1993. Inherent security problems made this option undesirable for many until 1995, when more effective security standards became widely available and were incorporated into browsers and Internet servers.

With the introduction of secure-payment protocols, you can now offer secure credit card transactions on the Internet. Will this help reduce customers' fears and facilitate more widespread transactions? Although no solution can be guaranteed 100 percent, current and anticipated secure-payment approaches suggest that the Internet will indeed enable widespread secured transactions over the next few years. For example, Netscape Communications, through its Merchant System and Istore products, provides commercial Internet storefronts that securely support credit card transactions.

Visa, MasterCard, Netscape, IBM, and Microsoft are all active in developing secure-payment mechanisms for the Internet. In 1995 Visa allied with Microsoft and began developing the Secure Transaction Technology (STT) protocol, while Netscape and MasterCard began developing the Secure Electronic Payment Protocol (SEPP). After some time, both groups recognized the need to work together on a single solution.

The combined standard is referred to as the Secure Electronic Transaction (SET) protocol. SET takes credit card security a step farther than the prior standards. While STT and SEPP reveal the customer's credit card number to the merchant, SET sends this information only to the merchant's bank. In this sense, Internet credit card transactions with SET may be more secure than paying a restaurant bill with a credit card. It appears that this standard will be a driving force in the widespread consumer adoption of the Internet and its integration into everyday practices.

Several other types of payment methods have been developed to foster secured Internet transactions.

ECash is a digital payment method from DigiCash. An ECash transaction requires client and merchant software and an ECash bank account in supporting banks. When users open an account and deposit actual money, they receive a copy of the required ECash software. The ECash process requires the user to transfer money from the ECash account onto a computer hard drive for use in transactions.

When purchasing from a merchant who accepts ECash, the user transfers the required amount from the ECash digital money stored on the computer's hard drive to the merchant's server. The merchant can deposit the money into its ECash account or keep it on its hard drive for future use.

CyberCash is similar to ECash. It too has three components: (1) the client (referred to as the wallet); (2) the merchant (with the CyberCash server); and (3) the verifying party. Both client and merchant must have CyberCash accounts in one of the supporting banks. The transaction mechanism is similar to ECash.

Both ECash and CyberCash offer digital cash payment mechanisms to eliminate the need for credit cards for small transactions. It also opens the Internet commercial market to people without credit cards.

FirstVirtual Bank Accounts generate a virtual link between credit cards and transactions. On opening an account with FirstVirtual, a personal identification number (PIN) identifying your account is assigned. To make a payment to a supporting vendor, the user simply provides the PIN. This PIN number, the nature of the transaction, and the amount are automatically sent to FirstVirtual by the merchant computer. FirstVirtual then sends a confirmation request by e-mail. If the purchase is confirmed, the account is debited by the transaction amount. Using PINs avoids sending credit card number over the Internet.

Additional secured payment solutions are being planned. One notable effort is a joint venture between Oracle Corp., a leading developer of database software, and VeriFone, Inc., maker of credit card swiping systems. The Oracle-VeriFone product will be a secure Web payment system for consumers and businesses, integrating

Oracle's WebServer software with VeriFone's secure payment software. This will allow real-time credit card authorization over the Internet through standards like SET. Standards are also being developed to cater to microtransactions, which may become more prominent in the future. Engineers at Carnegie Mellon University are developing NetBill as an architecture to securely handle microtransactions.

NOW THE HARD WORK: HOW TO INTEGRATE

Putting aside all the hype and speculation about the Internet, the vision of an online future is often accepted with little regard for the scope and complexity of the work. People read about the Internet in a book or see a demonstration and say, "Well, the Internet is here, it's a fait accompli. What's next?" Even if you agree with Nicholas Negroponte, director of the Media Lab at MIT and author of *Being Digital,* that the Internet may be the only development in history in which reality exceeds the hype, what's next is a lot of hard work.

Getting internal systems to work together is the job of systems integration specialists. The systems integrators are your IT group. They must look beyond the Internet hype and make the business vision a reality. The role of the system integrator must be periodically revisited, changed, and reinvented. As the marketer's is, the system's integrator's role is integral to the success of the Internet effort.

To achieve systems integration, IT staffers need to review their traditional assumptions, including sourcing approaches, traditional development time frames, and application revision schedules. For example, due to user workstations' platform independence, development and deployment time frames can be reduced. Theoretically, operational costs for this new paradigm will be reduced, given that there is no longer a need to distribute and install software locally. Java applets (Internet-enabled client/server applications) are not only platform independent but also deployed on a single server.

As business strategies and innovation cycles evolve more quickly, software flexibility becomes paramount for business success. Businesses must be equipped to respond to this change. As software is the engine that moves information, it follows that the role of software technology will grow dramatically.

Particularly in the service sector, success depends on the selections, utilization, and modification of software. The challenge faced by business processing software today is very different from that of 20 years ago. In the past, software was an accessory, a subordinate tool of the hardware infrastructure. Today, software is the enabler of change, the tool that permits service-based industries to meet the demands of a rapidly changing business environment. To fulfill this role, the nature and properties of the software needed by organizations will be very different from what they were in the past.

Table 7.6 summarizes common assumptions that should be revisited with the advent of Internet business strategies. Use this table to rethink your current IT assumptions.

WHAT ARE THE SOURCING OPTIONS?

Over the last several years IT organizations debated the value of outsourcing—the distribution of responsibility for defined activities to an outside entity. For example, many organizations outsource computer center or communication network operations to companies like IBM and EDS. This is commonplace, but many businesses choose to continue insourcing these functions.

With the advent of Internet technologies and systems, IT organizations are again faced with the sourcing question. This will be a critical issue for your business: Should you outsource your Internet technology responsibilities to an outside entity and, if so, to whom? Your answer depends on many factors, including (1) strategic importance of the Internet to your business, and (2) your success level with your current sourcing partner.

The more integral the Internet is to your business, the less likely you are to outsource. The more problems you have had with outsourcing vendors, the less likely you are to outsource.

Internet projects have narrow time frames and often only vague and transient requirements for integration into business and marketing functions. The technology strategy must be flexible. This is important to recognize because existing outsourcing arrangements may be criticized for impairing flexibility. They are written for projects and operations that can be clearly scoped out for the benefit of both parties involved. The outsourcing company wants assurances that certain activities will be accomplished within a given time frame. The vendor receiving the outsourcing contract wants to be assured it can fulfill the terms of agreement without encountering unexpected delays, cost overruns, and technical obstacles. In other words, the focus may shift from what is desirable to what is doable within the constraints of time and money.

The success of outsourcing has been widely overstated. Outsourcing contracts can be limiting to the business and difficult to construct flexibly. The Internet makes outsourcing even more difficult. With the rate of technological change in this field, it is virtually impossible to predict future requirements in any meaningful detail. Moreover, the typical amount of change required to establish and maintain an Internet presence is much greater than that needed for traditional outsourcing tasks such as payroll administration and data processing. Incorporate flexible terms and conditions—or a mechanism for drafting them—into your outsourcing contracts.

Think about the paradigm shift that has occurred. In the past it was easier to outsource IT systems and functions because they were not strategic foci for business management. A core competence in technology skills was not essential for business; cost containment was. Today technology plays a growing role in business strategy and is no longer an ancillary issue. It not only supports the business operations, it enables the business strategy.

It may be imprudent, then, to rely on an outside party to provide Internet skills. Keeping these functions in-house allows you to draw upon the expertise of employees with both technical skill *and* intimate knowledge of your business. In short, there may be no sharp demarcation between business functions and technology. An integrated approach requires you to consider them together; you cannot apportion mission-critical tasks in piecemeal fashion. Figure 7.4 illustrates this distinction. The lefthand side represents the common perspective of the last several years; the righthand side represents a model in which the business and technology are completely integrated.

Table 7.6 *Systems Integration Model*

Systems Integration	Old Model	New Model	General Implementation Observations
Sourcing	Outsourced focus	Insourced recognized	Systems groups are more integrated with marketing groups and business groups. Integration seen more as a highly strategic asset of an organization.
Model	Client/Server	Network-centric	Focus in the future will be on effectively integrated and networked servers and clients, seamlessly linked to appear as a single server to the user. Applications developed independent of customer platforms, unlike traditional client/server development.
Design Focus	Efficient, functional	Flexible, able to adapt to continually changing business strategies	Software flexibility clearly seen as the differentiator across all industries, as quicker innovation cycles mean faster changes are critical.
Typical Development Time Frame	Greater than 6 months	Much less than 6 months	The business imperatives require reducing development time frame.

(continued)

Table 7.6 (*continued*)

Systems Integration	Old Model	New Model	General Implementation Observations
Operational Costs	High	Moderate (relative to old model)	Given the platform independence of the technology, configuration management issues should be less significant. (However, managing distributed servers may be more significant.)
Relationship to Business Units	Varied	More integrated and networked relationship with business groups, especially marketing	Business success factor increasingly becomes better systems integration.
Upgrades/Application Revisions	Major revisions focus/ semiannual	Incremental revision focus/ monthly	Mindset shift from major application revisions to incremental revisions. Given the nature of Java development, application deployments can occur more rapidly than traditional deployments.
User Interface	Graphical user interface for clients	Multimedia interface	New multimedia capabilities require retraining and rethinking by IS executives.
Technical Architecture	Basic client/server Applications	Distributed object model	Object-based software architectures will be a key part of the future. Objects will be distributed among servers and deployed as applications on Web servers. Oracle, Netscape, and Microsoft are all focused on this approach. *(continued)*

Table 7.6 (*continued*)

Systems Integration	Old Model	New Model	General Implementation Observations
Primary Success Factor	Functionality for specific point in time	Software flexibility, and personalization	Software must be flexible because the operating reality is changing more rapidly: competitors, customers, laws, regulations, etc.
Target Audience	Internal employees	End customers, business partners, and internal employees	IT must recognize that the changes are no longer simply to internal employees; the design audience now includes customers and business partners.
Data Location	Internal to business	Internal and external	The IT challenge now includes the need to manage the external data. For instance, the business intelligence of the company depends on the degree to which external data can be internalized.

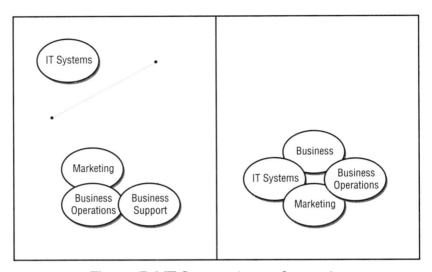

Figure 7.4 *IT Outsourcing vs. Insourcing*

CRITICAL FACTORS FOR SUCCESS

A new class of business processing software must be conceived to handle constant change. Rather than simply emulating in electronic form what humans would do manually, this class of software applications needs to take advantage of the supreme malleability of software as a raw material—its ability to adapt to new market conditions without being rebuilt from scratch.

Most organizational information systems disappoint managers because the structures are inflexible artifacts meant to model organizations that are by nature dynamic. Businesses cannot predict the future, stabilize their organizational structures and product sets, and then define their software based on that forecast. Rather, they can adopt flexible ways of operating that allow them to react quickly when markets shift by introducing new products, services, and features, as well as tailoring them to the most attractive customer segments. This reach can be truly global because software technology is practically unbounded by distance.

For many firms, a primary task is to develop systems and software that will enable the customer to take on design and testing responsibilities heretofore reserved to the company. Netscape puts some of the responsibility for product beta testing in the hands of its customer base. Developing significant revisions to its products every three months, Netscape offers a new product to the public for a beta testing period and can receive more feedback than it would by testing in-house. For the Netscape Navigator version 3.0 beta testing, customers were downloading the software at the rate of 50,000 copies per hour. Netscape offers incentives for customers to test new security features and attempt to break them.

During Internet system design, try to identify how the systems can be leveraged to effect complete, automated fulfillment. Using technology systems to process and fulfill requests offers significant value to the customer. A new customer value may be guaranteed fulfillment and timeliness. Automated systems can help achieve these potential priorities.

Commercial Internet applications are not as mature as other applications because of the need to deliver information quickly to multiple users. The Internet network itself is built on a reliable protocol in use since the late 1960s, but commercial applications for the Internet are a relatively recent phenomenon, and vendors are constantly trying to cut development.

Finding the right product solution is important, but perhaps the more important consideration is determining the standards you want to follow and ensuring that the products you purchase follow them.

The design and implementation time frame should not be longer than three months; anything greater than this has a much greater chance of failure, according to statistics. Emerging Internet technology capabilities and business drivers will force you to change your technology assumptions and strategies.

Develop a phased technical architecture approach appropriate to your business based on the strategy outlined in Chapter 5. A phasing approach has several benefits including: allowing the launch of Internet solutions earlier than if you wait until the final strategy can be implemented; providing you with customers in a short time frame; and building operational and architectural expertise to refine later phases of development. Last, a phasing approach allows the corporate Internet site to attract and build a customer base.

The Internet introduces several maintenance issues into the business equation. Internet computing includes maintaining the links between your site and outside resources. As sites evolve, they often contain hyperlinks to other resources within the site or in other sites. These links break when the resources they are directed to are relocated or removed. Serveral third-party tools provide this type of site management. Ensure that the appropriate management tools are in place at your site to limit this common problem.

The emergence of Sun Microsystems' Java programming language changed the staffing requirements of Internet service industries. Java is used to develop applications for customers to communicate directly with your business. The need for skilled C++ language programmers, designers, analysts, and architects will grow. Java is discussed in greater detail below. Microsoft's ActiveX environment is different from Java in that programmers do not need to learn a new language. With the introduction of ActiveX, Microsoft will allow current Microsoft-savvy developers to leverage existing knowledge of their different environments, and still maintain many of the advantages of Java.

Table 7.17 outlines success factors to consider in the Internet era.

Table 7.7 *Critical Success Factors*

Category	Traditional Model	Internet Model
System Focus	Internal systems focus	External systems focus
IS Development Model	Client-centric development	Network-centric development
IS Development Focus	IS-developed	IS- and customer-developed
IS Product Focus	Nonintelligent systems with limited interactivity	Expert systems with high interactivity
IS Design Focus	Business-designed, customer-generic formats	Customer- and business-designed customer-specific formats

(continued)

Table 7.7 *(continued)*

Category	Traditional Model	Internet Model
Sourcing Strategy	Outsourcing focus	Insourcing and partnering

TAKING ADVANTAGE OF THE INTERNET COMPUTING REVOLUTION

The issues of the client/server revolution included:

- new architecture models

- legacy system integration issues

- new, nonexistent, or evolving standards

- immature (version 1.0 or earlier) programming languages, standards, and development environments

- limited marketplace programming skills and design expertise

- new, immature IT vendors

- new security issues

The business and technology challenges of Internet computing, like the client/server revolution, are significant. Nevertheless, the Internet technology offers many opportunities.

JAVA IMPLICATIONS

The pace of Internet commercialization was greatly accelerated by the introduction of Java, an object-oriented, platform-independent computing language. On May 23, 1995, California-based Sun Microsystems, Inc., formally introduced Java. It might have been dismissed as just another computer language but for two things: Sun's assertion that the language was tailor-made for the Internet with the promise of platform-independent interactive computing; and Netscape Communication Corp.'s corresponding announcement that its popular browser would support Java.

Until recently, Hypertext Markup Language (HTML) was the de facto standard for developing information delivered through the World Wide Web. Although HTML is useful, it is far from a full-scale programming language that can provide architecturally sound integration with enterprise business systems. Moreover, HTML is only one of many technologies required to develop a public, community, or private Internet presence. HTML is the visible part of the iceberg. The more invisible IT systems components are much more complex.

Currently, most Web pages that integrate with back-end databases rely on Common Gateway Interface (CGI) programs, which are executed on Internet servers. CGI, however, is a limited architecture solution presenting several problems for experienced technical architects familiar with high-transaction volume, high performance, and mission-critical system elements. CGI's specific shortcomings are:

- It increases network traffic, as every client request is transmitted to the server and every response transmitted to the client. Although it is necessary to communicate with the server from time to time, most computations and screen updates could be performed on the client computer or through more limited server interactions.

- Because all the processing is handled by the Web server, its load is unnecessarily high.

- The output of any process must be presented in HTML format; thus, the look of finished products is limited.

Java was introduced to address these problems. It derives from a language called C++. With Java, developers create pieces of code called applets. These can be transported over the Internet and run on client computers, performing various kinds of client functionality.

Applets can be deployed to reside on Internet servers, and then transparently downloaded to customer workstations when browsers request related functions. For instance, when a Web page is requested by a client workstation, the applet is also sent along, transparently, to the user. When it arrives at the client machine it is interpreted and run by the Java interpreter, which is bundled with the Internet browser. Java applets perform activities on the client machine, thereby reducing the processing load on the Web server. The Java interpreter scans the code before it executes, to make sure it does not include security leaks.

Sun developed a set of Application Programming Interfaces (APIs) called Java Data Base Connectivity (JDBC) to provide connectivity to a wide range of existing corporate databases from a Java applet. Some software vendors provide programming tools to get directly from Java to databases.

Java has the potential to dramatically increase Internet business by making interactive business applications more intuitive and easy to use. Although initial Java applications represent 3-D animation, it is anticipated that Java applets capable of performing more traditional business applications will be available in the future, including:

- **Information Gathering**—surveys, questionnaires, forms, expert system front ends, registrations, and analysis front ends. An information-gathering applet's main purpose is to utilize client machine's processing capabilities to provide a more interactive and robust interface for information gathering.

- **Information Processing**—number-crunching functions that are transparent to the client workstation but occur there. An information-processing applet's main purpose is to utilize the client workstation's processing power to decrease the traffic between the client and the server, thus decreasing the load on the server.

- **Information Analysis**—statistical, financial, forecasting, mathematical, and scientific tools. An information-analyzing applet's main purpose is to utilize the client workstation's processing power and presentation capabilities to deliver interactive valuable analysis tools to the client. The amount of network traffic is also much lower than traditional HTML/CGI traffic, as the amount of data exchange between client and server systems is minimized.

- **Information Presentation**—tables, simulators, and graphic generation, animation, and customization tools. An information-presenting applet's main purpose is to use the client machine's processing power to generate better-looking and more functional data presentations.

Java still has design limitations; nonetheless, it is likely be an integral element of your Internet computing strategy. Java has the potential to be a crucial component of the distributed server–centric architecture.

Businesses should monitor other Java-based applications to stay on top of potential function capabilities and ideas for your business. This can be done by linking to business sites that link to Java applications.

THE INTERNET AND LEGACY SYSTEMS: LEVERAGING YOUR EXISTING INVESTMENTS

The critical information assets of businesses are often maintained on what are commonly referred to as legacy systems. Most current Internet-based implementations are Internet server–centric, meaning they exist on a new server. The business challenge is to make information maintained in existing corporate databases and applications available on the Internet. Many legacy system–Internet integration strategies rely on the duplication of legacy data in servers outside the firewall. This is generally performed manually or through file transfers. Several problems occur with this type of implementation; businesses need more robust and secure solutions.

To be fully accepted and integrated by businesses, Internet technologies should address issues of legacy system connectivity and integration: First, duplication of the data on Internet servers is not a long-term solution. Internet applications should be able to access back-end legacy systems directly, seamlessly, and securely. Second, access should be secure and integrated with the existing corporate security structure. Third, access control mechanism should be in place and allow several layers of access to system.

Sun's JDBC APIs, discussed above, are among the first major developments in this field. JDBC provides the Java developer with a set of functions for database connectivity, data query, and data retrieval. Several companies are working closely with Sun on the APIs to ensure that they provide the elements required for an architecturally robust and integrated solution.

NOTES

1. Moore, Geoffrey A., Inside the Tornado, (New York: Harper Collins, 1995).

2. Hayashi, Alden M., *Reality Behind the Hype,* Application Development Trends, (February 1996):78–85

CHAPTER 8

JOBS, PEOPLE, AND MANAGERS: HOW THE INTERNET/INTRANET SHOULD TRANSFORM YOUR ORGANIZATION

Many organizations have succeeded in incorporating the Internet into their overall business plans. Several themes are common to these companies. They maximized the Internet's capabilities to offer innovative products valued by customers. They built customer bases and won allegiances early, generated new revenue streams, and tested new products and services.

Here is the biggest executive challenge: how to transform your business in order to thrive with the Internet. The organizational steps to take to best achieve your vision follows.

WHY ORGANIZATIONS HAVE TO CHANGE

First, review why you need to rethink your organizational assumptions. Most executives only subconsciously recognize the Internet's impact on their organizations, but the more you are conscious of it, the better off you and your organization will be.

In the future, organizations will have to cope with heretofore unknown levels of change and uncertainty. If you are conscious of the Internet's impact on your organization, defining current and future roles will be easier. For example, Twentieth Century Mutual Funds realized through focus groups that it needed a new organizational role, a navigation specialist to be responsible for guiding customers through its electronic systems.

Many companies are considering establishing a new position in the corporate hierarchy: a chief knowledge officer (CKO) with responsibility for the management of knowledge capital. The role of a CKO becomes even more critical when one considers that the Internet pushes organizations to focus on their differentiators—often, information.

In general, communication shapes the relationship between customers and business organizations. In particular, the Internet shapes the way businesses communicate with customers, partners, and interlinkers because it empowers them with information.

All of these parties are important, but it is the customer who is likely to provide the most pertinent information. Customers can give valuable insight into how your organization should be structured to grow and evolve.

The successful Internet-based company is customer-oriented rather than internally oriented. The most successful companies genuinely understand the difference. This is at the heart of your need to consider organizational change.

On a theoretical level, you must consider the borderless quality of the Internet environment and the fundamental paradigm shift in the concept of the modern organization. It is moving from a business world, where the individual company is at the center of the universe, to a more fluid, interlinked environment, where each company is but one point in an extended network of equals.[1] The Internet's impact on the organization and its processes will be dramatic.

NINE ITEMS FOR THE TRANSFORMATION AGENDA

FOSTER EARLY LEARNING, EXPERIMENTATION, AND CREATIVITY

Does your current organizational structure foster creative thinkers, idea merchants, and, ultimately, a learning organization that experiments with new ideas? Successful Internet companies do. They must. This is a key function of their organization. Fresh ideas and approaches to presenting your competencies and customer solutions are vital to business success.

The most difficult challenge of your Internet strategy will likely arise when you attempt to strike a balance between fostering creative thinkers and managing the ideas into a successful execution. An environment of total creativity with no follow-through is just as disastrous as one with total follow-through but no creativity.

It is a given that the coming decades will be a time of uncertainty. The companies that ultimately succeed will do so by recognizing that they cannot predict the future and therefore must be creative, experiment, and learn. They know that they do not, and cannot, know everything. Hence, they will pursue multiple technological options and organizational approaches.

One electronic information database business prides itself on the mistakes it makes. It believes that if it is does not encounter the occasional failure, it is not being sufficiently experimental.

Creativity must be encouraged. This is an enormous challenge, given the legacy of business's suspicion, if not downright hostility, toward creativity. Consider the famous study on creativity conducted several years ago by George Land. Land examined a group of five-year-olds for NASA and rated 97 percent of the youngsters as highly creative. Several years later, the same children were reevaluated; only 30 percent rated highly creative. When Land revisited the subjects as adults, he found that the number had dropped to 2 percent.

Where did the creativity go? It didn't just leak away—it was buried by rules and regulations; by multiple choice tests and rigid lesson plans; by boring jobs; workplace politics; and the tacit pressure to conform.

Creativity within an organization can help in the development of new business models. Polaroid, the Massachusetts-based optics and advanced technology company, has on staff a creatologist. To Polaroid, a creatologist is a professional dedicated to the art and science of rekindling the inventive spirit, imagination, and intrinsic motivation of people engaged in creating the future.

Suzanne Merritt, the senior creatologist at Polaroid, notes, "Stifled creativity is particularly evident in the corporate world, where executives are terrified of getting off the track to success. They've been trained to follow the rules rather than make them up." Merritt counters the herd mentality by organizing creativity sessions for executives. "Right now, I'm looking for science fiction writers to participate and act as facilitators," she adds. "They have incredible imaginations and combine fantasy with true scientific genius."[2]

If the first rule of building Internet business strategy is to embrace the Internet strategically, organizationally, this must be rewarded by learning, experimentation, and creativity.

Microsoft made this the theme of its Internet strategy. At the December 1995 Internet Strategy Workshop, chairman Bill Gates made the company motto "Embrace and extend." Microsoft intends to adopt whatever ideas are hot in the software marketplace and fold them into branded products, if necessary buying up the talent or company that created the idea in the first place. But Microsoft realizes that it cannot simply embrace and extend other peoples ideas. It needs in-house creativity, where it can get first crack at new ideas. Microsoft maintains a team focused on creative solutions.

Many of the companies discussed in previous chapters foster environments in creativity, learning, and experimentation. GE Plastics was able to be creative and take risks within the structure of one of the largest corporations in the world. DealerNet was one of the first companies to experiment with Internet banner advertising. It began experimenting with Internet marketing in August 1994; today the company consistently achieves 8 percent click-through rates. Lombard Brokerage Inc. is a learning-oriented organization. Everything is a process, not a project. "Everything we do is neverending," says its president, Eric Roach. "The management then must foster this type of a learning process."

ORIENT YOUR BUSINESS EXTERNALLY

Being externally oriented is to center your organization around serving and responding to the customer. In other words, your business organization is structured to serve customers' needs and desires, rather than internal interests.

In most cases, serving customers' interests results in the adoption of a customer-centric organizational model. For example, each of DealerNet's sales teams centers around an account manager, who serves as the single point of contact for each client.

It is important to note that DealerNet's account managers serve two sets of customers. As aggregators, or infomediaries, they interact with thousands of end customers each day as well as the auto dealers who pay to advertise. The company found that the most effective arrangement is a cross-functional team supporting an account manager. Peter Wilson, cofounder of DealerNet, notes, "The biggest thing I learned was there are a wide spectrum of customers out there with the Internet. Recognizing and responding to this must drive your business organization and influence all your organization's decisions."

Wilson's insight helped shape the company. In its first few months of operation, DealerNet was basically a regional firm, working with a handful of auto dealers based in the Northwest. It soon decided that it needed to go national and find dealers across the country, because that's where end customers are.

Orienting your business externally means getting close to customers, but that is often not a part of standard organizational practice. While many businesses now understand the concept of customer closeness, they are not yet equipped to implement it. Consider the following questions: What processes are in place to identify customers new expectations? How will data gleaned from customers be used to improve products and services?

A survey done by the *Harvard Business Review* World Leadership Conference indicates that only about one-third of respondents "always" or "often" involve their suppliers and customers in product planning and design. Another 27 percent admit to "never" involving customers, and 17 percent report that they don't involve suppliers.

The findings are especially troubling because in the very same survey executives tagged quality and customer service as businesses' top success factors. But how can they expect to achieve high levels of quality and customer service if they do not also have high customer and supplier involvement?[3]

What are the organizational implications of orienting your business externally? You need to become more conscious of the international market. Even if you are not a global company, consider the value of including a person with an international perspective on the Internet project team. Remember that, by default, a public presence on the Internet provides your business with an immediate market in over 100 countries.

DealerNet was surprised by the makeup of its end consumers. Roughly one-third were from outside the United States. Dealers in the United States found themselves shipping equipment as far away as Japan and Iceland because of information customers found on the DealerNet site. As noted earlier, Amazon.com had customers in 26 countries in its first month of business, and Sausage Software was selling in more than a dozen countries immediately upon offering products.

Figure 8.1 illustrates the understanding your team should have towards the customer.

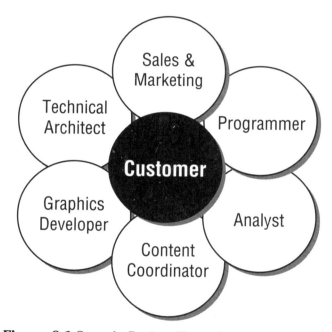

Figure 8.1 *Sample Project Team Organizational Chart*

MANAGE BY VISION

Business leaders must step forward to understand, educate, and prepare their company for the new business, technology, and marketing models enabled by the Internet. To do this, they must have an Internet business vision. Warren Bennis, a noted scholar on the characteristics of leadership, suggests that a leader can be defined as having two key characteristics: (1) knowing where you want to go; and (2) articulating and communicating this vision to your employees. The first part is about the vision itself. The second part is about managing that vision.

You, as an Internet strategist and leader, must empower your employees and provide them with your Internet vision. You are there to define the vision, nurture it, and help it evolve. You must help employees understand that vision.

It is not essential that every detail be clear at the outset, but what is absolutely necessary is an understanding of your role. You are not there to micromanage project activities. The Internet is changing such that you must focus on the bigger picture—the forest, so to speak. Above all, you must foster creativity, learning, and experimentation in employees.

The organization of the future will be staffed by knowledge specialists, which means that it will be managed in a new way. Leading the organization requires you to act as an orchestra conductor. You coordinate the performers (i.e., knowledge specialists). While they have different roles and functions, they share a common goal or vision. This will be the critical success factor for your organization.

Look at Microsoft's management style. "We don't practice a hands-off management style," says Nathan Myhrvold, group vice president for applications and content. "We want to know what's going on. On the other hand, you don't want to be in people's shorts all the time, either. It works both ways. People here know that if you have a neat idea, you don't have to fight through layers of middle managers who probably know nothing about research; you only have to convince Bill [Gates] and me. Here the product vision is driven from the very top of the company."[4] Microsoft found a balance between micromanagement and empowerment. That is your goal.

ELIMINATE THE MANAGEMENT GAP

The successful organization of the future will be led by front-line executives, those who best anticipate the customer's changing priorities and expectations. They will have their fingers on the pulse of the customer. Although this has always been important, it is essential with the Internet, because more competitors can respond more quickly to customer demands with innovative solutions.

But while the Internet drives the momentum for organizational shifts, many companies are slow to move. Hierarchy still rules many industrial organizations, and the split between the upper-level manager and the work force is as large as ever. Why? Companies are reluctant to embrace the mandate of technology—more specifically,the Internet—and bridge the chasms that separate levels of management.

Front-line business, sales, marketing, and technology managers together must be involved in the company's Internet business strategy because the need is greater than ever to eliminate the disparity between senior business managers' perceptions of the Internet and its actual capabilities.

The management gap can be characterized as the difference in perceptions of those who monitor and implement the latest technologies, sales techniques, and business trends, and the senior business management and leadership, who take a macro approach to the organization. As technologies continue to have an increasing impact on business models, the more important it is to recognize and eliminate this gap.

Gerhard Schulmeyer, who runs a large division of Siemens Nixdorf International (SNI), launched a planning initiative. The idea was radical and innovative: provide young people, those most enthusiastic about new technologies and closest to the company's next generation of customers, with a genuine voice in shaping corporate strategy. Beginning with four days of debate in a British castle and continuing through field trips to Silicon Valley and meetings with industry gurus, the FutureScape Team has been shaking things up. "Our role is to challenge the board," says Stacy Welsh, who at 29 is one of the youngest members. "The management board is saying, 'We don't understand the buying patterns of 16-year-olds, the kids who are watching MTV. We're nowhere near that generation.' They look to us for perspective."

The future is too important to be left to top executives unless the management gap is bridged. "The young generation has a different model of how it thinks about things," says SNI's Richard Roy. "FutureScape gives the board views it would not otherwise get. It also gives people in the organization a greater chance to influence the board." Mark Maletz, the architect of SNI's change efforts, says approvingly, "There is a new sense of dialogue in the company. People are more engaged with the direction and future of SNI." "FutureScape members are 'sparring partners for the board,' says Roy. "They should challenge us to look beyond today's boundaries and shape our thinking about the market, technology, social change."[5]

SHAPE YOUR BUSINESS WITH PARTNERSHIPS

A key attribute of the successful organization is its recognition of the value of identifying and maximizing interlinked global partnerships. As discussed in Chapter 2, these are opportunity-defined and not necessarily formal, equity-based relationships. They are fluid and opportunistic, and can be both internal and external to your industry.

Shape your organization around business partnerships that enhance and promote your Internet solutions. You can no longer afford to be provincial or to go it alone. You often cannot provide a complete solution or as innovative concept in a short time.

"Leaders must become cosmopolitans who are comfortable operating across boundaries and who can forge links between organizations. Leaders must take their ability to craft visions, inspire action, and empower others and use it to encourage people from diverse functions and disciplines. Cosmopolitans are leaders with open minds and outreach to partners."[6] This may require business partners with disparate global experiences. These alliances will produce, in effect, virtual organizations capable of forging solutions with alluring functionality or that have not yet been imagined by customers.

It is easy to say that you are going to shape your business around true partnerships but another to actually carry out the plan. Tom Peters, in his analysis of strategic alliances, notes, "We have many miles to go in translating slogans like 'strategic alliances' and 'borderless company' into competitive reality."

"Although many organizations *think* that they have partnerships, when it comes to the specific managerial practices that make partnership real, the [*Harvard Business Review*'s World Leadership Conference] survey suggests a very different story. Consider the subject of sharing information, which is arguably the clearest indicator of a company's intent to open the gates—both within and without the organization. Until information becomes widely available, all other aspects of partnership remain stuck at the stage of lip service or less."[7]

Ask the following questions to test how you have shaped your business and are planning to shape your business around business partners:

- Have you pursued any interlinking recently?

- If so, how will you ensure that the partnership will be effective for both you and your partner?

- How much do you trust your partners, and how will you integrate them into your information systems?

- What is your business objective for developing strategic partnerships?

Look everywhere for potential partners—even among your current competitors. Coopetition, a hybrid relationship encompassing aspects of cooperation and competition, has been a feature of the business landscape for a long time and will become even more prevalent in the future. You need to prepare your organization for its impact. As companies attempt to identify strategically what specific businesses they are in, they will end up competing with their partners in some situations. Consider the Netscape–Sun Microsystems relationship. In several ways they compete (both sell and market browser software) as well as cooperate (on devising and marketing compatible Internet server solutions). In fact, Netscape almost singlehandedly made Sun's Java a dominant force in the Internet industry by supporting it with its browser. This type of coopetition is widespread throughout the IT industry.

Businesses suited to flourish in this environment are optimally prepared for the new challenges. The Japanese refer to an ideal operating environment as *wa*, or harmony. Kenichi Ohmae says, "We largely miss the organizing logic of Japanese management: to protect companies worldwide; to provide government direction, but just enough to free private companies to develop; to compete fiercely but also to cooperate closely. The ultimate goal of all these activities is to create harmony," *Wa* in the business world might relate to the concept of coopetition. Your learning organization must embrace the notion of coopetition to flourish.

BUILD INTEGRATED TEAMS

Your Internet team structure must become more integrated with your customer. In successful companies, technology people become more involved with business and marketing people, business people may become more involved with technology, and so on. In fact, the difference between business and technology becomes indistinguishable. In the past, technology could be isolated. Companies had data processing groups, that performed computer functions necessary to support business functions. IT departments performed nonstrategic technology functions that could be clearly defined and were often outsourced. Now technology is more integrated with all aspects of business, so the Internet team must be integrated.

How much integration is enough? A learning organization requires that the individuals and teams comprising it be more integrated than ever before. Almost all companies highlighted here exhibit this characteristic. Because each element of the Internet business strategy is interdependent, the groups within your organization should be integrated in a close team to exploit synergies.

The integrated team model features people sharing a common goal, possessing complementary skills and knowledge, and holding themselves mutually accountable for results. In a sense, this is a virtual team, one that comes together whenever needed and as long as needed—to conduct a process, solve a problem, or respond to an opportunity—without necessarily being together physically or even belonging to the same organization.

Virtual teams transcend the boundaries that traditionally separate members of different departments and enterprises. As organizations and teams become more integrated around functions, they become knowledge specialists—and that is your goal. As Peter Drucker notes in *The Coming of the New Organization*, "to remain competitive— maybe even to survive—businesses will have to convert themselves into organizations of knowledgeable specialists. . . . The business 20 years hence is more likely to resemble a hospital or a symphony than a typical manufacturing company. . . . These teams must be driven to work together, as in a symphony or surgical ward."[8]

This is a departure from traditional business, technology, and marketing perspectives; finding the personnel with the necessary knowledge and skills may be difficult and expensive. Look for people with these characteristics:

- able and experienced in thinking outside the box

- technologically inclined (appreciative of new technologies)

- able to think creatively

- willing to take risks (create new models)

- able to cope with change

- comfortable working in an unstructured environment

Seek individuals who make the Internet part of their lives. As Executive VP of Marketing for Twentieth Century Mutual Funds, Gordon Snyder notes, "The technology, business, and marketing models are rapidly changing. You must make them a part of your daily life to understand their implications." Unless dedicated and passionate team members are involved, companies will not keep up with new capabilities and will be unable to develop innovative products. Individuals that make the Internet a part of their daily business and personal practices may be best at determining how to integrate these technologies into the business.

The following groups should be a part of the Internet team.

- senior business decision-making team

- empowered representatives from constituent groups

- business partners

- information technology management

- related business projects (i.e., reengineering)

- international offices

- marketing groups

- business support groups

- operations

- public relations

- multimedia groups

- legal counsel

- sales representatives

- customer liaisons

In the context of your current organization, your strategy team might look like Figure 8.2.

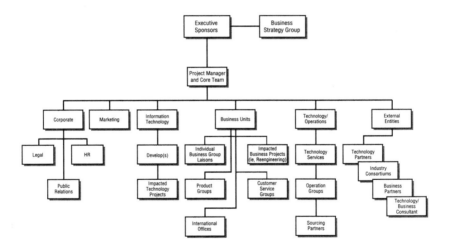

Figure 8.2 *Sample Internet Representatives*

INCORPORATE VIRTUAL COMPANY CONCEPTS

The Internet's integration into business will influence the business organization model of the future by fostering the virtual company, which is vastly different from current models. Even if you ultimately do not adopt the paradigm, you must be familiar with aspects of it. Even the widespread downsizing of the 1990s may not prepare companies for the organizational upheaval of the next five years.

To fully realize the Internet, you must focus exclusively on relevant core competencies and identify optimal business partners and strategic alliances. These will form the virtual corporation. The methods and processes a virtual organization uses to reach its goals can be quite different than those of traditional organizations.

The ideal virtual organization is highly adaptable and agile in its organizational structure. A virtual organization is an opportunity-derived entity, integrating its core competencies from a distributed set of real organizations.

Finding people on demand is essential. DealerNet's Peter Wilson says that his company was able to grow quickly because of resources available in the Seattle area that comprised his virtual team. For a long period DealerNet had no more than seven full-time employees. It leveraged needed skills from several other groups. Seattle and its environs had an early core of Internet-based companies, that provided technical, graphical, marketing, and other skills.

The benefits of virtualization can be high. Few organizations, however, have embraced all of its concepts and therefore have rarely realized its benefits. In general, by entering into cooperative, perhaps interlinking, relationships, each company can focus its efforts on those activities which its resources best fit. More specifically, the authors of *Agile Competitors and Virtual Organizations*, suggest that "alliances among companies with complementary resources and expertise reduce sunk costs and risks at the same time that they reduce development time. Alliances expand the pool of available human and physical resources. They increase the profitability of success and create interdependence on which to build future collaborations and continuing participation in the creation of multiple generations of successful product families."

Goldman et al. define a virtual organization structure as "an opportunistic alliance of core competencies distributed among a number of distinct operating entities within a single large company or among a group of independent companies." The underlying idea is "almost trivially obvious and far from new," they note: "Organize a group of people with relevant abilities into a team focused on a well-defined problem. Motivate these people, give them access to appropriate resources, reward them on the basis of the value of the solution they create, and then stand back."[9]

Table 8.1 presents a path that an organization may take toward the virtual organization.

Table 8.1 Four-Stage Organizational Development

Stage 1	Stage 2	Stage 3	Stage 4
Downsizing	Rightsizing	Forming Strategic Organizational Alliances	Linking of Global Business Core Competencies (Virtual Organization)

Downsizing. The late 1980s and early 1990s were characterized by significant, often drastic downsizing, much of which resulted from reengineering efforts attempting to achieve immediate financial benefit. In this phase, companies became more streamlined.

Rightsizing. After the era of dramatic downsizing, companies' efforts shifted to the concept of core competencies and rightsizing, sometimes called smartsizing. The intent was to focus on core competencies and take a responsible approach at organizational staffing needs.

Forming Strategic Organizational Alliances. Organizational alliances are becoming more popular as businesses from a variety of industries form strategic partnerships. The focus is shifting from identifying rightsizing to reviewing business alliances. For example, Microsoft and NBC, Westinghouse and ABC, and Intuit and Bank of America have entered strategic alliances. This phase is setting the stage for the interlinking of core competencies among more global and diverse business partners, resulting in a more global virtual corporation.

Linking of Business Core Competencies. In this fourth stage, businesses become fundamentally realigned with their most effective global business partners. The final stage is the full realization of the virtual organization. Theoretically, the businesses that passed through the prior stages have the proper internal staffing of knowledge specialists, have defined and integrated with the right partners, have identified their core competencies, and thrive in this new business model.

DESIGN FOR SPEED AND CHANGE

Many of the companies explored so far lead us to the conclusion that being able to react quickly to customer changes, driven by rapid innovation cycles, and receptive to new perspectives are predicates for success. Because of this, your business must be designed for speed and change in the face of changing customer priorities and expectations. Customer expectations of the functionality provided through the Internet are likely to increase rapidly, given the business and technology drivers.

Consider Parr Ford Auto Group, which was the first Ford dealer that sold cars and parts through DealerNet, and perhaps the first auto sales company to sell over the Internet. Indeed, Parr had its Web site up and running before Ford Motor Co.'s site was even operational.

Parr is committed to customer service. That is why a customer in New York may choose to purchase Ford parts from Parr, located in Bremerton, Washington, over the Internet rather than turn to a local dealer. Parr's efficient fulfillment process allows it to better meet the needs of some of its customers. The company's marketing manager constantly communicates with clients via e-mail. So much of a sales transaction's preliminary work is conducted over the Internet that a car buyer usually spends only 30 minutes in the actual showroom, as opposed to the two or three hours that a traditional transaction can take.

This sort of orientation has forced Parr Ford to challenge its organizational structure. Some car dealers offer customers the ability to search for used and new cars in stock over the Internet. Parr Ford's owner, Rod Parr, and marketing director, Kevin Root, rethought this process and challenged the industry's current assumptions. Now Parr offers what has turned out to be a popular and successful service in which the customer defines what type of used car she wants. If Parr Ford has a match in stock, the company informs the customer via the DealerNet system. If there is no match in stock, Parr's used car buyers out on the road are alerted to the customer's request. There is no guesswork involved; the salespeople know exactly what the customer wants. Parr's salespeople like this because, first, they understand what the customer wants. Second, they can process the request much faster. Finally, they obtain more customers because of the nonconfrontational buying experience. Designing for speed and change means changing some of the traditional functions of the salespeople.

The same principles apply for larger companies. The Forrester Group, an IT industry analyst, notes that "Internet computing will completely recast the dynamics of the software industry and redefine application development in the Global 2000 [group of companies]. This emerging model will foster a new type of application—'transactive content'—that will tilt the playing field in favor of fast, innovative software creators and agile CIOs." This should not be a surprise, since many of the companies here are fast and innovative software creators.

How do you move dramatically faster? Steven Papermaster, CEO of BSG Consulting, says that the only way to move faster is to create a culture in which urgency is at the core of everything the company does. "Culture and values are at the root of our ability to move fast."

BSG holds meetings every three months, but they aren't quarterly meetings, Papermaster insists—they are annual meetings that occur every quarter. "The pace of our business is very fast," he explains. "For us, a year's worth of change occurs every quarter."[10]

BEGIN TO CHANGE YOUR EMPLOYEES' BEHAVIOR

All the issues discussed in this chapter boil down to the fact that you need to change your organization. At the heart of this task, is the need to change your employees' behavior. There is a saying that "technology is easy, people are hard," which highlights the significance of the problem. Not everyone wants to be empowered. Not everyone wants to change. Not everyone understands the impact.

With a widely deployed and populated Intranet, more information is available to an organization's employees. Many companies are not prepared for this change. Current organizational philosophies may not foster information sharing, and change will be halted at the Intranet stage.

Successful companies will increasingly recognize and reward the idea merchants of their business. These are the employees who can change their behavior. Optimizing processes will be seen as important, as always, but creating new ideas will be essential. Business decisions will be focused on by the front-line executives, those that best anticipate the customer's changing priorities and expectations. Business leaders must step forward to understand, educate, and prepare their company for the new models enabled by the Internet.

Table 8.2 highlights characteristics to consider as organizations mature into the new business models.

Table 8.2 *Organizational Characteristic*

Organizational Characteristics	Old Model	New Model
Structure	Hierarchical	Integrated/team-based
Creativity	Largely undervalued	Must be nurtured
Orientation	Internal	External
Management Gap	Large	Small
Learning, experimenting, and creativeness	Important	Essential
Group relationships	Vertically aligned teams	Integrated teams centered around the customer
Virtual corporation acceptance	Stage 1–2	Stage 3–4
Primary business organization design goal	Dominance	Driven by speed and ability to change quickly
Key success factors	Streamlined and matured internal structure, tight, well-organized internal procedures	Changing company behavior; changing reward structures, externally focused

NOTES

1. Ohmae, Kenichi, ed. *The Evolving Global Economy* (Boston: Harvard Business School Press, 1995).

2. Kane, Kate A., "Job Titles We'd Love to Have," *Fast Company* (April–May 1996):32.

3. Peters, Tom, "The Boundaries of Business Partners—The Rhetoric and Reality," In *The Evolving Global Economy*, ed. Kenichi Ohmae (Boston: Harvard Business School Press, 1995).

4. Downey, Roger, "The Prophet Margin," *Eastsideweek* (July 31, 1996):12.

5. Kane, Kate A., "Strategy is for the Young," *Fast Company* (April–May 1996):26.

6. Hesselbein, Francis, Marshall Goldsmith, and Richard Beckhard, *The Leader of the Future* (San Francisco: Jossey-Bass, 1996) 90–91.

7. Hampden-Turner, Charles, *The Boundaries of Business: Commentaries from the Experts* (Boston: Harvard Business School Press, 1995).

8. Drucker, Peter F., "The Coming of the New Organization," *The Harvard Business Review* (January–February 1988).

9. Goldman,Steven L., Roger N. Nagel, and Kenneth Preiss, *Agile Competitors and Virtual Organizations* (New York: Van Nostrand Reinhold, 1995).

10. Bryce, Robert, "At BSG, There's Only One Speed—Faster," *Fast Company* 1(April–May 1996):32.

CHAPTER 9

LEGAL AND REGULATORY ISSUES: PROTECTING YOUR BUSINESS FOR THE FUTURE

CURRENT LAWS AND REGULATIONS ARE BEING CHALLENGED

The Internet has many legal ramifications—legal, regulatory, governmental, and societal—because it radically expands communications and interaction capabilities and changes the concept of borders in the context of information. For example, gambling laws were not drafted with the borderless, global Internet in mind. Rather, they are specific to each state. But the Internet challenges these laws by making it possible to gamble at online casinos anywhere in the world. In fact, law enforcement officials are unclear how gambling laws apply to offshore Internet-based casinos offering services in different states.

In 1995 the U.S. Information Agency put its Voice of America news dispatches on the Internet, but it soon moved many of them from its U.S. site to "secret" foreign sites. This move was made in compliance with a 1948 law prohibiting dissemination of government-controlled news broadcasts and propaganda inside the United States. However, U.S.-based citizens can get to the Voice of America foreign Internet site without any obstacles. The only difference they will see now when they arrive is a warning that the site is foreign. The regulations that originally directed the philosophy behind the Voice of America were designed for an earlier age of telecommunications and cannot easily accommodate the new paradigm.

In the past, a government could erect information barriers by censoring print media and jamming radio and television broadcasts. Today technology bests such efforts. In 1993 a Canadian judge ordered a news blackout of the sensational details of the Karla Homolka murder case. However, U.S. media organizations were free to report on the case, and Canadians eventually got the news through the Internet and in American newspapers brought across the border.

The tension between the Internet and traditional forms of control is highlighted in the Communications Decency Act. Concerned about the availability and dissemination of pornography on the Internet, the U.S. Congress passed the measure, which was signed into law by President Clinton on February 8, 1996. Under the Act, a person who intentionally transmits indecent materials or makes them available to minors online may face criminal fines of up to $25,000 and up to two years in prison.

One of the sponsors, Senator Daniel Coats (R-Indiana), said the measure was necessary because "our technology races beyond our ability to stop and reflect." He added, "We are left with a very dangerous gap, a period of time when society is unprepared to deal with the results of such rapid change. That is the situation we face with the Internet."

Immediately after the bill was enacted, a coalition of 20 organizations, including the ACLU and an AIDS treatment advocacy group, filed suit in a federal appeals court in Philadelphia, seeking to block the measure. Hearings began before a three-judge panel in March 1996. On June 11 the court unanimously struck down the Act, saying it violates the First Amendment and the due process protections of the Fifth Amendment. (In particular, the court found the term *indecent* is unacceptably vague.) To make its point about technology, the court distributed the text of the ruling on a 3.5-inch floppy disk.

In one of the three separate opinions, Appeals Judge Stewart Dalzell noted, "The Internet has achieved...the most participatory marketplace of mass speech that this country—and indeed the world—has yet seen....Any content-based regulation of the Internet, no matter how benign the purpose, could burn the global village to roast the pig."

It is likely that the U.S. Supreme Court will hear the matter. Both sides agree on one thing—that the Internet poses new and thorny questions. "We're facing the frontier of the law," notes Peter F. Harter, public policy counsel for Netscape Communications Corp. As Henry H. Perritt, Jr., a professor at Villanova University Law School, observes, "We need new institutions that match the characteristics of the Net. We have to modify the rules to fit the new technology."[1]

Well-intentioned efforts have collided with existing rules and regulations. As noted in Chapter 1, the New York–based Spring Street Brewery Co. had to delay its Internet-based initial public offering after the Securities and Exchange Commission intervened. Federal regulators approved company-specific regulations, and Spring Street's IPO was carried out. To date, general guidelines for IPOs on the Internet have not been developed.

On March 1, 1996, Spring Street Brewery launched Wit-Trade (named after the company's popular wheat beer), which allows buyers and sellers to post bids and offers for the company's stock on its Web site, thereby saving investors broker fees. While the SEC gave Spring Street a conditional green light for its Internet trading system, the commission asked the company to use an independent agent to receive checks from buyers of securities and to publish warnings on its Web site about the fact that the shares are not traded on an exchange.

This new method of buying and selling stock is poised to become tremendously popular. "There will be an avalanche of firms," notes David Loring, president of Interactive Holdings, which followed in Spring Street's steps and went public on the Internet. "I have a long list of companies calling and asking how to do it."

In addition to buying and selling stock, many companies are finding the Internet a useful tool for shareholder relations. Colgate-Palmolive's Web site lists the daily highs and lows of the company's stock over the past five years. Bell & Howell took questions via e-mail during its annual meeting in May 1996. According to Anne Crawford, director of investor relations at Colgate-Palmolive, the

Web is a conduit for potential shareholders. She notes, "We are probably getting inquiries about the company that we might not otherwise have gotten, for instance, from investment clubs that saw our site." Inquiries have come from as far away as Hong Kong and Malaysia.[2]

The lesson in these examples is that the Internet does not respect traditional legal and regulatory regimes. You can take steps to lessen your risk. You need to learn about new technologies that can protect your business, carefully identify your Internet business partners, and ensure that you get customer feedback easily. These and other steps are discussed below.

TAKE STEPS TO PROTECT YOUR BUSINESS

How can you protect your business, considering all of these challenges, and still position yourself to exploit the opportunities that the Internet offers? There are no sure-fire ways, but you should consider the following ten steps:

1. Learn, monitor, and incorporate new technologies.
2. Follow, participate in, or initiate industry consortia.
3. Continually update and validate your content.
4. Integrate and coordinate with legal representatives.
5. Select your interlinking partners consciously and carefully.
6. Adopt appropriate disclaimers and international strategy.
7. Ensure that users view current content.
8. Provide customers with an easy feedback loop.
9. Take internal steps to limit your risk.
10. Monitor misuse of your information and functionality on the Internet.

LEARN, MONITOR, AND INCORPORATE NEW TECHNOLOGIES

Educate your legal staff about emerging Internet technologies that can potentially protect your business. Technologies protecting copyrights may be essential to your Internet business strategy. Pertinent technologies to learn, monitor, and potentially incorporate include copyright protection and watermark technologies, (e.g., secured containers), digital and authorized signature technologies, and electronic notaries.

IBM's InfoMarket is a search engine that combines data retrieval with payment and rights management. It accomplishes this with technology called the cryptolope, which IBM invented as an electronic means to guarantee payment and copyrights. A cryptolope is a secured electronic envelope containing copyrighted material, intellectual capital, or other sensitive documents. With this mechanism, only the paying customer can electronically unlock the document. If the paying customer forwards the document, it cannot be opened until the creator is notified, approves, and provides the key to unlock the material.

Efforts are underway to develop electronic watermarks, whereby unique electronic symbols are embedded in each copy of a product, allowing illegal copies to be traced to their source.

A few states, including Washington, have already enacted legislation approving the use of digital signatures in electronic transactions. One measure, known as the Washington Electronic Authentication Act, provides a secure and convenient way for businesses to electronically transfer contracts, letters of credit, payments, and formal documents that in the past required a written signature. The law authorizes businesses and organizations to obtain a special digital code for use as a signature in electronic transactions. The Secretary of State in Olympia licenses private vendors to verify the codes upon receipt of an electronic document. Many other states are in the process of ratifying similar legislation.[3]

A committee of the American Bar Association has been studying the legal requirements for documents transmitted internationally via the Internet and is developing guidelines for electronic commerce and certification of the authenticity and validity of electronic transactions. Cybernotaries, individuals with legal or commercial status, would fill a gap by attesting to the validity of the code used to verify the identity of a document's originator.[4]

Some software companies already build cybernotary authorities into their products. For example, Virtual CA, part of GTE Corp.'s series of online certification services, provides subscribers with a tailored home page for certificate data entry, and issuing, renewal, and revocation services as well. The product is intended for organizations that require a certification authority capability but do not seek to assume the administrative burdens that attend certification ownership.

As the world gets smaller and more integrated because of the Internet, and individual ease of access increases, digital assaults and online harassment become easier to commit. In a recent case, a doctoral student in California was expelled after university officials charged him with sexually harassing his former girlfriend via e-mail. The student denied authorship of the e-mail messages, and as they were not authenticated from the sender there was no way to prove electronically that he actually sent them. In fact, one message with the student's name on it had actually been sent as a joke by the woman's new boyfriend in Salt Lake City. In the future, digital signatures, time stamps, and authentication standards may help address these problems.

FOLLOW, PARTICIPATE IN, OR INITIATE INDUSTRY CONSORTIA

A fundamental question which will shape the Internet for business is: Who will regulate the Internet—state and federal governments or industries themselves? While various proposals for the regulation of cyberspace make their way through Congress, Internet businesses are eager to provide their own solutions to avoid government regulation. It behooves business organizations to either follow, participate in, or initiate action in consortia or industry associations in order to craft beneficial solutions. By participating you protect your company's and your customers' interests, sending a message that responsibility for regulation of the Internet should rest with industry, not the government.

A group composed of Internet technology vendors, online service providers, and content-oriented businesses, developed a standard called Platform for Internet Content Selection (PICS), the result of a collaboration between the World Wide Web Consortium (W3C), a university-sponsored group, and the Information Highway Parental Empowerment Group (IHPEG), an organization formed by Microsoft, Netscape, and Progressive Networks. Essentially, PICS is a filtering utility, to be distributed as freeware, that is programmed with an agreed-upon industry rating system. With these standards, parents using any popular Web browser or major commercial on-line service connected to the Internet have their choice of PICS-compatible rating systems for controlling their children's access to Internet content. Tim Berners-Lee, inventor of the World Wide Web service, predicts that PICS will become the global platform on which most access control systems are built. PICS was developed as a practical alternative to global governmental censorship of the Internet. The participating companies would rather shape their collective future by establishing standards than rely on governmental regulation. It is important to note that PICS is not—and will not become—a rating service. It is a technical platform that empowers individuals, groups, and organizations to develop their own rating systems, distribute labels for Internet content, and create label-reading software and services.

Today, browser companies, online services, access-control companies, and publishers are currently working on PICS-compatible strategies. "With so much new content being added to the Internet daily, it is impractical, and certainly not desirable, for any government to attempt to control or censor that flow," notes Berners-Lee. "The practical, workable solution is to give end users the tools to control what ultimately flows into their homes. This noncensorship approach works not only on a national, but on a global, basis as well. I'm encouraged by the rapid acceptance and deployment of the PICS platform in the United States. If this trend continues at the international level, PICS could become a global platform in the next 12 months [March 1997], and hopefully allay governments' desires to censor this incredible growing medium that is the Internet."[5]

Other associations are being formed to help shape their business's and industry's future operating environment. While the Securities and Exchange Commission has been proactive, much work remains. It is apparent that the hurdles to be conquered are greater than any one entity can achieve alone. It will take the cooperation of many people and organizations to fully develop the parameters within which this new market will operate. The National Internet Securities Association (NISA) was formed with this in mind.

NISA is dedicated to contributing to the progression of the securities industry's Internet segment by educating investors and issuers of securities about the Internet securities marketplace. Its mission is to provide a forum for the exchange of ideas and issues pertaining to this emerging market and to help establish guidelines for these activities on the Internet. Among NISA's founders are forward-looking leaders in the Internet industry, including IPO Net, IPO Trade, and Web IPO, which provide services to companies planning to going public. NISA's goals are:

- To develop a forum whereby individuals and entities can discuss and analyze the key issues facing this new industry.

- To disseminate information about the Internet to the investing public and to companies interested in tapping new capital markets.

- To develop a regulatory structure for the efficient and secure exchange of stocks through the Internet.

- To develop a World Wide Web site for educating investors and issuing companies.

You should also follow developments in federal agencies as they prepare for the future of the information superhighway, known as the National Information Infrastructure (NII). Bruce Lehman, Commissioner of the Patent and Trademark Office and chairman of the NII Working Group on Intellectual Property, says, "We are recommending some limited but important changes to the copyright law." These changes include:

- New penalties for any individual or organization pirating works valued at more than $5,000. This benchmark provides a safe harbor for customer mistakes or inadvertent violations.

- Criminalizing the use, manufacture, or importation of technology designed to circumvent or destroy copyright protections.

A group of IT companies, including Hewlett-Packard, AT&T, Eastman Kodak, and Netscape Communications, are banding together to launch a service for policing Internet commerce. The Council of Better Business Bureaus, concerned about the proliferation of fake and illegal Web sites and swindling schemes, has announced a new online service to monitor the online performance of businesses and help resolve complaints. The service, called BBBOnline, will be operational by early 1997. Once the BBB's service is running, users will be able to go to a participating company's or organization's site and click on a BBBOnline seal to receive reliability reports.

CONTINUALLY UPDATE AND VALIDATE YOUR CONTENT

Beyond the strategic business reasons to continually update your content and functionality for your customer, there are compelling legal reasons as well. A major European airline was fined $14,000 by the U.S. government for keeping an expired fare posted on a public Internet site. The airline had posted an accurate special fare offer but had inadvertently failed to remove it after the sale period expired.

Yet some leading companies see the Internet as a mechanism to *reduce* liabilities. As Rick Pocock of GE Plastics explains, posting the most updated product use information available is not only a customer benefit, it is a legally sound measure. The more information a customer has, the less likely it is the product will be used improperly or cause harm and result in legal action.

INTEGRATE AND COORDINATE WITH LEGAL REPRESENTATIVES

Information posted to the Internet public is available to a global community immediately. Although an Internet presence can be continually updated with new content, including sales and marketing data, the process must be integrated and coordinated with your legal representatives.

You must be careful about the content you provide. Is it strictly informational, or could it be construed as "advice"? Keep in mind that the dispensing of formal advice or opinions must adhere to industry, state, and federal regulations. Most states have stringent laws regulating the dispensing of medical, financial, and legal advice by nonlicensed persons. Giving advice on product labeling could bring an investigation by a number of federal agencies, including the Food and Drug Administration and the Federal Trade Commission.

SELECT YOUR INTERLINKING PARTNERS CONSCIOUSLY AND CAREFULLY

The interlinking partners with whom you do business are a reflection of your business values. When you direct a customer to another site through a link, the customer may think that you endorse the content and functionality of that site. As connections from one site to another can appear transparent to customers, they may not realize that they are actually at a new, independent site. Even if they do, you still are providing the directions and encouraging them to link there. Thus you are responsible not only for your own Web site but also sites with which you maintain hyperlinks.

This is more than a simple issue of reputation. Under federal copyright law, your business could be liable if you link to sites that violate copyrights. In particular, forum operators have been held liable for contributory infringement when unauthorized copyrighted material is posted to them. Concern over this issue mounted in late 1995, when a federal judge in California ruled that Netcom Online Communications Services, operator of a bulletin board service, could be tried for contributory infringement after it failed to remove copyrighted material that had been illegally placed on one of its servers by a dissident of the Church of Scientology. Netcom and the Church of Scientology later resolved their dispute out of court.

ADOPT APPROPRIATE DISCLAIMERS AND INTERNATIONAL STRATEGY

Consider placing appropriate disclaimers in key sections of your Internet presence.The potential legal implications of failing to include disclaimers can be significant. Disclaimers should be in a highly visible location, such as a customer sign-up page, and should be carefully worded. The assistance of your legal department or outside counsel may be required.

As you adopt appropriate disclaimers, you should also consider the legal implications of being a global company. Your reach now extends to other countries with other legal systems, and the potential for friction is there. In a far-reaching example of international Internet censorship, CompuServe blocked access by its subscribers in the United States and around the world to more than 200 sex-oriented computer discussion groups and picture databases; a federal prosecutor in Munich had warned that the material violated German pornography laws. The action underscores the extent to which diverse national, cultural, and political values come into conflict with the borderless technology of the global Internet computer network. As a CompuServe spokesman noted at the time, "We do business in hundreds of countries. It's a huge global market and in order to play in each country we have to play by their rules." In sum, adopt both a domestic and an international legal perspective as part of your Internet business strategy.

ENSURE THAT USERS VIEW CURRENT CONTENT

Internet browsers usually save Internet content on the user's hard drive, a process referred to as *caching*. When a customer attempts to navigate to the site again, the browser checks to see if the content has been saved or cached locally from a prior visit. If it has been saved on the hard drive, it can be retrieved locally. If not, the user must log on to the Internet to find it. Naturally this takes more time than accessing a cached version. Additional performance-enhancing techniques are used by Internet providers so that your site is not hit for the data.

While there are performance advantages to this, it is important to ensure that users have the current content and functionality. This can be done by adding expiration tags and other design techniques to your WWW pages, thereby forcing the user's browser to update the content. If you do not employ updating techniques, users may unknowingly view outdated or superseded material. This may be more than simply embarrassing—it can have financial and legal consequences as well.

PROVIDE CUSTOMERS WITH AN EASY FEEDBACK LOOP

Ensure that customers are able to easily provide feedback, which can illuminate nascent potential issues, concerns, and customer desires. For example, customers may warn you that your content is not updated or that they have seen your copyrighted materials on another site.

Make sure you save and archive these communications. As the legal environment of the Internet is still evolving, many companies are taking no chances. For example, Lombard Brokerage Investors is not sure if the SEC's requirement to maintain copies of correspondence with customers also relates to e-mail. Playing it safe, the company is saving all e-mail messages from customers.

TAKE INTERNAL STEPS TO LIMIT YOUR RISK

A corporate Information Services (IS) compliance, or legal departments can take internal steps to shield its business's liability. They can write Internet usage policies that forbid certain statements or improper uses of the Internet. It can exploit technologies, such as digital signatures, cryptolopes, and encryption, to limit risks. IS groups can also take more aggressive action by shutting off access to nonbusiness portions of the Internet behind the firewall through proxy servers and Web filtering technologies. Firewalls and layered access are discussed in Chapter 4.

Tools and services like Secure Computing Corp.'s BorderWare WebTrack can help you enforce your policies and provide monthly categorized site usage reports, which you can then use to limit employees' access to particular sites. You do not want your employees going to sites that could place your business in an awkward legal position.

MONITOR MISUSE OF YOUR INFORMATION AND FUNCTIONALITY ON THE INTERNET

It is difficult to enforce copyright regulations in cyberspace, given the borderless nature of the Internet. While media companies, authors, and artists are trying to get greater control of their content on the Internet through strengthened copyright protection, representatives of academic, library, and civil liberties groups argue that changes to existing law would hamper the free flow of information.

Until the advent of a worldwide protection regime—if indeed such a program could ever be agreed upon and implemented—you need to develop strategies for monitoring information on the Internet that infringes on your content rights. Some Fortune 500 companies have hired full-time individuals to surf the Internet and identify misuse of the companies' copyrights and services, or inappropriate employee actions. These monitors also identify sites containing inaccurate corporate information.

This process can be facilitated with the use of software agents, which can be programmed to search the Internet for potential misuse of your copyrights. One large domestic securities broker even has dedicated Internet surfers to search for brokers moonlighting after business hours.

Beyond the potential for content and copyright violation, it is possible for other sites to exploit your functionality. Your public presence functionality is available to all interested parties. If a customer is viewing Internet site A, which may appear to present stock quotes, for example, that site may in fact be transparently linking to Site B to get the quotes and pull them to Site A. Monitor your Internet access logs to help identify this type of activity.

HOW ARE GOVERNMENTS RESPONDING?

Governments are at a defining point where they must determine whether they will limit the dissemination of information or be proactive in the Information Age. This is because the global knowledge economy is becoming more apparent and unstoppable. A government's approach to the advances of the global knowledge economy will directly influence that country's economic performance. A restrictive government approach, or even one slow to adapt, may place a country in a disadvantageous position. As Kenichi Ohmae notes in *The Borderless World*: "Governments can, of course, try to deny these facts or keep them from us. At the same time, they recognize that the capacity to generate wealth is no longer based on the richness of what lies on or under the soil, or on their legal ability to tax or on their military stead, but on the hard and dedicated work of well-trained and well-educated people. And such people will, by definition, be knowledgeable about events elsewhere in the interlinked economy."[6]

Some governments play an active role in the global knowledge economy. In his essay, "Singapore Invests in the Nation-Corporation," Rajendra S. Sisodia explains that "Singapore's story demonstrates the capacity of a country with almost no natural resources to create economic advantages with influence far beyond its region. It represents one scenario for what can happen when a government assumes an instrumental position in shaping and managing the economic environment." The phenomenal growth of the city-state's economy, a star among Asia's tiger economies, "underscores the importance of identifying and investing in certain key capabilities. The Singaporean government determined that if it invested enormously in technological and human capabilities, it could create an economy where both individuals and organizations would be more likely to flourish."[7]

The U.S. government has taken some proactive steps. It initiated the National Information Infrastructure (NII) project. This effort addresses technological, legal, and societal issues that must be rethought in the Information Age. The NII is made up of working groups that examine actual and presumed effects on industrial sectors, individuals, and communities.

Some federal government agencies identified methods of capitalizing on the Internet as part of an overall attempt to reinvent government. The Internal Revenue Service provides a variety of materials, including answers to FAQs, on its Web site. The office of the U.S. Trade Representative maintains a site containing information about trade missions, export opportunities, and official proceedings. The National Trade Data Bank provides leads that are collected by U.S. Commerce Department offices all over the world.

Other examples of governments positively leveraging the Internet can be seen on the state level. Florida has placed some of its most important legislative documents on the World Wide Web. Interested parties can browse through and search state statues, texts of bills, and legislative calendars. Information and hyperlinks are updated daily. Senate President Jim Scott notes, "Our plan is to begin with this basic information on the Internet for the citizens and then revise and expand the service over time, depending on the public's preferences and changing technology."

One can envision a situation in which governmental responses to individuals are customized as they are by successful businesses using the Internet. The traditional approach of addressing individuals as numbers could change to a responsive, citizen-centric, holistic approach in the future.

While the United States, Australia, and the Scandinavian countries have made good progress in integrating the Internet in government and business affairs, other countries have been slow to embrace the technology. Excessive Internet access charges are partially to blame. However, interest in the Internet is growing exponentially in countries throughout the world. At a 1995 Internet seminar in Turkey, hundreds of attendees were highly knowledgeable about Internet capabilities even though they had little or no access. Turkey currently has only a single, low-speed Internet connection that is shared by all users in the country.

Traditionally, a government's role was to represent its people's interests, serve their purposes, and protect them from external military and economic threats. Over time and with new technologies, people have become more informed and clever as a consequence of living in a global information era. Some governments have become the major obstacle to truly free and open trade.[8]

TARIFFS

Tariffs may push government's reinvention in the Information Age more than anything else. The government's ability to monitor the flow and accumulation of value and its ability to apply taxes, tariffs, and trade controls is based primarily on the concept that value is derived only from tangible assets.

How, then, does a government control and tax value when it is represented by information arranged in bits? This is even more challenging when these bits have been integrated to form a product or solution from multiple interlinked global partners. Many state and local agencies are levying taxes in complicated ways; taxing the use of online services is different from state to state. Most tax laws do not explicitly cover electronic services. Determining what is taxable and who should pay is therefore a significant challenge. The agencies levying the taxes often use laws that originally governed telecommunications or the sale of tangible assets.

Online purchasing is treated differently in each state. California and South Carolina, for example, both tax merchandise that is delivered by mail but do not if the merchandise is delivered online. Thus, someone who purchased software by downloading it from an

Internet site or receiving it as a file would not be taxed, but if he ordered software on a CD-ROM and it is sent through the mail, he would be. "Of course, companies should be keeping good records and stay abreast of government activities. They may also want to forge a closer relationship with regulators to help them craft equitable rules," says Kent Johnson of KPMG Peat Marwick.

How will governments react? Nathan Newman of the University of California at Berkeley's Center for Community Economic Research believes one of two trends is likely to emerge as electronic commerce explodes and sales tax revenues shrink. "You either keep raising the rate to increase revenue, which just accelerates the process (of more people choosing online commerce), or maybe you realize that this just isn't the tax and you begin to get that revenue from an income tax," he notes. "The Internet is not about decentralization; it's about globalization. Your average sales, purchase, or work-to-work relationship could be anywhere in the world. With these local tax issues, the problem is that local governments try to deal with global commerce, and everybody loses."

DEFENSE

The national defense establishment is beginning to recognize the increasing need to protect U.S. commercial and military information sites from theft and sabotage. Damaged or violated commercial sites have increasing significance to a nation's interest. Senior U.S. military officials have said that the likelihood of enemy attacks against domestic information systems is mounting. They warn that both military and private sectors may not be prepared for the threat of future wars, which could be waged as much with bytes as with bombs. Indeed, Internet was originally conceived as a decentralized computer system that could withstand nuclear attack.

The Pentagon acknowledges that it is developing electronic weapons to attack the information systems of its adversaries. This effort highlights the increasing importance of protecting electronic communications. Assistant Secretary of Defense Emmett Paige, Jr., notes, "We do have offensive capabilities, and we are working on others."

This recognition of the role information systems play in national activities is changing military strategy. "There's the potential for major breakthroughs in the conduct of war based on information technology," says General Ronald R. Fogelman, chief of staff of the U.S. Air Force. "In the future, we'll engage enemy information systems in a variety of ways. Instead of bombing the central telephone switches in Baghdad, we may leave it so we can exploit it."[9]

Some suggest that the military's review of these issues is occurring too slowly. The U.S. military is ignoring the commercial information systems on which it depends, according to Winn Schwartau, author of *Information Warfare—Chaos on the Information Highway*. He notes, "Wall Street and others in non-defense industries are crucial economic assets of the United States, and we need to incorporate a means for their defense in an overall policy," adding, "Right now, the private sector is sitting there all alone, and the weapons coming our way today are more sophisticated than a couple of guys writing viruses in Bulgaria."[10] Schwartau is lobbying for a national information policy to address these problems. A national policy must be capable of addressing two of the most important questions, according to Schwartau: (1) Are industrial secrets the equivalent of military secrets?; and (2) Should U.S. intelligence agencies spy on foreign corporations?

BORDERS

The significance of interstate and international borders, crucial for managing traditional forms of commerce, wanes in the cyberspace environment. The classic paradigm simply does not fit in the Information Age. Moreover, countries that erect electronic borders will limit themselves in the global knowledge economy.

Since nation-states were created to meet the needs of an earlier historical period, they do not have the will, incentive, credibility, tools, or political base necessary to play an effective role in a borderless economy. The bottom line is that they have become unnatural—even dysfunctional—actors in a global economy, because they are incapable of putting global logic first in their decisions. Nation-states are no longer meaningful units in which to think about economic activity. In a borderless world, they embody the wrong level of aggregation.

WEALTH

Access to information will increasingly define prosperity in the coming decades. Many governments are aware of this and are working to bring information parity to their citizens. Singapore, once noted for stern censorship and heavy-handed control of news, now realizes that advancing economic and social well-being depend, in large degree, on a free flow of information. "Technology such as the Internet will make it increasingly difficult to suppress information," states Cheong Yip Seng, group editor-in-chief of Singapore's *New Strait Times*. "What one newspaper suppresses will re-emerge in another. The process will be accelerated by economic development and mass education. There is, in fact, no stopping the spread of information and cultural exchange."[11] Similarly, President Clinton believes that information technology will be the "great equalizer" in the classroom. Poor and rich children must have equal access to information.[12]

Table 9.1 summarizes how successful governments may evolve in the Information Age.

Table 9.1 *Where Are Successful Governments Heading?*

Government/National Characteristics	Old Model	New Model
Relationship to Business	Nonsynergistic government and business relationships	Business and government sponsoring and partnering; opening up and disseminating information
Tariffs	Derived solely from tangible assets	New models need to be developed
Defense	Physical defense focus	Recognition of the need for electronic defense of military and commercial Internet sites

(continued)

Table 9.1 (continued)

Government/National Characteristics	Old Model	New Model
Borders	Physical borders recognized	Borders become more logical than physical; global knowledge economy becomes the focus
Approach to Citizens	Departmental approach	Individual and holistic approach
Wealth and Poverty	Economically rich/ economically poor	Access to information increasingly influences wealth and poverty

SOCIETAL AND CULTURAL CONSIDERATIONS

Many technology theorists suggest that the Internet will have a more profound impact on society than any other prior technological advancement. As with prior revolutions, there are societal and cultural implications. Understanding the Internet's impact on the business world is not enough; to understand fully requires an appreciation of the Internet's social and cultural effects.

It is to your business advantage to anticipate societal reaction to new technologies. A 1993 survey by Dell Computer Company indicated that 55 percent of Americans said they either '"didn't like" or "hated" electronic devices such as personal computers, cellular phones, and digital clock radios. According to a Dell spokesman, "fear of technology may be the phobia of the 90s."

Many information technology companies set about to make their organizations and products more user-friendly. Gateway 2000 developed a PC model that integrates with a standard entertainment center, such as a stereo/TV system. Several other companies, including Apple, Dell, Oracle, and Sony, are addressing the phobia by designing computer products that function more like traditional household appliances. Known as Internet appliances, they are effectively pretuned computers that do not have the feel of the traditional PC. Eventually they will drive ubiquitous computing,

which, unlike what most people believe, is not about placing a computer in every person's hands. Ideally, computing will be om-
nipresent but invisible—so integrated that it is seamless.

The Internet may also accelerate the reward of entrepreneurial
endeavors. Commerce itself may change as the Internet's ability to
handle microtransactions brings products and services to heretofore inaccessible markets. With the global pool of customers and
the ability to charge tiny fractions, specialized micromerchants
may become more popular. Thus, you must understand the value
proposition of a greater number of smaller transactions.

Given the Internet's ability to navigate amidst information in a
nonlinear fashion, educational systems are likely to embrace interactive learning. In fact, hypertext (the common language of the Internet) was developed by Xerox as a more natural way to foster
learning with children. Several national governments have begun
initiatives to incorporate the latest Internet technologies into their
schools. Taiwan plans to spend $114 million on computers for
schools by 1998. President Clinton has suggested that every school
and library have access to the Internet by the year 2000. A society
with this type of environment, with a younger generation comfortable with technology and receptive to new ideas, is indeed a strategic asset to society, serving as an agent of change.

"There is no question that technology drives culture," says Pas-
tora Caffert, a cultural historian at the University of Chicago. "But
during the time that culture is being changed by technology, there
is very little assessment of the positive or negative consequences of
its use, especially unintended and unexpected consequences."[13]
Computer networks return information, but they emphasize the
product over the process and sometimes strip information of its
context. Thus, educational institutions may be exposing students
to "information of unknown pedigree and dubious quality, since little of the Internet has been refereed or reviewed."

Consider how the Internet will affect employment. Sociologists
suggest that there will be a fundamental shift in the business employment structure. Social futurists point out that 60 percent of today's 12-year-olds will be working at jobs that have not yet been
defined and that will be largely information-centric.

Table 9.2 summarizes how the Internet and information technology may influence society.

Table 9.2 *Potential Social Effects of the Internet*

Social Characteristics	Old Model	New Model
Geography	Societies are primary geographically located and bound; individualism is less recognized	The physical boundaries of societies disappear; paradoxically, individualism increases
Commerce	Large work force orientation	Entrepreneur orientation
Education	Structure and theory drivers	Interactive and practical
Employment Scenarios	Moderately changing employment scenarios	Dramatically changing employment scenarios

NOTES

1. Yang, Catherine, "Law Creeps Onto the Lawless Net" *Business-Week* (May 6, 1996).

2. "Companies Reach Investors Via the Net," *New York Times,* 23 September 1996, sec. D, p. 6.

3. "Digital Signature Law Signed," *The Seattle Times,* 7 April 1996.

4. Murphy, Kathleen, "Sending Legal Documents Overseas Can Be Tricky, But Cybernotaries' May Help" *Web Week 2,* no. 2 (February 1996).

5. Ek, Brian, "PICS Picks Up Steam" *Business Wire* Cambridge, MA March 16, 1996.

6. Ohmae, Kenichi, *The Borderless World (New York:* HarperPerennial, 1995).

7. Naisbitt, John, *Megatrends Asia* (New York:Simon and Schuster, 1995).

8. Kenichi, Ohmae, ed., *The Evolving Global Economy* (Boston: Harvard Business School Press, 1995).

9. "Info Warfare Risk Grows," *Computerworld* (May 22, 1995):16.

10. Schwartau, Winn, *Information Warefare: Chaos on the Information Highway.*

11. Naisbitt, John, *Megatrends Asia* (New York:Simon and Schuster, 1995).

12. U.S. President William Jefferson Clinton, Speech at Shoreline Community College (Shoreline, Washington: February 24, 1996).

13. Griffith, Jean Latz, "Time Out for Reflection," *Seattle Times* (11 February 1996).

CHAPTER 10

BUSINESS RISKS AND BARRIERS: OVERCOMING THE OBSTACLES THAT COULD LIMIT YOUR SUCCESS

It is important to understand the risks and barriers to success that accompany a strategic embrace of the Internet. If not anticipated and managed properly, they can limit your business success. Risks are discussed in the context of the consequence of actions that can impair your overall effectiveness and therefore must be the object of conscious management. By contrast, barriers may keep you from even reaching the point of adoption.

BUSINESS RISKS

In this section, nine business risks that may impede your success are discussed:

1. The bureaucratic impulse.
2. Lack of trust in a virtual business world.
3. Immature Internet software and hardware.
4. Securing the insecure.
5. Bad first impressions.
6. Legal troubles.

7. Technology infrastructure limitations.
8. Risks of empowerment.
9. Underestimating project costs.

THE BUREAUCRATIC IMPULSE

Once you have accepted the Internet strategically, be nimble. Do not become a bureaucracy. You risk losing customers to faster and more innovative competition. You must be able to quickly respond to customer requests for more functionality, education, content, information, interlinks, and integration into your information systems. If your business is unable to meet these expectations quickly, then competitors will. Businesses that are organized to respond to customer expectations and can resist the urge to bureaucratize can take advantage of this opportunity.

Eric Roach of Lombard Institutional Brokerage, Inc. believes that the greatest management challenge is resisting the organizational urge to bureaucratize. To be successful, you need to maintain a dynamic and innovative working environment. Lombard does this by empowering all echelons of the company and ensuring that management by proxy is rare. Roach notes that he has personally spent all-nighters with the programmers. The technology people must have quick access to the business end of Lombard, and vice versa, and Roach takes pains to make it happen.

LACK OF TRUST IN A VIRTUAL BUSINESS WORLD

To be successful, you need to be agile. To be agile, you must have fluid, loose, informal, opportunity-based relationships. For these relationships to work, you need to trust your partners. As you become specialized in your own core competencies, you must find trustworthy business partners with complementary skills.

The Red and White Company, a Hong Kong–based wine merchant, sees itself as a virtual company in many respects. It exploits the resources of worldwide business partners (i.e., wine producers) to offer products on the Internet. However, Red and White must trust its business partners—one of its biggest risks. The ability to develop trust becomes more important and at the same time more difficult because partners may be global, less known, and maintain only opportunity-based relationships.

How can a business trust key partners with whom it has never worked? How is trust developed in a virtual organization? Are employees rewarded for trusting business partners? You must first find mutually beneficial partners and then carefully nurture relationships. Your business cannot grow quickly and remain nimble without them. You must get beyond the risks of bureaucracy, reacting too slowly, and a lack of trust.

IMMATURE INTERNET SOFTWARE AND HARDWARE

As time to market decreases, the risk of immature hardware and software products increases. Netscape intends to offer new versions of its products every quarter. Microsoft says will match it. Still others may beat it. Although Internet product development is the fastest-growing segment of the computer hardware and software market, the products are often far from mature. In many cases, the first version of Internet-enabled hardware products is just slightly different than the non-Internet version. This situation should improve over the next 12 to 18 months as hardware and software specifically tuned for the Internet becomes widely available. CUC International, the online shopping company, believes one of its biggest risks was that of immature software available to build its online shopping experience. But because it was an early innovator, it had to take risks. CUC felt this was a cost of doing business on the Internet, but they consciously managed this risk.

SECURING THE INSECURE

Security of information assets during interactions with customers and business partners represents a constant and significant risk. Insecure systems can compromise your business and your customer's allegiance. According to the Computer Security Institute, one of every five companies suffers an unauthorized break-in (hacking), with one in three break-ins occurring after a firewall is installed.[1] According to federal law enforcement estimates, online thieves steal more than $10 billion worth of data in the United

States annually. Law enforcement officials admit that so far they are fighting a losing battle. The director of the CIA, John Deutch, says the United States will set up a defense center to combat the growing threat of computer sabotage and theft.[2]

While new and more mature technologies continue to address gaps in security, they will never eliminate all the risks. Security risks are a part of doing business, and Internet security risks are a part of doing business online. Many security steps can be taken to reduce the risks. A thorough security approach must become an integral part of business decisions.

Many businesses hire outside security experts to attempt to break into their systems. Well-implemented 'firewall' systems and a variety of other security precautions may provide an effective infrastructure for business. Many security considerations are outlined in Chapter 7.

CUC launched its Internet site only to find that it had underestimated the volume of credit card fraud. Development of new information systems was imperative. Gordon Snyder of Twentieth Century Mutual Funds says that fear of fraud, whether legitimate or irrational, is an enormous handicap for your Internet business strategy. If customers do not believe your business is secure, they will be reluctant to disclose private information.

BAD FIRST IMPRESSIONS

Amazon.com, the online bookstore, believes that the most important thing it did when establishing its service was having an extensive beta test period. A beta software product is a preproduction test version used for debugging and assessment.

Exhaustive beta testing can greatly reduce the chance that an immature or technically unsound product reaches customers. As Jeff Bezos, president of Amazon.com, notes, "You don't get a second chance with a lot of customers." Quite simply, your presence on the Internet must be a polished performance, not a dress rehearsal. Bad first impressions are seen by a large audience. Internet customers are largely unforgiving. CUC's Rick Fernandes, observes, "In this business you can't afford to make a bad first impression because the Internet is all about developing customer allegiances. Customers are too busy to come back to revisit if you don't impress them the first time."

LEGAL TROUBLES

Businesses assume legal risks with an Internet business strategy.

Legal action by regulators. Consider your legal requirement of updating and continually validating your Internet presence. A major European airline was fined $14,000 by the U.S. government in 1995 for continuing to advertise an expired airfare on the Internet. Although it indicated that the mistake was not an attempt to misinform the public but rather was the result of a maintenance error, the airline was still required to pay the fine.

Legal action by competitors. You are a global company on the Internet and need to respect international laws. In Germany, for example, comparative advertising is illegal. Competitors can present legal action if ours-versus-theirs advertising is used against their product.

Legal action from employees' conduct. Employees may not be conscious of their company's policies regarding the Internet. An employee of an online company was fired for linking his personal home page to the employer's Internet site without prior approval. Management argued that the link implied that its business supported the content appearing on the employee's home page, and that the information was inconsistent with the company's philosophy.

Legal action by foreign countries. The laws of foreign countries may limit your ability to carry out sales and marketing over the Internet. Playboy Enterprises cannot market its magazines in several Middle Eastern countries. In a well-publicized case, CompuServe pulled more than 100 of its sex-related Internet newsgroups off its service for fear of legal action by the German government.

Legal repercussions due to customer action. Current or potential customers may perceive harm from a service or product you provide over the Internet. Consider the impact of providing inaccurate financial advice, information systems, or other professional advice. Customers may post information on your site that harms another customer.

As noted in Chapter 9, legal risks are significant and profound. The chief Internet strategist for one of the largest entertainment companies recently noted, "The greatest risk in the legal realm concerns politicians and governments who may make a play in asserting political control over the Internet. Since the general public doesn't really fully understand the Internet, they are susceptible to demagoguery which trades on fears they create to win support for intrusive laws and regulations."

TECHNOLOGY INFRASTRUCTURE LIMITATIONS

Technology infrastructure may impair your ability to quickly respond to customers' changing priorities. A poor technology infrastructure may result in the inability to leverage existing business systems in new ways, with significant consequences. For example, if your ability to reply to customer Internet requests is hemmed in by your infrastructure, you may lose business. Remember, your customers have other options.

Imagine the situation at Charles Schwab, which was processing an average of 81,500 trades per day in February 1996. As the brokerage moves toward conducting more of its business via the Internet, the demands of performance and availability become all the more critical. Their infrastructure becomes key.

RISKS OF EMPOWERMENT

The ability of the Internet to empower your employees requires new forms of management. An electronic deployment manager at a large high-tech manufacturer notes, Internet technologies are scattered throughout the company. The Internet is not just another technology, like the PC or mainframe computer, and it cannot be managed as if it were.

It is forcing us to reconsider the meaning of production servers, which in the past were tightly monitored and controlled in the operational glass house, a central control facility with round-the-clock operational and technical support. Before the Internet became commonplace, the number of computer systems requiring monitoring and control was manageable and a central node was sufficient.

Now, with the introduction of Internet technologies, new applications are developed and run by users on systems outside the glass house. The data most critical to the company is dispersed throughout the organization. Thousands of workstations on user desktops may need to become production servers.

In one instance, a manager had posted key data on his desktop and made it Web-accessible. Several months later the manager's computer crashed while he was on vacation. The users had become reliant on the data stored on it, and they called the production support team to report the problem, but the production support personnel knew nothing about it. It was not physically within their walls, was not built by an MIS manager, and was not registered.

These problems have become more widespread throughout many companies as users Web-enable their applications. You need to carefully determine your policy when empowering users. Where should the company's data reside?

UNDERESTIMATING PROJECT COSTS

A look at full implementation and operational costs can be eye-opening. Underfunding your Internet effort imperils your success. You may wind up lacking equipment, infrastructure, and personnel.

According to a December 1995 report issued by Forrester Research, the cost of launching and operating a simple promotional site can cost $304,000 per year. Launching and operating a content-based site may run to $1.3 million per year, while a fully transactional Internet site can cost $3.4 million. These costs are expected to increase 52 to 231 percent over the next two years.

Keep in mind that the purchase price of software is only a small fraction of total infrastructure costs. In many cases the network infrastructure and PCs need to be upgraded. Users and operational people need training and continuing education. Maintenance, application development, infrastructure, and migration costs must also be factored in. Many of these expenses require large up-front outlays.

As with the client/server computing revolution, industry analyst groups say that the most significant cost associated with the five-year total cost of system ownership is maintenance. The salaries of maintenance personnel account for a significant percentage of the total cost.

As the Internet evolves, it may address some of the maintenance and configuration issues that were introduced with the client/server revolution but introduce new cost areas. Perhaps these cost areas will result from:

- a high degree of involvement of top business management

- the effect of integration on current and planned projects

- the number of groups (i.e., legal, PR, marketing, IT) involved in the Internet project, and the associated personnel costs

- security architecture and management costs

- training costs required to stay on top of constantly emerging technologies

BUSINESS BARRIERS

The discussion of risks assumed that you have embraced the Internet strategically. What barriers might limit you from adopting it in the first place? There are several.

RESPONDING REACTIVELY

Business management often perceives the Internet as a fad promising large revenues and other business benefits that may not be possible. Because of this they respond reactively. But the risks of not accurately calculating the impact of the Internet, failing to identify new business models, and postponing the development of an appropriate strategy will jeopardize your business future.

You need to be a pioneer to be successful. Pioneers do not react; they act, ahead of their competitors. Look, for example, at Twentieth Century Mutual Funds, a company that manages more than $50 billion for 2 million investors.

Being the first mutual fund company to offer transactions on the Internet entailed certain risks. Twentieth Century worked with the mutual fund industry's insurance carrier, ICI Mutual, to craft the first insurance policy of its kind. For Gordon Snyder, the company's executive vice president of marketing and the driving force of the pioneering effort, Twentieth Century's focus was never on the competition but rather on bringing new and innovative services to current and potential customers.

With the advent and commercialization of the Internet, some suggest that the best way to stay abreast of trends and developments is to monitor the actions of the competition. As the discussion of the circle of influence in Chapter 5 demonstrates, focusing on your competitors is not effective. You can't control competition, and you don't want others setting your company's pace and agenda.

A reactive attitude with respect to the Internet generally starts with monitoring the competition. This approach is likely to end in failure. A strategic approach does not focus on the competition per se, but rather on what the customer values and what the Internet can offer the customer. Figure 10.1 outlines these two approaches.

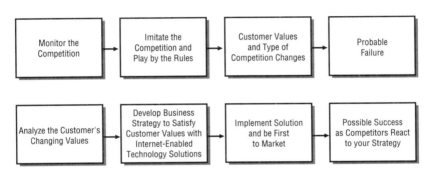

Figure 10.1 *Reactive Response (Top) vs.*
Proactive Response (Bottom)

TRADITIONAL OPERATING MODELS

Most business managers operate under traditional business models and find new approaches or templates threatening. Moving your company forward must involve a conscious effort to introduce employees of all levels to Internet technology and show them just how powerful it can be.

The walls set up in organizations—between managers and workers, organizational functions, between the workplace and home, and between company and society—constrain change, and managers are slow to dismantle them. Only when the walls begin to crumble do companies fulfill the potential of technology. Managers must understand, appreciate, and ultimately become a part of this deeper technological revolution. In the workplace, technology can precipitate revolutionary changes with dramatic impact on the content of work.

With telephones and fax machines, managers can communicate with anyone around the world as easily as down the hall. Everyone agrees that to ignore these technologies would impair a company's competitiveness. Yet the technology of the telephone, which has been around for more than a century, has not fundamentally changed management style or thinking. What could be a powerful tool to break down the walls between functions and levels in an organization, to share information and speed decision-making, is instead limited to enhancing the communications that already are a part of most managers' lives. Managers have used these technologies to wire the walls, rather than to remove them.[3]

Technology must be a core competency of the organization. CUC International realized this early and bought its Internet technology systems integrator. Twentieth Century Mutual Funds put together a SWAT team to implement Internet technology. Lombard organized the brokerage company around its technology specialists. But many organizations are unwilling to lead the pack and operate in these new models. They are waiting for competitors to explore the new medium before developing their own strategy. Successful companies of the future will seize a leadership position, create the new models, develop the new rules of business, and reap the potential rewards.

You should understand what models your customers expect you to be operating in. Twentieth Century Mutual Funds management recognized that its customers expected a new operating environment. In 1993, its survey revealed that more than 70 percent of its customers had a PC. This in itself was not a huge surprise. Twentieth Century is best known for its aggressive mutual funds and investment strategy, and caters to young, technologically savvy customers comfortable with higher-risk investments. Moving the company into electronic commerce was designated a priority, and the necessary organizational steps were taken to remove the barriers.

TOO MUCH CHANGE

The amount of change in business today can distract from focusing necessary energies on the Internet strategy. Downsizing, regulatory changes, global competition, reengineering, and other tasks can occupy a substantial amount of time, sapping your energy for developing and executing effective online strategies.

The successful Internet strategies presented in this book, such as those of Lombard Brokerage, GE Plastics, Twentieth Century Mutual Funds, Amazon.com, and Sausage Software, emerged from companies facing the same pressures as their competitors. In each case a pioneering individual or team saw the advantages of the Internet and spearheaded an effort through uncharted waters, during times where distractions could have easily taken away from their ability to rise to the occasion.

INERTIA

Inertia can be a significant business barrier hindering innovation, agility, and flexibility. It works against the characteristics that lead to success: nimbleness, agility, and innovation. Overcoming your business's ironclad beliefs is essential if the Internet is to have any chance of working for it. As Hamel and Prahalad comment in their essay, "Strategic Intent," "A company's strategic orthodoxies are more dangerous than its well-financed rivals."[4] You need to look honestly at your ability to be nimble. As Chris Argyris observes in *Interpersonal Barriers to Decision Making*, "the gap that often exists between what executives say and how they behave helps create barriers to openness and trust, to the effective search for alternatives, to innovations, and to flexibility in the organization."[5]

INFLEXIBLE FUNDING STRATEGY

Annual budgeting cycles do not reflect the dramatic change occurring in business, government, society, and technology. Technology advances will continue to occur more rapidly and have a growing influence on business. Budgeting cycles should reflect this need to be flexible, for it is very likely that your Internet initiative cannot wait 12 months until funding is approved.

Compared to traditional IS efforts, Internet projects may be difficult to budget because the technology changes frequently. "Today's management accounting information, driven by the procedures and traditional annual cycle of the organization's financial reporting system, is too late, too aggregated, and too distorted to be relevant for management's planning and control decisions," notes one study. "As companies are forced by competition to move towards agility, the problems caused by this flaw in management accounting systems will become even more serious."[6]

FAILURE TO RECOGNIZE THE VALUE OF STRATEGIC ALLIANCES

Interlinking business partners represent an important component in your overall Internet business strategy. However, there is often a lack of a management direction encouraging both global and strategy, as well as loose and informal interlinking alliances.

You must force yourself to understand both the requirements and the value of true strategic alliances. They must be effective and strategic to both partners. Most managers have little or no experience with business projects that entail shared control. Capitalizing on the benefits of interlinking alliances requires a shift from the old top-down mindset to an appreciation of a cadre of complementary interlinkers.

BAD IT REPORT CARDS

Management often perceives IT as failing to deliver promised dramatic improvements in business productivity. It is not difficult to figure out why. Consider the following:

- In the United States, 31 percent of IT projects are canceled before completion (80,000 projects in 1995), costing businesses $81 billion.

- Only sixty-one percent of all business functionality anticipated in IT systems efforts is included in the first version.

- Only 13 percent of all IT systems projects are considered successful by executives.

- More than 50 percent of all systems projects have a cost over-run of 189 percent or more, costing U.S. businesses $59 billion per year.[7]

This perception presents a difficult barrier to overcome. You must convince management that understanding the failures of the past can be a potent tool in planning for future upgrades and improvements. Failures can be addressed through more flexible systems, internal technology core competence, and closer integration of business units.

Moreover, most IS organizations have only a limited ability to think outside of the box. If technology is a business enabler, how much liberty are the technologists given to brainstorm new approaches to problems? What processes foster an environment in which the IS staff can explore new business models? Many businesses do not empower IS organizations for strategic decision-making; therefore, IS organizations do not think that they are responsible for providing direction.

MISEDUCATION

Incorrect or misguided information concerning issues, risks, capabilities, and benefits of the Internet is a common barrier to success. Even worse, understanding of the Internet is inconsistent among organizational levels. This lack of common understanding of the Internet across the business often results in an inappropriate focus, limiting timely and successful development of an Internet business strategy.

When unfiltered information about the Internet is provided to conservative executives, they often see only the potential problems, not the opportunities. As an advocate of the Internet, you must prevent key decision-makers from being swayed by irresponsible and unfounded rumors and half-truths. Many people believe the Internet is rife with problems, often centering on security, performance, and lack of ownership. Do not sweep skeptics' concerns under the rug. Present solutions grounded in the most accessible technologies and practices, and emphasize the inherent evolutionary quality of the Internet.

BANDWIDTH

Make no mistake: bandwidth *is* a limitation to offering a rich set of graphics-intensive services to your customers. However, successful companies are not letting this stunt their online efforts.

Graphics are not the be-all and end-all. When Twentieth Century Mutual Funds held a series of focus groups in which customers were asked about what services and features they would like to see on the Internet, functionality and ease of navigation emerged as the most desirable qualities. Customers recognize the appeal of graphics but are more concerned with ease of use, comfort in navigating a site, and self-service.

It is possible to innovatively bypass bandwidth problems. Amazon.com's Author Search sends e-mail to a customer when the online bookstore's search engine finds new books by authors in whom the customer indicated an interest. This minimizes the time the customer must navigate the Web and presents a new service while bypassing bandwidth limitations.

CONCLUSION

These are the risks and barriers to consider as you develop and implement your Internet business strategy. Recognize those that apply to your business and develop a management approach. Remember: The barriers limit you from taking the first step of an Internet business strategy. After reviewing the barriers and potential risks, you may discover that some can be managed with proper education. Others may require fundamental organizational change.

NOTES

1. Wilder, Clinton and Bob Violino, "Online Theft," *Information Week,* 28 August 1995.

2. Panettieri, Joseph C., "Security," *Information Week,* (27 November 1995):23.

3. Jaikumar, Jay, "The Boundaries of Business: The Impact of Technology," in *The Evolving Global Economy;* ed. Kenichi Ohmae (Boston: Harvard Business School Press, 1995):93.

4. Hamel, Gary and C.K. Prahalad, "Strategic Intent," *Harvard Business Review* (May–June 1989).

5. Argyris, Chris, "Interpersonal Barriers to Decision Making," *Harvard Business Review* (March–April 1996).

6. Johnson, Jim, "CHAOS: The Dollar-Drain of IT Project Failures," *Application Development Trends* (January 1995).

7. Johnson, "CHAOS."

CHAPTER 11

MEASURING SUCCESS: ASSESSING YOUR POSITION REALISTICALLY AND ANALYZING RESULTS

The first ten chapters of this book presented dozens of concepts and practical steps, challenged traditional assumptions, and explored real-life examples, thus laying the foundation for an effective Internet strategy. There are two more concepts: (1) assessing your current position and (2) measuring your success. These final activities put the finishing touches on this exploration of Internet business strategy.

AN INTERNET GAP ANALYSIS

An Internet gap analysis helps assess where you are relative to where you want be. Perform the analysis after developing your strategy through the ten steps discussed in Chapter 5. The gap analysis will help with six key tasks:

1. Analyzing where you are currently positioned.
2. Understanding where you can be positioned.
3. Recognizing the business benefits offered by different levels of adoption.

4. Identifying where you want to be, and within what time frames.
5. Determining the necessary implementation steps.
6. Articulating your vision of where you want to be.

ANALYZING YOUR CURRENT POSITION

Before setting a course for the future, you must first assess where your organization is at the present. In this section, five levels of adoption are presented and explained.

FIVE STAGES OF EVOLUTION

Consider the stages of Internet technology adoption. This model illustrates that acceptance of the Internet (or, more broadly, network-centric computing) occurs in five stages, each representing a different level of adoption of the Internet technologies into the business strategy, each progressively more strategic. The five stages are:

1. general company information sharing
2. establishment of initial Internet presence
3. provision of initial value-added services
4. moderate integration of systems with customers and partners
5. full integration of systems, services, and industries

The Internet adoption spectrum in Figure 11.1 suggests that most businesses are in stages 1 and 2. Some leading businesses, such as Lombard Brokerage, GE Plastics, Amazon.com, and CUC International, are in stages 3 to 5. Most Internet technology companies, such as Netscape, SGI, and Microsoft are already in stages 3 to 5.

80% of Businesses   20% of Businesses

Stage 1   Stage 2   Stage 3   Stage 4   Stage 5

Figure 11.1 *Internet Adoption Spectrum*

General Company Information Sharing. This stage is characterized by an organization's acceptance of the importance of general
electronic-based information sharing within the company. This usually includes the adoption of a local area network (LAN) as the business's first foray into electronic communications enablement.

LANs become the technical foundation for Stage 1 companies.
Although LAN and related communications technologies emerge,
they are seen as a supporting element of the business. While the internal IT group supports the business, it is not perceived as an enabler of additional business opportunities.

In this phase business managers endorse and encourage the
sharing of general information in the office automation capacity.
Files are shared across a LAN; computers can network and, therefore, share printers. This stage often includes deploying technologies to enable document management. A Lotus Notes application
may provide basic workgroup collaboration. The typical target user
group for this technology is the internal business employee. In-
teroffice network communications may be implemented for information dissemination and information sharing. Applications like
internal e-mail become more popular. LANs also became the basis
for client/server computing, where applications run partly on an
employee's personal computer and partly on a centralized LAN
server or mainframe.

Over time costs become significant, especially the cost to support and operate the environment. The last ten years have seen the
widespread adoption of this technology. It provides a starting point
of the Internet evolution because it is the basis of managers' treatment and perception of network technologies and how the business
organizes to incorporate these technologies.

Establishment of Initial Internet Presence. This stage of evolution features the business's tactical, reactive, and almost defensive approach to the amazingly rapid commercialization and popularization of the Internet. Businesses tend initially to offer limited or no business functionality beyond marketing content, annual reports, and general public material. They use existing brochures, press releases, and similar materials for the Internet's public presence. The focus and underlying success criterion is presentation style (i.e., graphics and other multimedia elements) rather than business functionality. Initial Internet presences are often referred to as public vanity sites. Because of the rapid commercialization of the Internet and the associated hype, employees whose companies do not have public sites lose pride in their organization. Stage 2, then, is almost a defense reaction to save face for a business. However, the technologies used can be leveraged from the first stage.

However, some important changes do occur in the mindset of business managers. The audience is suddenly recognized as global and external, even though the information or content presented on these first home pages is generic and not customized for the new audience in any way. Often led by the marketing group, the initial Internet presence is developed from a nonstrategic business perspective. Businesses do not recognize the Internet's ability to fundamentally alter business, technology, and marketing models as discussed throughout this book.

Why is this? The level of understanding of the Internet's capabilities differs dramatically across the organization in this phase. Most companies are confused by the phenomenon of the Internet. It is difficult for any business to see the forest for the trees. But early adopters who embrace it strategically quickly migrate to stage 3. In phase 2, however, the four steps an organization typically takes are characterized in Figure 11.2.

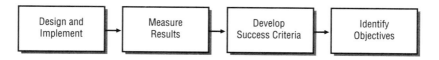

Figure 11.2 Typical Stage 2 Steps

The tendency in Stage 2 is to react to the hype by designing and implementing a generic marketing solution. Businesses are then challenged to measure the results of the project by senior management.

After companies measure results, they are then challenged to determine if the initial presence was a success. This forces the business to attempt to understand what the objectives were, or should have been. At this point it is recognized that the Internet team did not know what its objectives were in the first place. The Internet strategy was not aligned with their business goals or objectives. As businesses begin to question their Internet objectives they enter stage 3 and follow a different methodology, described below.

Many businesses have perceived the value of the Internet technology set by including human resources (HR) forms, phone lists, and other applications on an Intranet for internal employees. The internal application is the same as the external in the sense that the materials are generic and already available in paper form.

Departments begin to use Web browsers for obtaining information internal and external to the company, but this is not standard across the company because the commercialization of the Internet and the explosion of new technologies has happened so fast. The organization's technology standards group has not even had the time to understand where this fits into an organization's technology strategy.

Moreover, the capabilities of the browsers and other Web technologies offer dramatic new features and functions every few months versus every year. The technical services and IT groups are increasingly challenged by infrastructure issues to support a growing customer base. The users are now both internal and external to a company.

The new business models, however, are not clearly understood. Fundamental changes in business design are not widely recognized. Businesses employ profit models on the Internet, such as through advertising and subscription, rather than through more innovative models like micropayments or more complete product offerings. Webmasters are generally skilled graphics artists versus technical or business executives. Functionality loses priority to cool graphics. Many businesses outsource their systems to niche Internet content and service providers, as maintaining a competency in this area is not considered strategic during this stage.

Provision of Initial Value-Added Services. This stage brings a slightly more strategic attempt to incorporate Internet technologies into new business models. Businesses offer more customer services and functionality. Business, marketing, and technology representatives begin to recognize the expectations, needs, and interests of individual customers. Sites feature international language support; screens are built more dynamically and are customized for users.

In this phase, a few visionaries within the organization begin to more deeply appreciate and understand the new operating models by attempting to experiment with new value-added services. The majority of the business, however, still tends to question the value of the Internet and its associated technology set as it relates to their business situation.

Now the objectives are identified first. Some business leaders begin to recognize the underlying capabilities of the Internet and the need to create new business models. As stage 3 evolves, IT and business representatives move into leadership roles, while the marketing group's involvement becomes more integrated with these technologists. Figure 11.3 illustrates the typical steps taken in this stage. The order of the steps is aligned with an Internet strategy which is aligned in turn with business objectives.

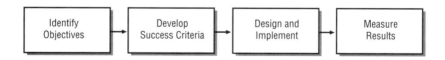

Figure 11.3 *Typical Stage 3 Steps*

New technologies, such as Java, promise cost savings for developing, configuring, and deploying Internet business applications. The overall business groups, however, still remain unclear about the Internet's business opportunities.

Perhaps 80 percent of businesses today are in stages 1, 2, or 3.

Moderate Integration of Systems with Customers and Business Partners. This phase features more significant integration of business and systems into the Internet strategy. Customer-specific applications become more prominent. Instead of utilizing the home page as a generic marketing tool, the business begins to utilize multiple servers that direct users to appropriate content based on the individual user's specifications.

The business begins to fundamentally change in this phase. It reinvents marketing, adopts the new technology standards, reengineers impacted business processes, and reorganizes the business structure. The Internet technology set is used to extend business systems to business partners, customers, and employees. New niche groups are created and targeted by marketers. New information systems are built on the network-centric computing paradigm.

At this point many companies no longer outsource their Internet business strategy and systems because the Internet is seen as essential and integrated throughout the organization. It is now recognized as the way to achieve the benefits of network-centric computing, where the network is inherent in *your* design and computer platform independence is achieved.

Businesses begin to respect changing customer values, needs, interests, and expectations by providing more complete solutions through integration and interlinking with business partners. IT architectures are extended in new ways to solve existing business problems and create business opportunities. Business virtualization concepts become more relevant, while fundamental trends of the global economy and widespread consumer access become more prominent. Businesses begin creating new business, technology, and marketing models, as companies in stage 4 are well into rethinking their business future with the Internet.

Full Integration of Systems, Services, and Industries. The final phase represents the organization's full realization of the Internet's capabilities. Complete acceptance and implementation of Internet services is integrated into the business strategy. Successful companies create business opportunities and adopt new marketing, systems, and organizational operating assumptions. Stage 5 companies fully exploit interlinking with business partners. Revenues are shared between business partners for interlinking. Global interlinking occurs in an opportunist fashion. These relationships are common and effective but loose and informal. Successful companies specialize more exclusively in their core competency than ever before.

Business leaders create new business, marketing, and systems models enabled by the Internet. In this phase, the business, technology, and marketing groups are clearly integrated and working together toward the most effective strategy.

The company has deep specialized skills and empowered knowledge workers. The concept of global localization is fully implemented through a network of virtual organizations focusing on customer values such as individualism and transparency. Most new applications are developed network-centrically. It is accepted that software architectures must be more highly and inherently flexible than ever before in order to adapt to rapid innovations in business designs. Technology is, to a large extent, driving or influencing the business strategy. Some IT companies, such as SGI, are moving into stage 5.

Figure 11.4 plots this range of adoption levels against their enabling business value.

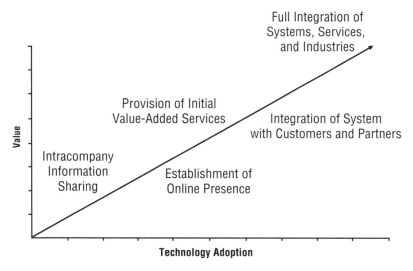

Figure 11.4 *Internet Strategy Continuum*

Review Table 11.1, which summarizes the five stages of Internet and business evolution.

Table 11.1 *Internet Positioning Assessment Model*

	Stage 1	Stage 2	Stage 3	Stage 4	Stage 5
Description	Intracompany Information Sharing	Establishment of Initial Internet Presence	Provision of Initial Value-Added Internet Services	Moderate Integration of Systems with Customer	Full Integration of Systems, Services, and Industries
Business Goals	Leverage internal knowledge capital and corporate information. Support **existing** internal business communications.	Create worldwide awareness on the Internet. Leverage company's paper-based marketing information over the Internet. Begin to understand the impact on systems, marketing, and other business units. The focus is on the public access layer application.	Identify **new** business opportunities by more leveraging and extending systems. Companies experiment with new innovative products and services.	Respond to customers' changing needs by more extensively communicating with new partners, customers, and employees more seamlessly.	Achieve complete integration with new business systems. Businesses communicate on all layers of interaction with customers, strategic partners, and employees.
Target Audience	Internal employees	Global public community	Customers and employees	Customers, business partners, and employees	Customers, business partners, and employees
Technology	Supports Business	Supports Business	Enables Business	Enables Business	Enables Business

(continued)

Table 11.1 (*continued*)

	Stage 1	Stage 2	Stage 3	Stage 4	Stage 5
Enabling Technologies and Standards	LANs, Ethernet	HTML, HTTP	CGI, SSL	Java, ActiveX, SSL 3.0, Microtransactions, Digital IDs	VRML, SET, cable modems, ADSL
General Phase Characteristics	Sharing of files and print services across a company. Basic e-mail across a company's WAN.	Static and informative marketing material. Focus is on graphics and visual appeal.	Customization is recognized. Realization of interactive functionalities becomes more essential. Initial transaction processing, light nonstrategic integration into back-end databases.	High-level interaction, greater user control, acceptance of the Internet as a two-way interactive medium with Java business functionality allowing integration into enterprise systems. High-level transactional processing.	Agents, electronic consultants, robots become prominent. Focus on expert systems and tight integration with multiple global business partners' systems.
IT Summary	Internal workgroup collaboration	Limited integration with the Internet	Light integration, network-centric perspective	Moderate integration	High integration; network-centric applications become the standard.
Principal Risks and Questions	Technical (Will it work?)	Financial (Can we make money?)	Security (What security mechanisms are in place now that we are opening up our systems?)	Business Partner Strategy (Do I have the right interlinking business partners?)	Global Competition (Have I found my niches and my specialization?)

USING THE GAP ANALYSIS TO ACHIEVE YOUR STRATEGIC GOALS

You need to determine at least two things: (1) where you are; and (2) where you want to be. You will then be able to determine what steps to take or what areas to focus on.

Consider a fictitious organization, Company A, which manufacturers and sells consumer packaged goods. Company A has implemented an Internet public presence (public access layer) and introduced some applications available only to a more select group. A brief analysis of Company A's current situation is given below.

First, identify activity associated with each level of the Internet access model. For this example, accept the interaction model introduced in Chapter 4. Each application will be discussed through this model.

1. **Public access characteristics**. Company A's publicly available functions include:

   - an audio message from the CEO that can be downloaded

   - a static corporate overview section

   - an employment opportunities section with direct e-mail to the HR department

   - a section providing relevant educational materials with interactive trivia

   - an online questionnaire that collects marketing information and customer feedback about the company's products

   - press releases

   - a FAQ section

2. **Community access characteristics**. These functions include:

   - static pricing and availability regarding Company A's products

   - an expert utility that helps customers identify the right product for their needs

   - a tracking system to identify visitors to the Company A site

3. Integrated access characteristics. Business partners and strategic customers have no access to information.

4. Organizational access characteristics. Neither remote nor local employees have access.

5. Strategic access characteristics. No strategic information is available.

Company A is between stages 2 and 3. It has taken a reactive approach to the Internet business situation. Although it offers marketing content and other general company material online, the strategic business value of the Internet is not recognized in its internal processes. This may be due to a reaction of the rapid commercialization of the Internet. The audience is viewed as global and generic. Information is in no way customized. Company A has not recognized the Internet's ability to fundamentally alter business, technology, and marketing models.

However, Company A has begun to value business functionality over graphics by providing an expert utility, and it has developed an interaction access layer application for customers. The overall business management, however, is not clear on the value of the Internet to their business situation. In this phase, the business objectives are probably not identified first.

Overall, Company A has made a mild attempt to market with traditional marketing techniques and may or may not be on the path to recognize the value of the Internet to its business design. Relevant core competencies have not been explored. No applicable value proposition has been defined. Customers do not service themselves other than through pricing and availability information, and the solutions offered are not innovative. The business has simply assumed that the new models of business would be as relevant as the old ones.

Company A should aggressively launch applications beyond the public access layer. These applications may include:

- supply chain management
- product planning with customers and partners
- client/business partner—specific information services

- joint project development with interlinked global partners

- strategic knowledge/information sharing

- private information sharing between executives and selected outside partners and customers, such as banks, insurance companies, legal entities, government and financial institutions

The business applications table in Chapter 7 provides more ideas on application strategy.

This positioning assessment activity is used to identify a business's position in relation to the opportunities offered by the Internet. The value of this five-stage model is its illustration of where you are and what your business environment, challenges, and opportunities may be as you move forward. When you understand where your business is positioned and where you could be, you are better prepared to determine where you want to be.

IS YOUR STRATEGY SUCCESSFUL?

One more activity rounds out this comprehensive exploration of Internet business strategies: determining success criteria so that your success can be measured.

The success criteria for your Internet business strategy should be measurable and critical to your business objectives. For example, you may need a communications infrastructure to give your employees access seven days per week, 24 hours per day, anywhere in the world. In this case, high network availability would be necessary for success.

Identifying a wide range of success criteria is an effective exercise when developing, implementing, and maintaining your strategy. In fact, identifying criteria for each business unit results in a better understanding of each group's needs, strengths, and weaknesses. This is important because as businesses become less hierarchical and more networked, the more critical it will be for all team members to understand what constitutes a success for the whole company.

Success criteria should be identified after the objectives are clear but prior to the design, implementation, and experimentation phases of your strategy. For example, if your business objective is to register more subscribing customers, your success criterion may be to use the Internet to attract and register new members, and this will influence your design, implementation, and experimentation. Refer to Figure 11.5 for the strategic sequence. Relative to the defensive approach, whereby objectives are reviewed after results are measured and success criteria estimated, this approach is proactive and strategic. This approach takes the business on the offensive.

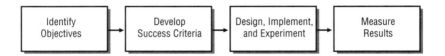

Figure 11.5 *Offensive Internet Strategy*

Most business success criteria center around growing revenues and increasing profit. However, other criteria can benefit a business. In addition to generating revenues, Lombard's success criteria also center on being recognized as a leading-edge solution for investors because Lombard must convince individual investors that its high-tech Internet-based solutions are a better choice for individual customers than common brokers.

Many sites offer free stock quotes (with a 15–20 minute delay) during the trading day; Lombard's quote server also offers complete option montages on any stock with outstanding options. This feature is extremely popular. Lombard's technology allows people to create customized charts and graphs live, online, and in real time. Customers who want to place an order simply pull up an order ticket in another window and execute the trade online.

The Lombard site draws one million hits per day. Although the company profits from the trading of shares from its customer base, its success criteria include: (1) being high-tech and (2) being a part of their customers' daily practices (having a high hit rate). Lombard received a prestigious technology innovation award, which helps it more quantitatively measure its success criteria.

CUC's initial success criteria were less about generating revenue and more about learning about their customers. As Rick Fernandes, executive vice president of CUC Interactive Services, notes, "Although we have 18 years in the interactive and online sales business, we need to keep learning about our customer's needs. Why? For CUC, the success criteria used recognized that you have one chance to make a first impression for customers."

Although developing success criteria is important for all business and technology projects, it has special significance for the Internet business strategy because:

- An inconsistent understanding of the Internet's capabilities across the business will yield a suboptimal Internet strategy.

- Internet architecture technical design changes may be necessary to measure success criteria.

- Business processes may need to be defined or reengineered to effectively measure criteria.

- Each group needs to clearly understand the others' potential impact in a networked organization.

- A variety of groups is impacted by the Internet.

- The new business, marketing, and technology models enabled by the Internet technology are better understood when success criteria are laid out.

HOW TO IDENTIFY SUCCESS CRITERIA

Identifying and measuring success criteria is a challenging process because it may be easier to agree on a definition of failure than to agree on what constitutes a success. Essentially, failure is an event, whereas success is a state. Your success criteria will evolve as you identify better ways to measure your objectives. Additionally, technical capabilities will change, offering more ways to measure success.

It is important to remember the interaction model because you need to consider success from the perspective of employees, business partners, even customers. See success through their eyes. Galt's NETworth site has links from more than 1,000 others, Playboy from more than 10,000. These linkages might indicate success because advertisers like to see them.

A variety of internal success criteria should be evaluated. Consider identifying success criteria from the perspective of customers, business management, IT and systems delivery, business partnerships, marketing, sales, production services, IT operations, legal and regulatory departments, engineering and R & D, internal services (e.g., mail and phone services), and human resources (e.g., recruiting and accounting).

Consider the underlying perspective of your success criteria. Review the initial criteria you identified. Is there a marketing bias? A technology bias? Ideally, the criteria should be comprehensive, aligned with business objectives, and balanced throughout the business. In addition, identify the phase in which the criteria can be met.

A MANAGER'S SUCCESS CHECKLIST

Table 11.2 outlines sample success criteria. Review the table and establish the applicability of each in your business environment. Challenge yourself to identify additional success criteria and ways to measure these results.

Table 11.2 Sample Success Criteria

Business Function	Sample Success Criteria	Possible Measurements Options
Customer	Incorporated into daily practice of customer.	Count number of hits per day, or number of customers that return to your site. Measure by customers that have your site bookmarked (Frank Russell Company and Pointcast)
	New customer solutions are created.	Measure new types of products or services created through suggestions and feedback from customers. These may include new interlinking partners. (Amazon.com)

(continued)

Table 11.2 (*continued*)

Business Function	Sample Success Criteria	Possible Measurements Options
Business Management	More efficient worldwide business management communication.	Count the number of Internet e-mails between management.
	Measurable customer closeness to business.	Measure via customer feedback and ability to develop to new products based on better understanding customers. (GE Plastics)
	Competition is constantly trying to keep up with or emulate your presence.	Measure via review of competitors' sites or industry innovation awards. (Lombard)
	Reduction in lead time to sale.	Measure the time between the initial inquiry and the sales closing. Compare it with traditional channels. (ONYX Software)
	A changed management mindset; clearly developed new business models for the industry.	Measure via questioning senior and middle management before and after Internet involvement. Review the new operating assumptions presented in this book for marketing, technology, and more. (Parr Ford)
	More experience with online business models to better define the company's operating environment.	Measure via questioning relevant personnel before and after the Internet involvement.
	Better understanding of clients, their profiles, knowledge, and concerns.	Measure via evaluation of the data collected by automated tools and online questionnaires. Measure by how many new niche opportunities you think you can create. (The Red and White Company)

(*continued*)

Table 11.2 (continued)

Business Function	Sample Success Criteria	Possible Measurements Options
	A long-term reduction in costs related to supporting customers.	Measure cost savings associated with the sales and customer support provided with the Corporate Web site. (FedEx and SUN Microsystems)
	Identification of revenue-generating opportunities.	Measure revenues generated by leads from corporate Web site. (Sausage Software)
	The high average time of qualified clients in online presence.	Measure through customized reports. (SeeDoo)
	Fewer forms (i.e., prospectus) sent through mail or fax; decreased paperwork.	Count quantity delivered electronically. (Fidelity)
	Flexibility/adaptability of a given business process in a given dynamic environment.	Measure in time required to repackage product/service.
Customer Support	Faster response time to customer.	Measure the average time between the initial inquiry and the response. Compare it with traditional channels. (ONYX Software)
	Reduction in the number of customer support representatives currently required.	Measure by comparing the average number of support cases handled by customers via the Internet versus traditional support personnel over time. (SUN Microsystems)
	Increased quality of customer service	Measure via feedback from customers. (Amazon.com)
	Provision of customer with more tools to better use the product or service.	Measure via feedback from customers. (GE Plastics)

(continued)

Table 11.2 *(continued)*

Business Function	Sample Success Criteria	Possible Measurements Options
	Reduction in communication costs by leveraging Internet infrastructure.	Count number of visits to Internet customer support site. Measure level of e-mail–based support.
Marketing and Sales	Increase in sales influenced by corporate Internet involvement.	Measure via feedback from sales personnel and actual sales generated and closed electronically. (Netscape)
	Internet results (sales, customer demographics) incorporated into decision-making business applications and procedures.	Measure via management feedback.
	Reduction in concept-to-cash-flow time frame leveraging Internet media for marketing, product distribution, customer feedback, etc.	Measure the time between material production to delivery on the Internet relative to traditional channels. (Sausage Software)
	Reduction in printing of sales and marketing literature.	Measure cost savings associated with electronically distributed material. (Netstockdirect.com)
	Better segmentation of target customer market.	Count number of responses received for electronically segmented campaigns versus traditional campaigns. (The Red and White Company)
	Exploited access to global markets.	Count number of global leads generated via Internet.
	Enhanced ability to customize sales and marketing approach.	Measure via the leads/visitor ratio on the Internet relative to traditional channels. (Cathay Pacific)
	Publicity regarding the innovative use of customer feedback.	Measure via quality/volume of press releases and technology. (Amazon.com)

(continued)

Table 11.2 (continued)

Business Function	Sample Success Criteria	Possible Measurements Options
	Exploited ability to provide more sales and marketing material via the Internet.	Measure via the information and content quality of online materials relative to that distributed through traditional channels. (GE Plastics)
	Provision of more educational information for targeted customer base.	Measure via customer feedback.
	Decrease in the expense of sales and marketing efforts worldwide.	Measure via cost comparison of the Internet marketing versus traditional global marketing.
Product Development	More customized products based on increased customer closeness.	Measure via customer and employee feedback. (Sausage Software)
Engineering R&D	Better and faster feedback from customers to improve quality of products.	Measure via customer feedback.
	Access to appropriate Internet information gathering for R&D.	Measure via employee feedback.
Internal Services	Reduction in cost of faxing, mailing, and other forms of distribution.	Measure the cost savings associated with electronically distributed material.
	Reduction in telephone expenses.	Count the number of e-mails sent and received compared to the traditional mail expense savings.
Business Partnerships	Better communication between partners.	Measure via the amount of information sent and received between the corporation and its partners via the Internet.

(continued)

Table 11.2 (continued)

Business Function	Sample Success Criteria	Possible Measurements Options
	Better coordination between partners.	Measure via feedback.
	Easier identification and leveraging of new or more optimal business partners throughout the world.	Count number of leads generated by the Internet.
	Better supply chain management flow.	Measure via the amount of data sent and received on the supply chain flow.
Information Technology Services and Operations	Publicity regarding the innovative use of technology in working with customers.	Measure via quality/ volume of press.
	No security breakthroughs that impact system performance, availability, or integrity.	Measure via logs.
	Lower operational costs than traditional proprietary architectures.	Measure via comparing alternative costs of the proprietary and open system designs in relevant areas.
	More integrated business and technology team collaboration.	Measure via employee feedback.
	Superior system availability, i.e., 99 percent up time.	Measure via system logs.
Systems Development	Leveraging existing and future Information Technology systems efforts.	Measure by tracking cost savings due to the open architecture of Internet technology.
	Shorter system time to market.	Measure time savings due to the open architecture of Internet technology.

(continued)

Table 11.2 (continued)

Business Function	Sample Success Criteria	Possible Measurements Options
Human Resources	Access to worldwide recruits.	Count the number of applications received and recruits hired via Internet.
	Reduction of recruiting costs.	Measure by comparing the recruiting cost per employee hired via the Internet versus the cost of hiring via traditional channels.
	Better and more qualified work force.	Measure by comparing the average qualifications of the recruits hired via Internet with those hired via traditional methods.
Legal and Regulatory	No legal action.	Measure volume of legal action caused by corporate Internet involvement.
	Better communication with legal and regulatory governmental groups leveraging Internet.	Measure via feedback from corporate legal associates.

MEASURING, ASSESSING, AND REPORTING THE RESULTS

Once your success criteria are identified, you need to determine ways to measure and assess them. Many businesses fail to consciously and continually perform this critical step because of the dearth of Internet-specific business processes and technology tools and a lack of integration between the few there are. It is very difficult to track successes and failures to particular business units; some departments may be very protective about their areas of responsibility.

If sales opportunities are generated through the Internet, sales representatives may feel their jobs are threatened. Results like this are not easily measured as statistical tools are not applicable. Instead, direct and indirect feedback from salespeople, customer service personnel, and others is used. Groups that are expected to identify successes and failures manually need to be specifically informed of their responsibility.

Tools are available to track usage information. This largely untapped Internet capability, if properly designed, yields a wealth of information about customers. Ensure that appropriate tools and procedures are in place to measure the results. Several software companies sell statistical and analytical tools for all platforms; refer to Chapter 7 for more information. Most Internet server software includes some level of analytical tools. Resulting data can be easily converted to graphical tables and figures.

Avoid underestimating success by failing to recognize the intangible benefits of your initial versions. These benefits can be especially substantial in the short term. Your analysis should consider more immediate public relations capabilities, familiarization of business executives with Internet-enabled business opportunities, more satisfied customers and distributors, and improved name recognition.

Ensure that every Internet project team member and business unit representative understands all of the success criteria, as they may need to measure the results—a real challenge. It is imperative that everyone thoroughly understand the criteria on which the results are based.

If results are poor, do not immediately cease activities, but reevaluate the strategy and implementation. Perhaps this is simply because of one or two minor elements that were not integrated into the strategy. The management mindset must shift from "we will do a pilot and if it fails we will drop it" to "we will do Phase 1 and if it fails we will find out why, make the necessary changes, and refine our approach, assumptions, and design until our business success criteria are met."

When developing your success criteria, consider Table 11.2. Do not, however, be limited by it. Instead, use the examples as starting points for each business group, and think outside the box to extensively develop the most relevant criteria for your organization. This exercise should result in a thorough understanding of and agreement in the objectives across all business units and support groups. Reassess the success criteria periodically.

RECAPPING THE STEPS TO INTERNET SUCCESS

This book analyzed ten essential steps of a successful Internet strategy, explored new marketing models, reviewed the technology, assessed the impact on the organization, visited the legal issues, developed an Internet gap analysis, and discussed several other activities to help achieve Internet success. Here is a summary and a potential order in which to carry out the process.

- **Develop Internet business strategy.** These ten steps are discussed in Chapter 5. The strategy must be early, experimental, customer-centric, and innovative. Your product or service must offer customers a well-thought-out value proposition, respecting their changing needs, interests, and expectations. Profit models must be tested. New business operating assumptions must be adopted and the Internet must be embraced in a strategic manner.

- **Identify and assess position.** Analyze your current position and understand where it can be in the future. This allows you to determine where you are heading and to recognize when you get there.

- **Develop marketing and legal strategies.** The marketing function itself must be reprioritized and reinvented. Marketing considerations are discussed in Chapter 6. Associated legal issues must also be addressed; many are explored in Chapter 9.

- **Assess technology and develop systems plans.** These activities are examined throughout Chapter 7.

- **Assess and refine affected business processes.** Business processes change with new business, marketing, and systems assumptions. Businesses must assess this impact and rethink the plan. This activity is reviewed in Chapter 8.

- **Identify new organization required.** New roles and responsibilities must be recognized for the proper definition, development, and fulfillment of the strategy. The proper team with a clear understanding of the objectives is critical. The organization must mature through proper management planning. Organizational considerations are offered in Chapter 8.

- **Develop success criteria.** These provide a way to measure the attainment of business objectives. Obtaining a consensus on success criteria ensures that the business managers clearly understand their objectives and goals. This exercise is outlined in this chapter.

- **Develop and implement plans.** Define a detailed phasing and implementation strategy by reviewing the business plans outlined in the ten essential steps.

- **Evaluate results.** Compare results to success criteria. Take appropriate steps to respond to the results.

The steps outlined here represent a process, not a project. It is important to continually revisit and refine the steps. Figure 11.6 outlines a process for the execution of an Internet business strategy. Review this approach and customize it for your business. Note that many of the tasks can be done in parallel.

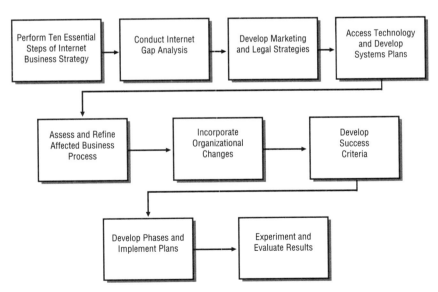

Figure 11.6 Execution of an Internet Business Strategy

RESOURCES TO HELP DEVELOP AND EXECUTE AN INTERNET STRATEGY

A DIRECTORY OF INTERNET BUSINESS STRATEGY RESOURCES

Anyone embarking on an Internet strategy is challenged with constantly reviewing the state of technology, and its associated business impact and new opportunities. This is not a simple task. In fact, it is not even a task—it is a process and a significant challenge. This resource appendix gives you a head start in filtering through the vast amount of resources available.

Useful information to aid in the development and execution of your Internet business strategy is highlighted. The following types of resources are included:

- innovative business strategy sites

- Internet business and technology background resources

- Internet business strategy information

INNOVATIVE BUSINESS STRATEGY SITES

To better understand the impact that the Internet will have on your business, examine a variety of sites taking a proactive and strategic approach. Think through the customer values these businesses are catering to. Think through the new assumptions and the ways they recapture profit. This exercise may provide you with ideas which may fundamentally alter the way you view your existing services or products. Table A.1 represents a limited but relevant list of insightful business strategies. Also review the sites described in this book, including GE Plastics, ONYX, Pointcast, NETworth, Netscape, Microsoft, Sausage Software, DealerNet, Parr Ford, CUC International, Sun Microsystems, Amazon.com, Netstockdirect.com, Lombard, and Silicon Graphics.

INTERNET BUSINESS AND TECHNOLOGY BACKGROUND RESOURCES

The following print and online resources provide valuable analyses of the Internet and emerging business models:

- *Web Week.* Referred to as "The Newspaper of Web Technology and Business Strategy." (www.webweek.com)

- *Interactive Week.* A highly informative publication detailing the industry's key weekly events and relevant business issues. Published simultaneously online and in print. (www.zdnet.com/~intweek)

- *Fast Company: How Smart Business Works.* A monthly business journal focusing on preparing businesses for the challenges of rapid and innovative business cycles. (www.fastcompany.com)

- *Internet World.* A monthly magazine focusing on Internet technology and business issues. (www.mecklerweb.com/mags/iw)

- *Wired.* A print magazine offering an alternative perspective on social, government, business, and consumer issues with respect to technology such as the Internet. The online version is called *HotWired.* (www.hotwired.com)

- *Application Development Trends.* Comprehensive and thor-

Table A.1 Business Strategy Example

General Industry	Business	Address*	Functionality	Analysis
Service	Alamo Rental Car	www.freeways.com	Provides renting and booking information along with travel tips, maps, weather reports, and forums.	• a complete customer solution offering more than simply car booking capabilities • educational buying experience • electronic booking over the Internet
Retail	DealerNet	www.dealernet.com	Valuable information service for car shoppers. It allows customers to search for a car that meets specified criteria. The service confirms price and provides local dealer information.	• self-educated selling • time and cost savings for buyer • more educated/informed customer • user-defined shopping experience • powerful search capabilities, such as "Show me all the cars under $12,000"
Entertainment	Discovery Channel Online	www.discovery.com	An array of educational information presented in a well-designed manner.	• new entertainment models • new educational models
Banking	Wells Fargo	www.wellsfargo.com	Personal banking with digital account capabilities.	• personal banking over the Internet

(continued)

Table A.1 (*continued*)

General Industry	Business	Address*	Functionality	Analysis
Service	Federal Express	www.fedex.com	Ability to track a package from anywhere in the world.	• customer-employee customer service model • leveraging of existing database and systems
Publishing	PR Newswire	www.prnewswire.com	Focused, timely news.	• customer pull capability for information retrieval • convenient, immediate service

* Note that businesses may periodically change Internet addresses. Use search engines if these are no longer valid.

ough monthly magazine objectively analyzing a variety of technology strategies, many in regard to Internet computing. (www.spgnet.com)

- *Convergence.* A monthly magazine for the interactive communications industry. Helpful in monitoring success stories and the state of the market in interactive technologies. (www.convergencemag.com)

- *Interactive Age Online.* Interactive industry news and developments, many related to the Internet. (techweb.cmp.com/ia/)

BUSINESS STRATEGY BACKGROUND INFORMATION

More high-quality Internet business information is available online, as highlighted in Table A.2.

Table A.2 *Internet Business Resources*

Resource	Address	Description
Internet Advertising Resource Guide	www.msu.edu/unit/adv/internet-advertising-guide.htm	Internet advertising comments. A starting point for marketing- and advertising-related resources.
Economics of the Internet	www.sims.berkeley.edu/resources/infoecon/	A perspective on the implications of Internet on the economy.
Project 2000	www2000.ogsm.vanderbilt.edu	Research information on the Internet and its impact on various models.
Gartner Group's @xpo	www.gartner.com	A directory that provides context and links to IT vendor sites.

Appendix B

BIBLIOGRAPHY

Argyris, Chris, "Interpersonal Barriers to Decision Making." *Harvard Business Review* (March–April 1996).

Clinton, U.S. President William Jefferson. Speech at Shoreline Community College (Shoreline, Washington) 24 February 1996.

"Companies Reach Investors Via the Net." *New York Times* (23 September 1996, sec. D):6.

Covey, Steven, *The 7 Habits of Highly Effective People*. (New York: Simon and Schuster, 1990).

Davidow, William H., and Michael S. Malone, *The Virtual Corporation*. (New York: HarperCollins, 1993).

Drucker, Peter F., "The Coming of the New Organization," *The Best of the Harvard Business Review*. (Boston: Harvard Business School Press, 1991).

Fites, Donald V., "Make Your Dealers Your Partners." *Harvard Business Review* (March-April 1996).

Foster, David F., *International Guide to E-Mail and EDI Products*, EDI Strategies, Inc. (1993).

Gates, Bill, *The Road Ahead.* (New York: Viking, 1995).

Goldman, Steven L., Roger N. Nagel, and Kenneth Preiss, *Agile Competitors and Virtual Organizations.* (New York: Van Nostrand Reinhold, 1995).

Hamel, Gary and C.K. Prahalad, "Strategic Intent." *Harvard Business Review* (May–June 1989).

Hardy, Charles, "Trust and the Virtual Corporation." *Harvard Business Review* (May–June 1995).

Hesselbein, Frances, Marshall Goldsmith, and Richard Beckhard, *The Leader of the Future.* (San Francisco: Jossey-Bass, 1996).

Jaikumar, Jay, "The Boundaries of Business: The Impact of Technology." In *The Evolving Global Economy*, ed. Kenichi Ohmae. (Boston: Harvard Business School Press, 1995).

Kanellis, Panagiotis, and Ray J. Paul, "Towards an Epistemological Framework for Measuring the Fit of Information Systems Under Perpetual Change," Uxbridge, Middlesex: Centre for Information Systems Department of Computer Science & Information Systems at St. Johns Brunel University, 1995. (An essay on the Internet.)

Martins, Tony, *Value Software for the Services Sector.* Claremont Technology Group, 1991. (Unpublished essay)

Moore, Geoffrey A., *Inside the Tornado.* (New York: Harper Business, 1995).

Naisbitt, John, *Megatrends Asia.* (New York: Simon and Schuster, 1995).

Negroponte, Nicholas, *Being Digital.* (New York: Vintage Books, 1995).

Ohmae, Kenichi. *The Borderless World.* (New York: HarperPerennial, 1995).

Ohmae, Kenichi ed. *The Evolving Global Economy.* (Boston: Harvard Business School Press, 1995).

Peters, Tom, "The Boundaries of Business Partners—The Rhetoric and Reality." In *The Evolving Global Economy,* ed. Kenichi Ohmae. (Boston: Harvard Business School Press, 1995).

Porter, Michael E., and Victor E. Miller, "How Information Gives You Competitive Advantage," *The Best of the Harvard Business Review* (Boston: Harvard Business School Press, 1991).

Rayport, Jeffrey F. and John V. Sviokla, "Exploiting the Virtual Value Chain." *Harvard Business Review* (November–December 1995).

Reichheld, Frederick F., "Learning From Customer Defections." *Harvard Business Review* (March-April 1996).

Sandler, Susan, "Cable's Big Breakthrough." *Convergence* (February 1996):21.

Schaaf, Dick, *Keeping the Edge—Giving Customers the Service They Demand.* (New York: Penguin, 1995).

Slywotzky, Adrian J., *The Value Migration.* (Boston: Harvard Business School Press, 1996).

Stoll, Clifford, *Silicon Snake Oil: Second Thoughts on the Information Superhighway.* (New York: Doubleday, 1996).

Tenebaum, Jay M., "The Internet as an Agent of Social Change." *Computer Technology Review.*

Zells, Lois, "Why do we need I/S?" *Application Development Trends* (Feb, 1996).

INDEX